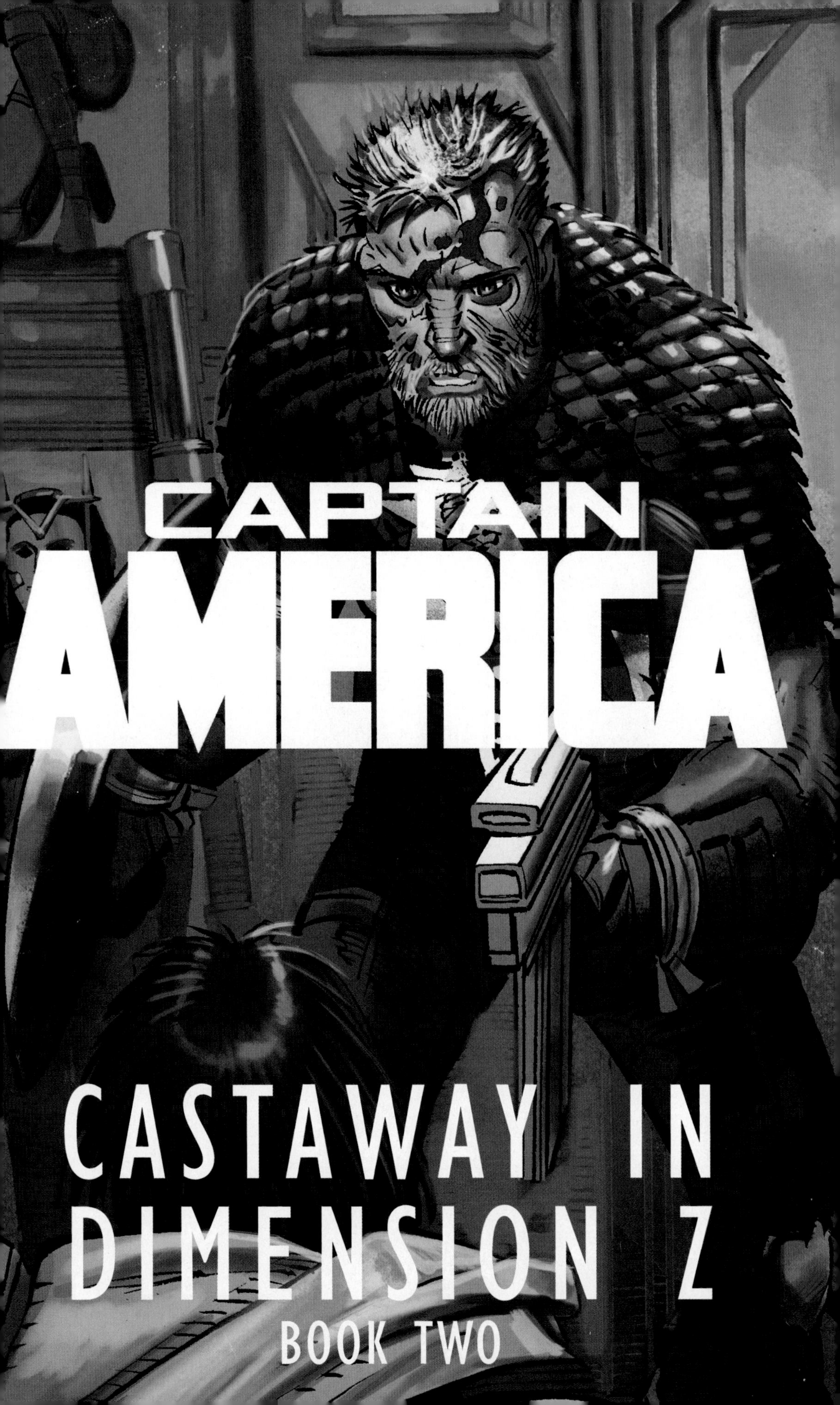

CAPTAIN
AMERICA
CASTAWAY IN
DIMENSION Z
BOOK TWO

CASTAWAY IN DIMENSION Z

BOOK TWO

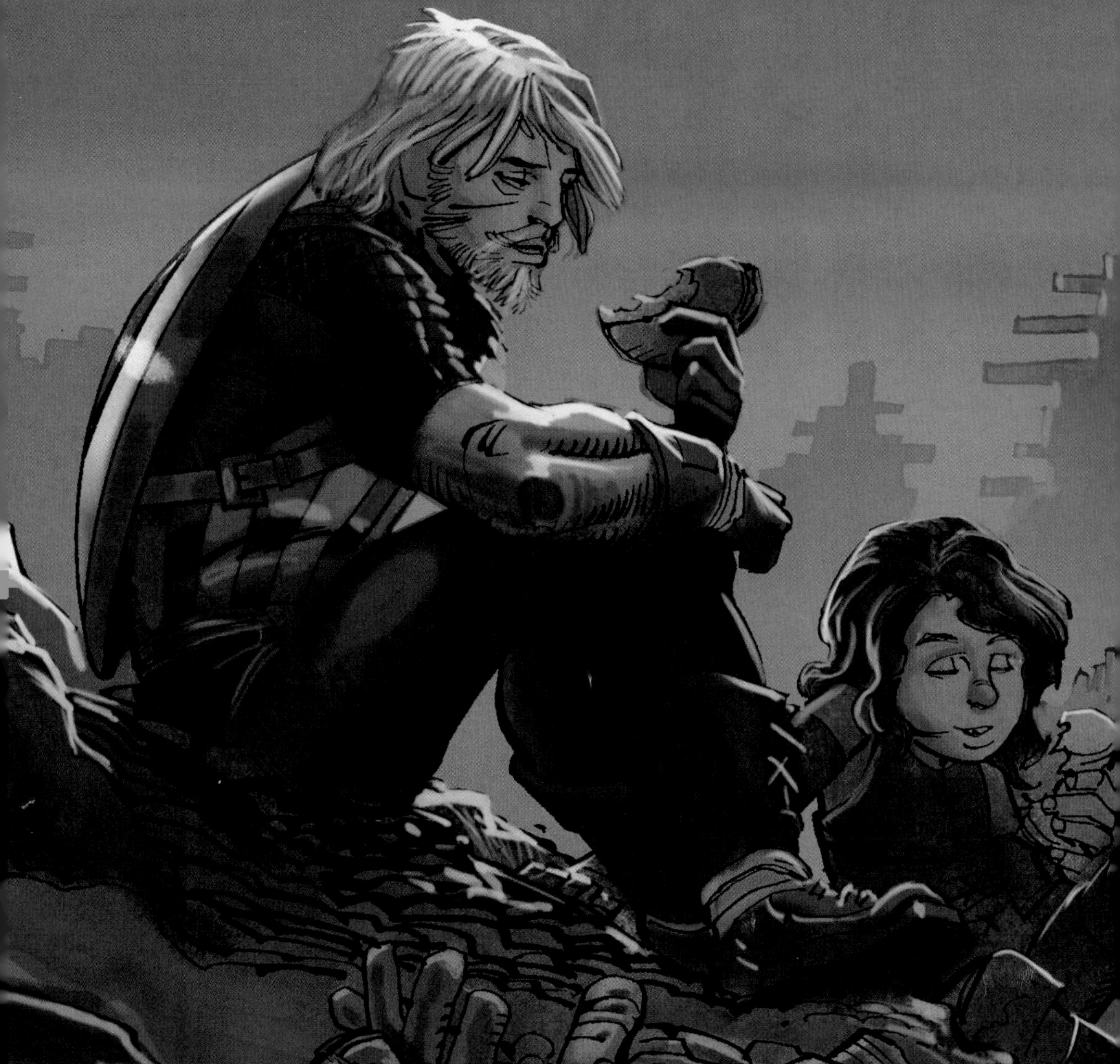

COLLECTION EDITOR
CORY LEVINE

ASSISTANT EDITORS
ALEX STARBUCK
& NELSON RIBEIRO

EDITORS,
SPECIAL PROJECTS
JENNIFER GRÜNWALD
& MARK D. BEAZLEY

SENIOR EDITOR,
SPECIAL PROJECTS
JEFF YOUNGQUIST

SVP OF PRINT & DIGITAL
PUBLISHING SALES
DAVID GABRIEL

BOOK DESIGN
JEFF POWELL
& CORY LEVINE

EDITOR IN CHIEF
AXEL ALONSO

CHIEF CREATIVE OFFICER
JOE QUESADA

PUBLISHER
DAN BUCKLEY

EXECUTIVE PRODUCER
ALAN FINE

WRITER
RICK REMENDER

PENCILER (#6-9) & BREAKDOWNS (#10)
JOHN ROMITA JR.

INKERS (#6-9) & FINISHES (#10)
TOM PALMER (#6-7 & #9-10),
KLAUS JANSON (#6-10)
& SCOTT HANNA (#6-10)

COLORISTS
DEAN WHITE
WITH RACHELLE ROSENBERG (#10)

LETTERER
VC'S JOE CARAMAGNA

COVER ARTISTS
JOHN ROMITA JR.,
KLAUS JANSON
& DEAN WHITE

ASSISTANT EDITOR
JAKE THOMAS

EDITORS
TOM BREVOORT
WITH LAUREN SANKOVITCH

CAPTAIN AMERICA CREATED BY
JOE SIMON & JACK KIRBY

CAPTAIN AMERICA VOL. 2: CASTAWAY IN DIMENSION Z BOOK 2. Contains material originally published in magazine form as CAPTAIN AMERICA #6-10. First printing 2013. ISBN# 978-0-7851-6827-0. Published by MARVEL WORLDWIDE, INC., a subsidiary of MARVEL ENTERTAINMENT, LLC. OFFICE OF PUBLICATION: 135 West 50th Street, New York, NY 10020. Copyright © 2012 and 2013 Marvel Characters, Inc. All rights reserved. All characters featured in this issue and the distinctive names and likenesses thereof, and all related indicia are trademarks of Marvel Characters, Inc. No similarity between any of the names, characters, persons, and/or institutions in this magazine with those of any living or dead person or institution is intended, and any such similarity which may exist is purely coincidental. **Printed in the U.S.A.** ALAN FINE, EVP - Office of the President, Marvel Worldwide, Inc. and EVP & CMO Marvel Characters B.V.; DAN BUCKLEY, Publisher & President - Print, Animation & Digital Divisions; JOE QUESADA, Chief Creative Officer; TOM BREVOORT, SVP of Publishing; DAVID BOGART, SVP of Operations & Procurement, Publishing; C.B. CEBULSKI, SVP of Creator & Content Development; DAVID GABRIEL, SVP of Print & Digital Publishing Sales; JIM O'KEEFE, VP of Operations & Logistics; DAN CARR, Executive Director of Publishing Technology; SUSAN CRESPI, Editorial Operations Manager; ALEX MORALES, Publishing Operations Manager; STAN LEE, Chairman Emeritus. For information regarding advertising in Marvel Comics or on Marvel.com, please contact Niza Disla, Director of Marvel Partnerships, at ndisla@marvel.com. For Marvel subscription inquiries, please call 800-217-9158. **Manufactured between 9/27/2013 and 11/11/2013 by R.R. DONNELLEY, INC., SALEM, VA, USA.**

10 9 8 7 6 5 4 3 2 1

During WWII a secret military experiment turned scrawny Steve Rogers into America's first super-soldier, Captain America. Near the end of the war Rogers was presumed dead in an explosion over the English Channel.

Decades later Captain America was found frozen in ice and revived. Steve Rogers awakened to a world he never imagined, a man out of time. He again took up the mantle of Captain America, defending the U.S. and the world from threats of all kinds.

PREVIOUSLY...

Twelve years ago, evil scientist Arnim Zola trapped Captain America in Dimension Z to run genetic experiments on him. Steve escaped Zola's fortress, absconding with an infant he named Ian. He raised Ian among the Phrox, Dimension Z natives who oppose Zola's reign. After a bloody battle between the Phrox and Zola's Mutates, led by his deadly daughter Jet Black, Zola took Ian and blasted Steve off a cliff.

Steve survived, and swore an oath of retribution. He's coming for his son.

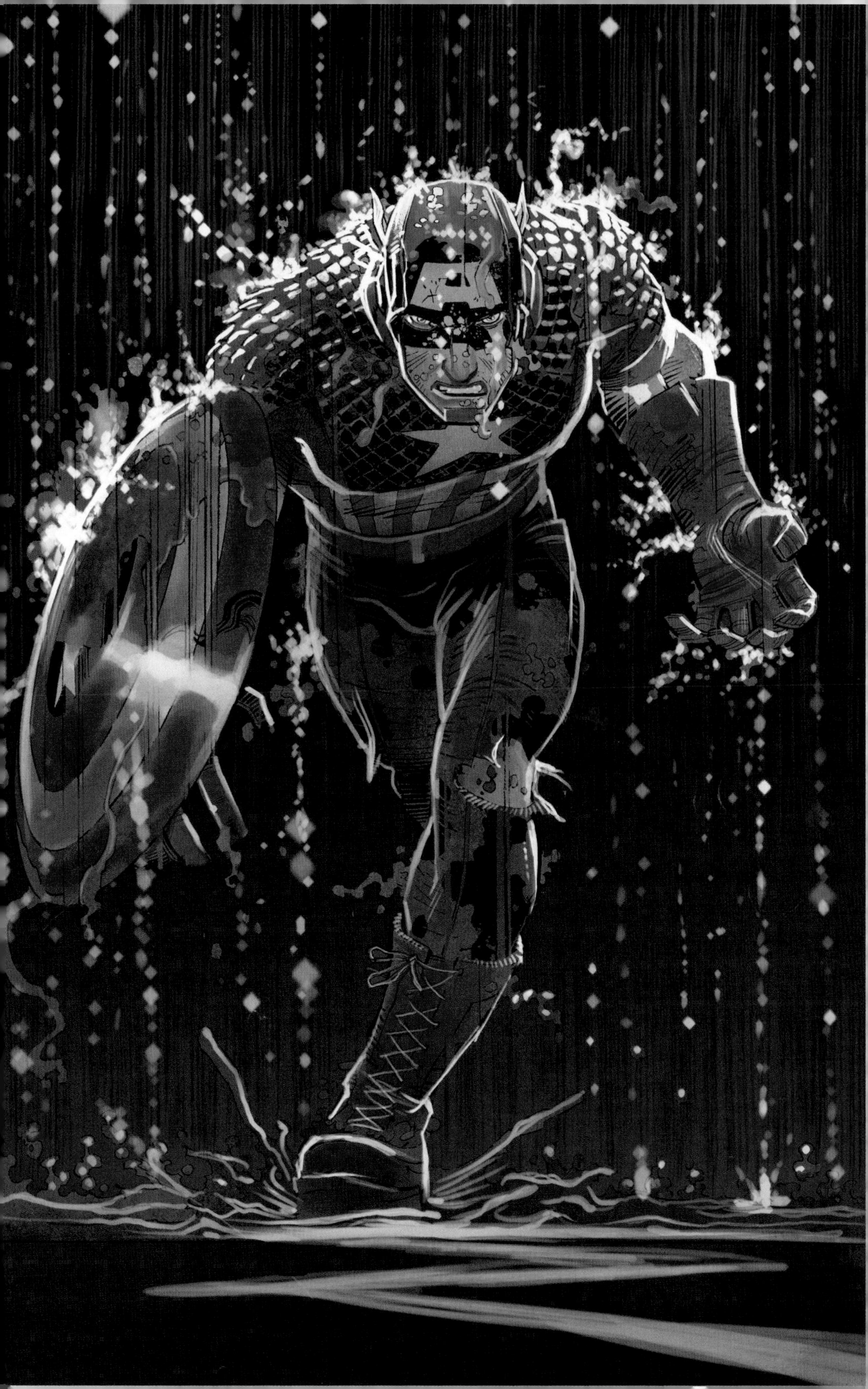

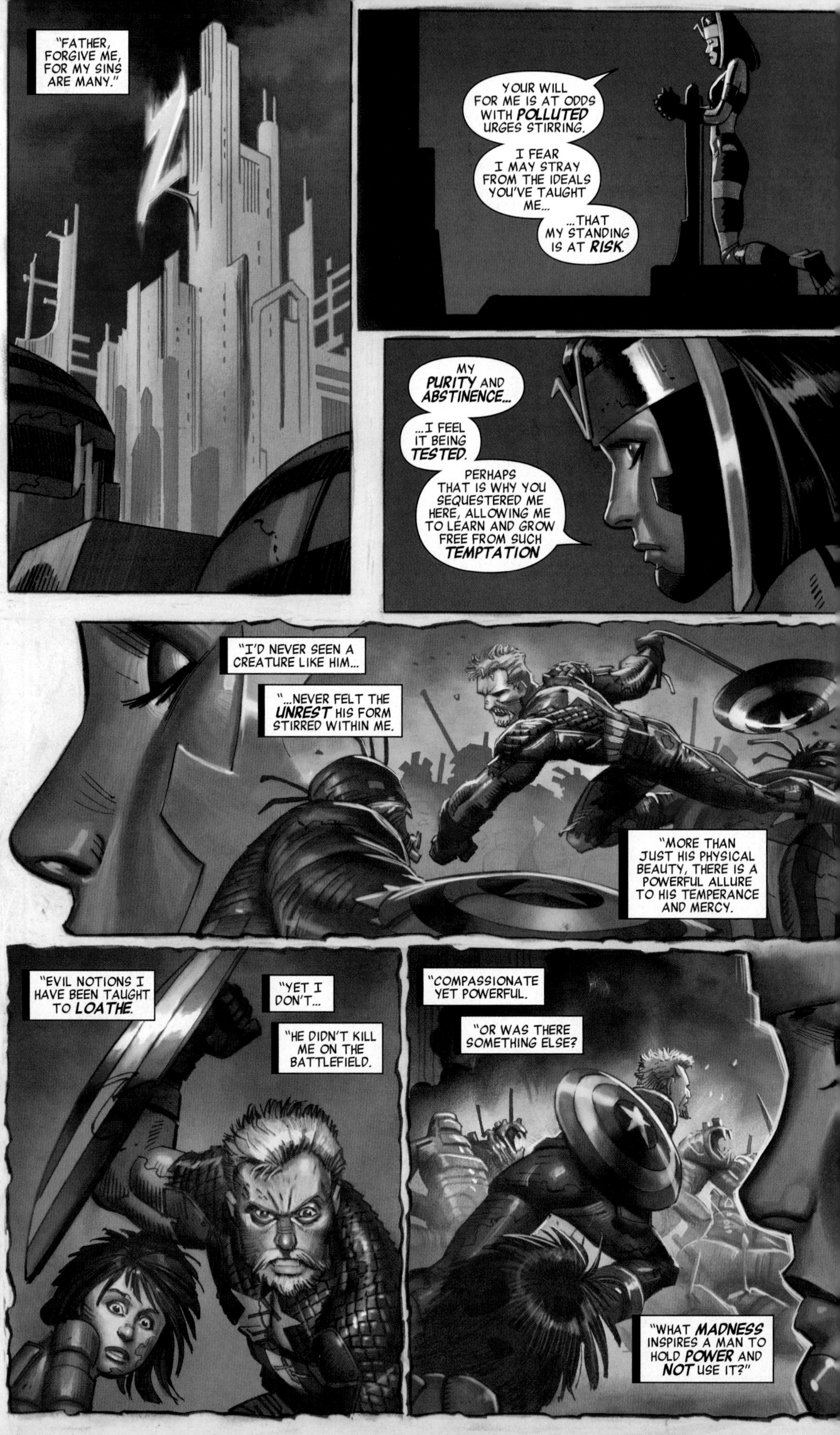
"FATHER, FORGIVE ME, FOR MY SINS ARE MANY."
YOUR WILL FOR ME IS AT ODDS WITH POLLUTED URGES STIRRING.
I FEAR I MAY STRAY FROM THE IDEALS YOU'VE TAUGHT ME...
...THAT MY STANDING IS AT RISK.
MY PURITY AND ABSTINENCE...
...I FEEL IT BEING TESTED.
PERHAPS THAT IS WHY YOU SEQUESTERED ME HERE, ALLOWING ME TO LEARN AND GROW FREE FROM SUCH TEMPTATION
"I'D NEVER SEEN A CREATURE LIKE HIM...
"...NEVER FELT THE UNREST HIS FORM STIRRED WITHIN ME.
"MORE THAN JUST HIS PHYSICAL BEAUTY, THERE IS A POWERFUL ALLURE TO HIS TEMPERANCE AND MERCY.
"EVIL NOTIONS I HAVE BEEN TAUGHT TO LOATHE.
"YET I DON'T...
"HE DIDN'T KILL ME ON THE BATTLEFIELD.
"COMPASSIONATE YET POWERFUL.
"OR WAS THERE SOMETHING ELSE?
"WHAT MADNESS INSPIRES A MAN TO HOLD POWER AND NOT USE IT?"

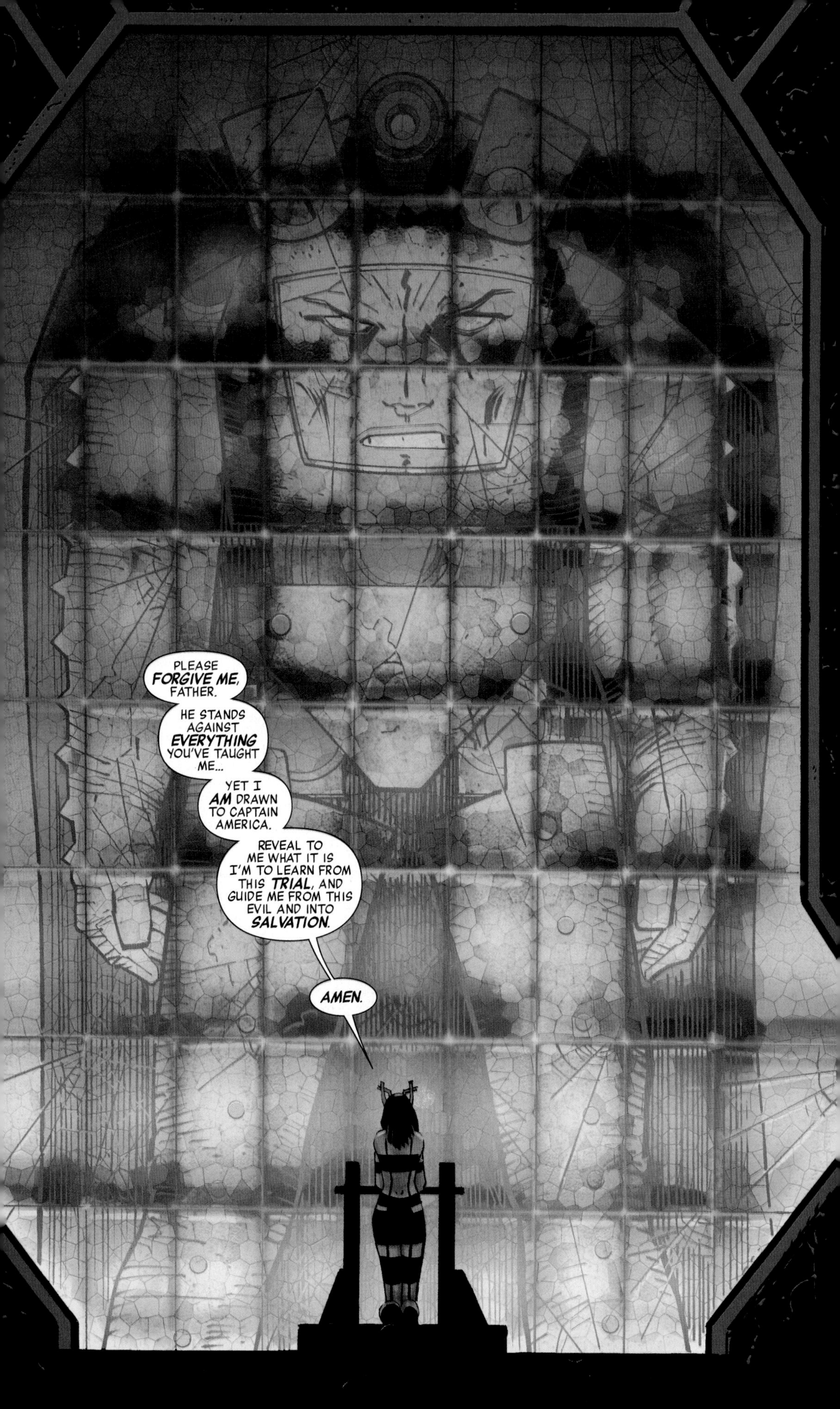

PLEASE FORGIVE ME, FATHER.
HE STANDS AGAINST EVERYTHING YOU'VE TAUGHT ME...
YET I AM DRAWN TO CAPTAIN AMERICA.
REVEAL TO ME WHAT IT IS I'M TO LEARN FROM THIS TRIAL, AND GUIDE ME FROM THIS EVIL AND INTO SALVATION.
AMEN.

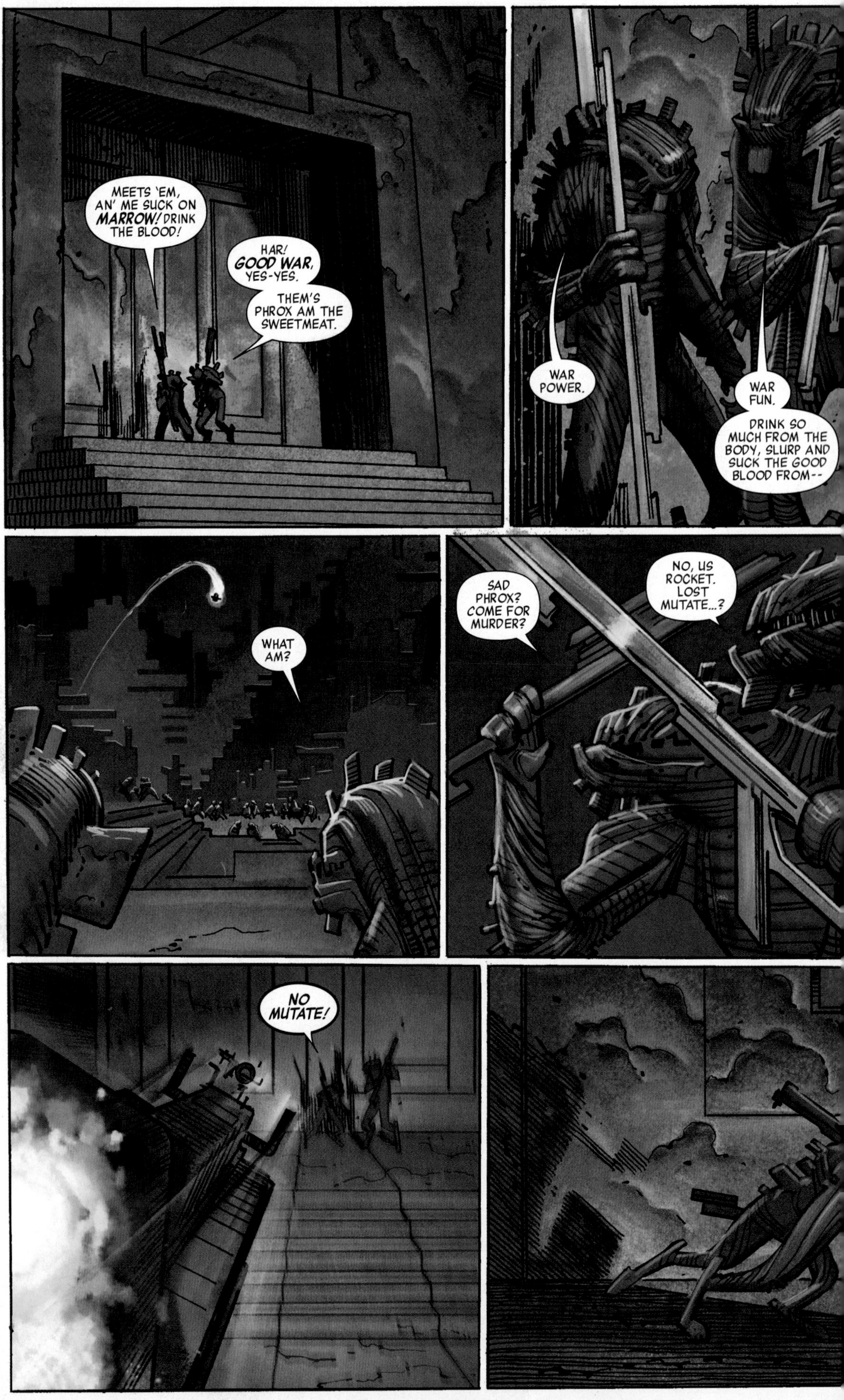
MEETS 'EM, AN' ME SUCK ON MARROW! DRINK THE BLOOD!
HAR! GOOD WAR, YES-YES.
THEM'S PHROX AM THE SWEETMEAT.
WAR POWER.
WAR FUN.
DRINK SO MUCH FROM THE BODY, SLURP AND SUCK THE GOOD BLOOD FROM--
WHAT AM?
SAD PHROX? COME FOR MURDER?
NO, US ROCKET. LOST MUTATE...?
NO MUTATE!

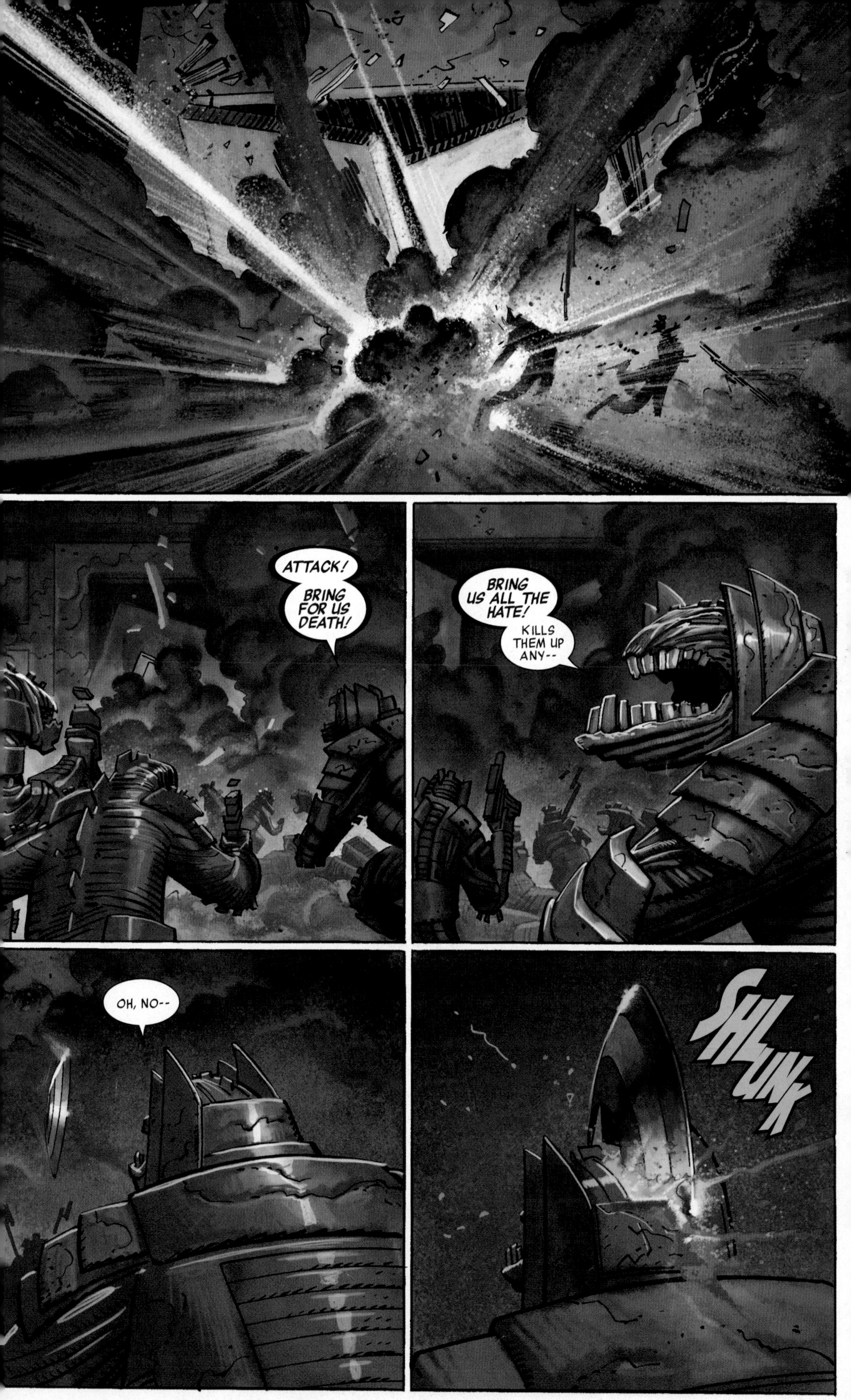
ATTACK!
BRING FOR US DEATH!
BRING US ALL THE HATE!
KILLS THEM UP ANY--
OH, NO--
SHLUNK

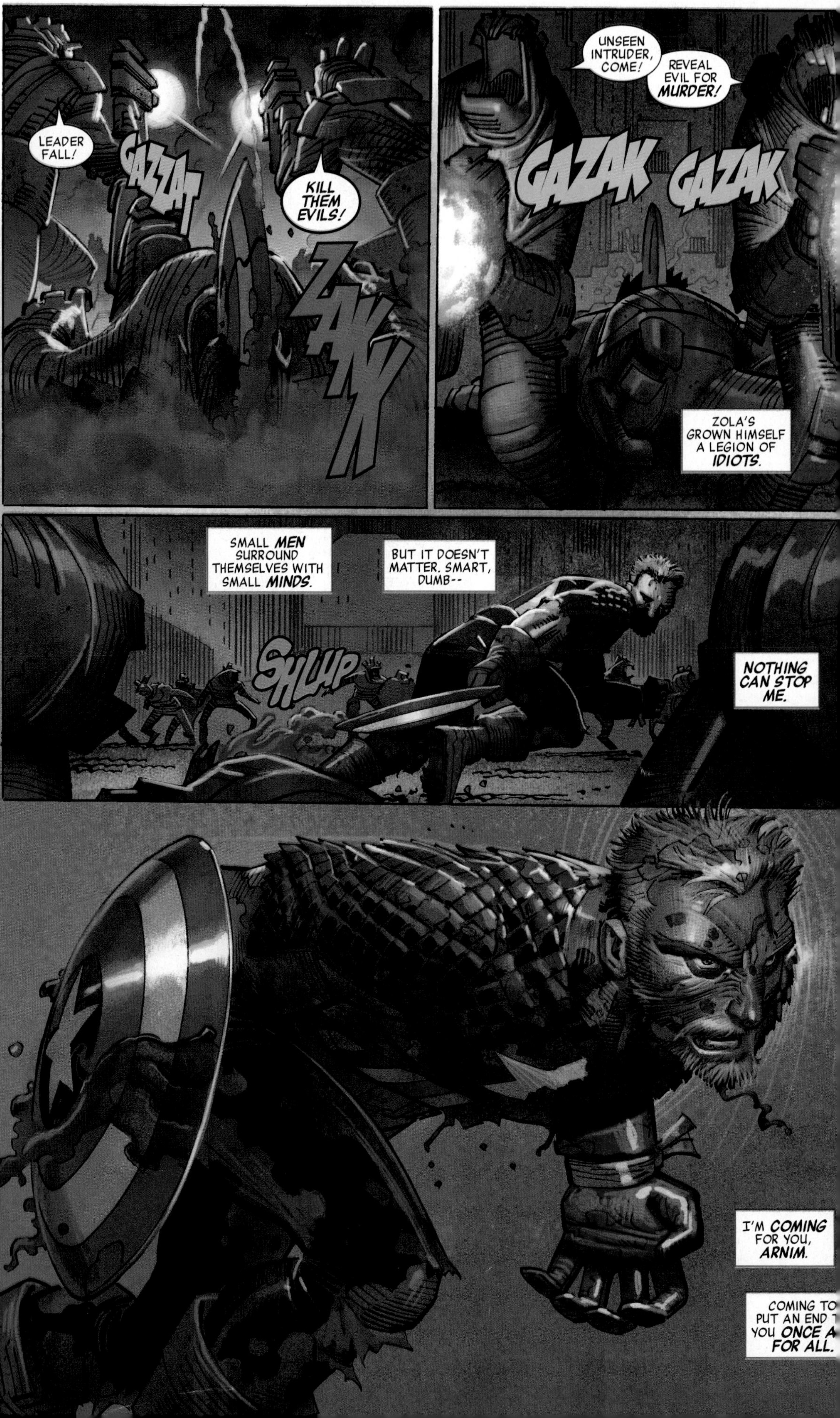
LEADER FALL!
GAZZAT
KILL THEM EVILS!
ZAKK
UNSEEN INTRUDER, COME!
REVEAL EVIL FOR MURDER!
GAZAK GAZAK
ZOLA'S GROWN HIMSELF A LEGION OF IDIOTS.
SMALL MEN SURROUND THEMSELVES WITH SMALL MINDS.
BUT IT DOESN'T MATTER. SMART, DUMB--
SHLUP
NOTHING CAN STOP ME.
I'M COMING FOR YOU, ARNIM.
COMING TO PUT AN END YOU ONCE A FOR ALL.

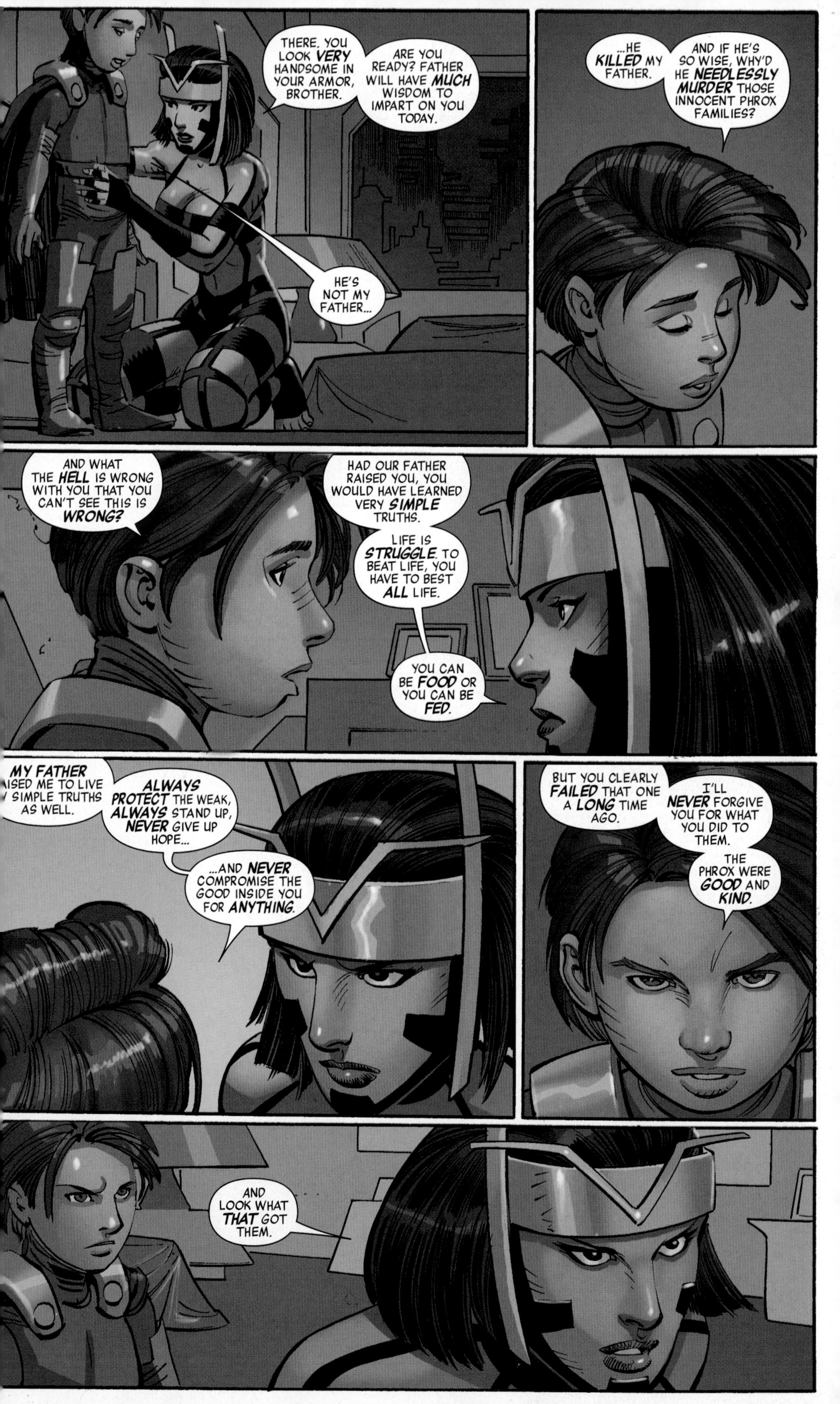

THERE. YOU LOOK VERY HANDSOME IN YOUR ARMOR, BROTHER.
ARE YOU READY? FATHER WILL HAVE MUCH WISDOM TO IMPART ON YOU TODAY.
HE'S NOT MY FATHER...
...HE KILLED MY FATHER.
AND IF HE'S SO WISE, WHY'D HE NEEDLESSLY MURDER THOSE INNOCENT PHROX FAMILIES?
AND WHAT THE HELL IS WRONG WITH YOU THAT YOU CAN'T SEE THIS IS WRONG?
HAD OUR FATHER RAISED YOU, YOU WOULD HAVE LEARNED VERY SIMPLE TRUTHS.
LIFE IS STRUGGLE. TO BEAT LIFE, YOU HAVE TO BEST ALL LIFE.
YOU CAN BE FOOD OR YOU CAN BE FED.
MY FATHER
AISED ME TO LIVE
SIMPLE TRUTHS AS WELL.
ALWAYS PROTECT THE WEAK, ALWAYS STAND UP, NEVER GIVE UP HOPE...
...AND NEVER COMPROMISE THE GOOD INSIDE YOU FOR ANYTHING.
BUT YOU CLEARLY FAILED THAT ONE A LONG TIME AGO.
I'LL NEVER FORGIVE YOU FOR WHAT YOU DID TO THEM.
THE PHROX WERE GOOD AND KIND.
AND LOOK WHAT THAT GOT THEM.

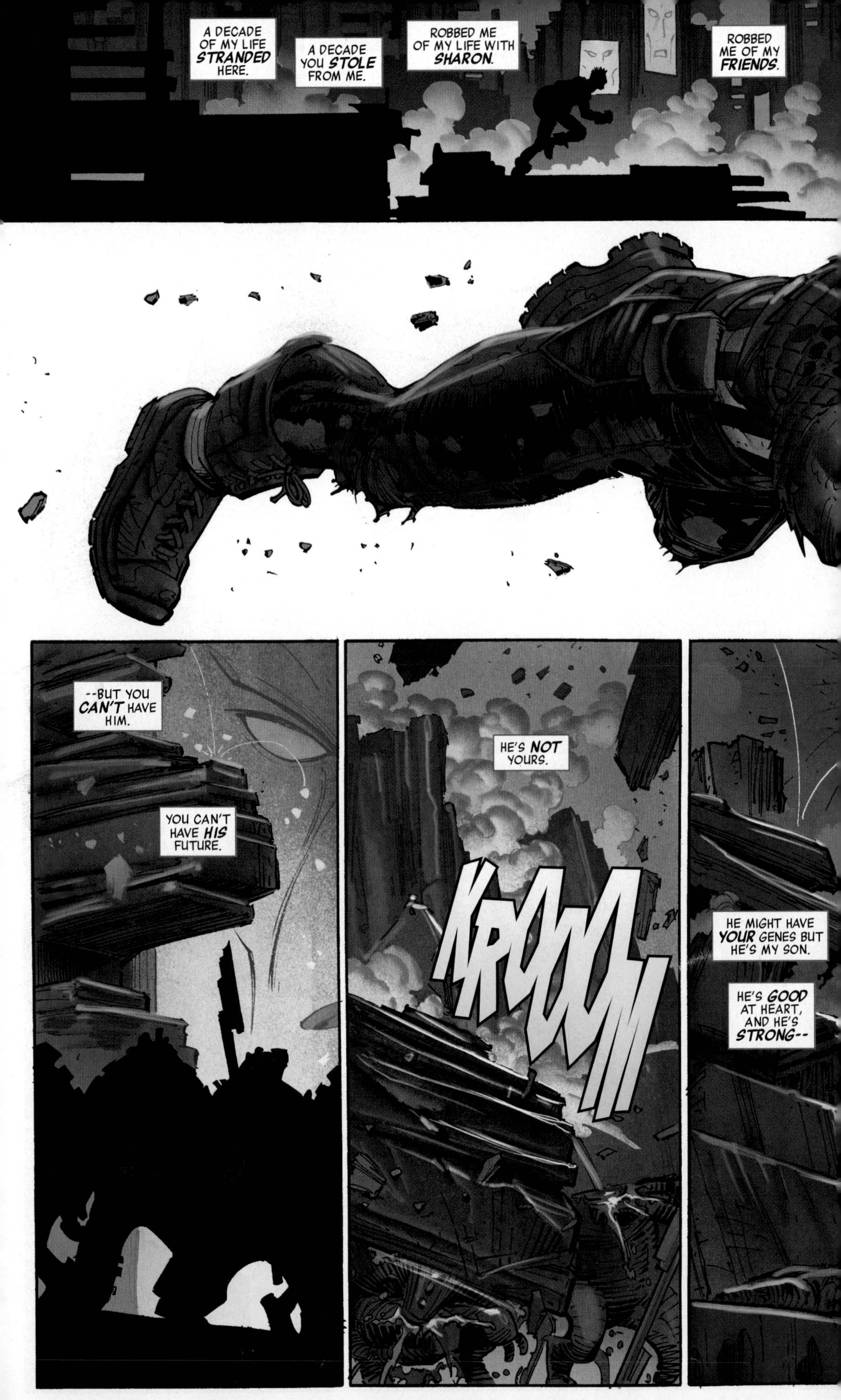

A DECADE OF MY LIFE STRANDED HERE.
A DECADE YOU STOLE FROM ME.
ROBBED ME OF MY LIFE WITH SHARON.
ROBBED ME OF MY FRIENDS.
--BUT YOU CAN'T HAVE HIM.
YOU CAN'T HAVE HIS FUTURE.
HE'S NOT YOURS.
KROOOM
HE MIGHT HAVE YOUR GENES BUT HE'S MY SON.
HE'S GOOD AT HEART, AND HE'S STRONG--

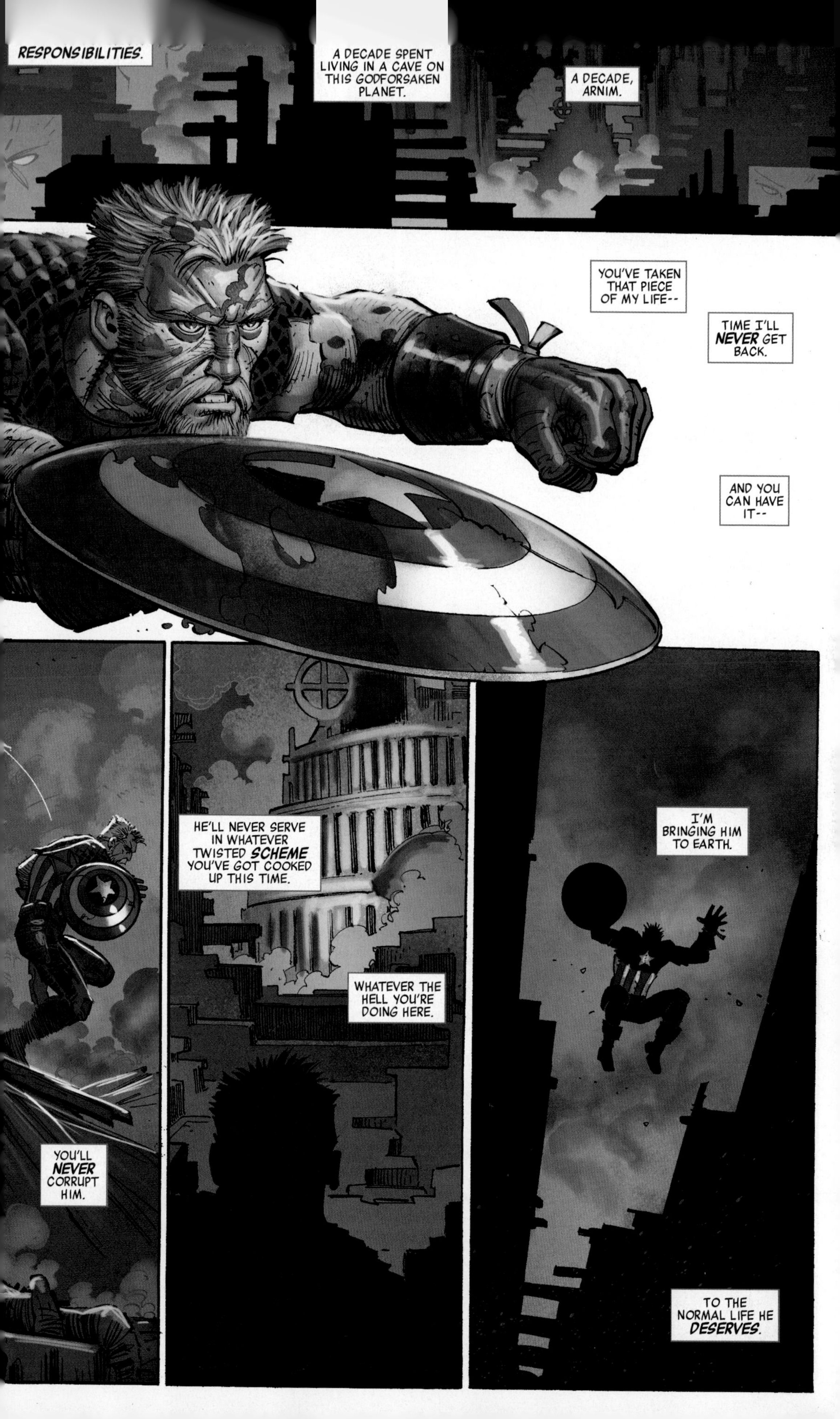
RESPONSIBILITIES.
A DECADE SPENT LIVING IN A CAVE ON THIS GODFORSAKEN PLANET.
A DECADE, ARNIM.
YOU'VE TAKEN THAT PIECE OF MY LIFE--
TIME I'LL NEVER GET BACK.
AND YOU CAN HAVE IT--
YOU'LL NEVER CORRUPT HIM.
HE'LL NEVER SERVE IN WHATEVER TWISTED SCHEME YOU'VE GOT COOKED UP THIS TIME.
WHATEVER THE HELL YOU'RE DOING HERE.
I'M BRINGING HIM TO EARTH.
TO THE NORMAL LIFE HE DESERVES.

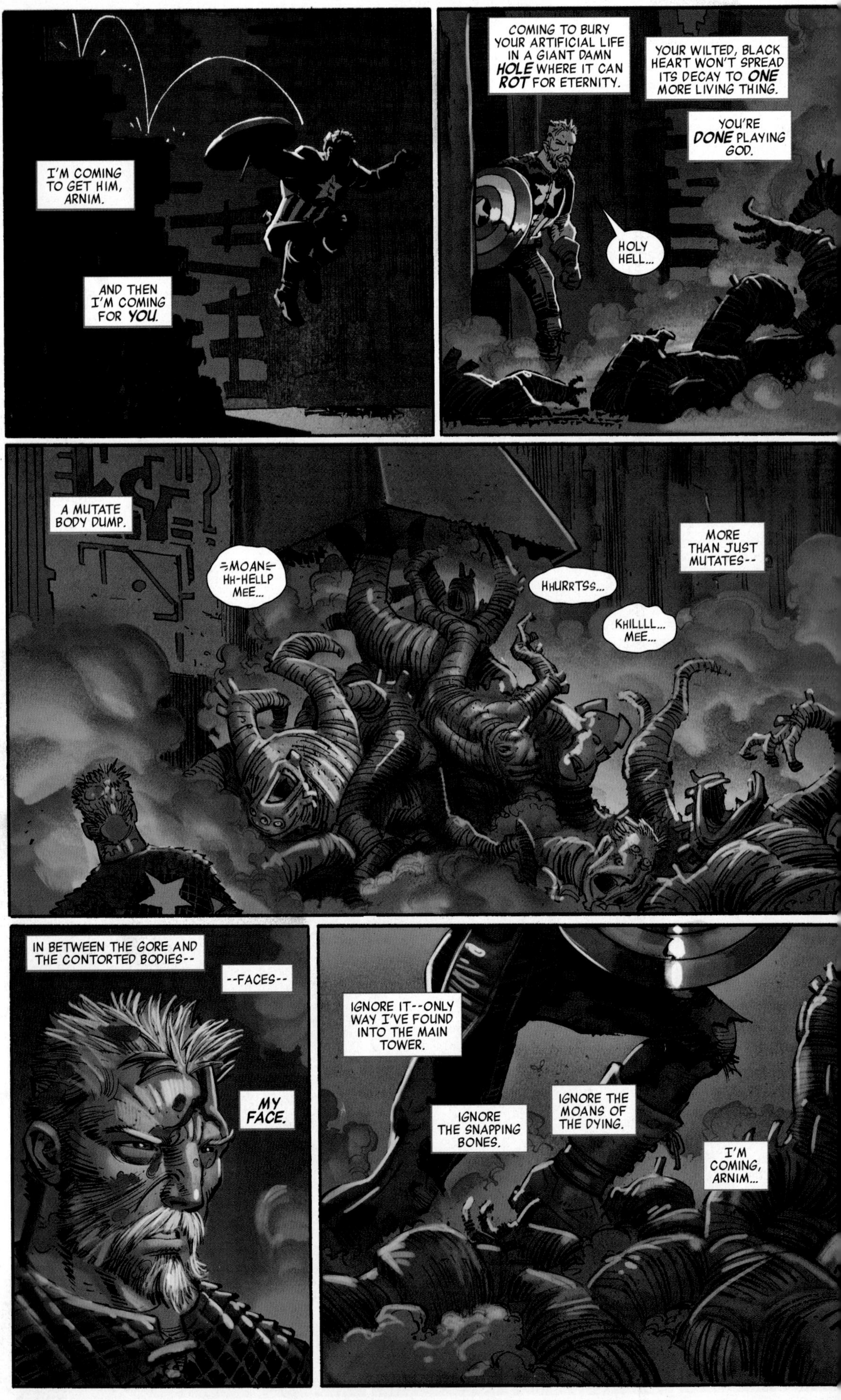
I'M COMING TO GET HIM, ARNIM.
AND THEN I'M COMING FOR YOU.
COMING TO BURY YOUR ARTIFICIAL LIFE IN A GIANT DAMN HOLE WHERE IT CAN ROT FOR ETERNITY.
YOUR WILTED, BLACK HEART WON'T SPREAD ITS DECAY TO ONE MORE LIVING THING.
YOU'RE DONE PLAYING GOD.
HOLY HELL...
A MUTATE BODY DUMP.
=MOAN= HH-HELLP MEE...
HHURRTSS...
MORE THAN JUST MUTATES--
KHILLLL... MEE...
IN BETWEEN THE GORE AND THE CONTORTED BODIES--
--FACES--
MY FACE.
IGNORE IT--ONLY WAY I'VE FOUND INTO THE MAIN TOWER.
IGNORE THE SNAPPING BONES.
IGNORE THE MOANS OF THE DYING.
I'M COMING, ARNIM...

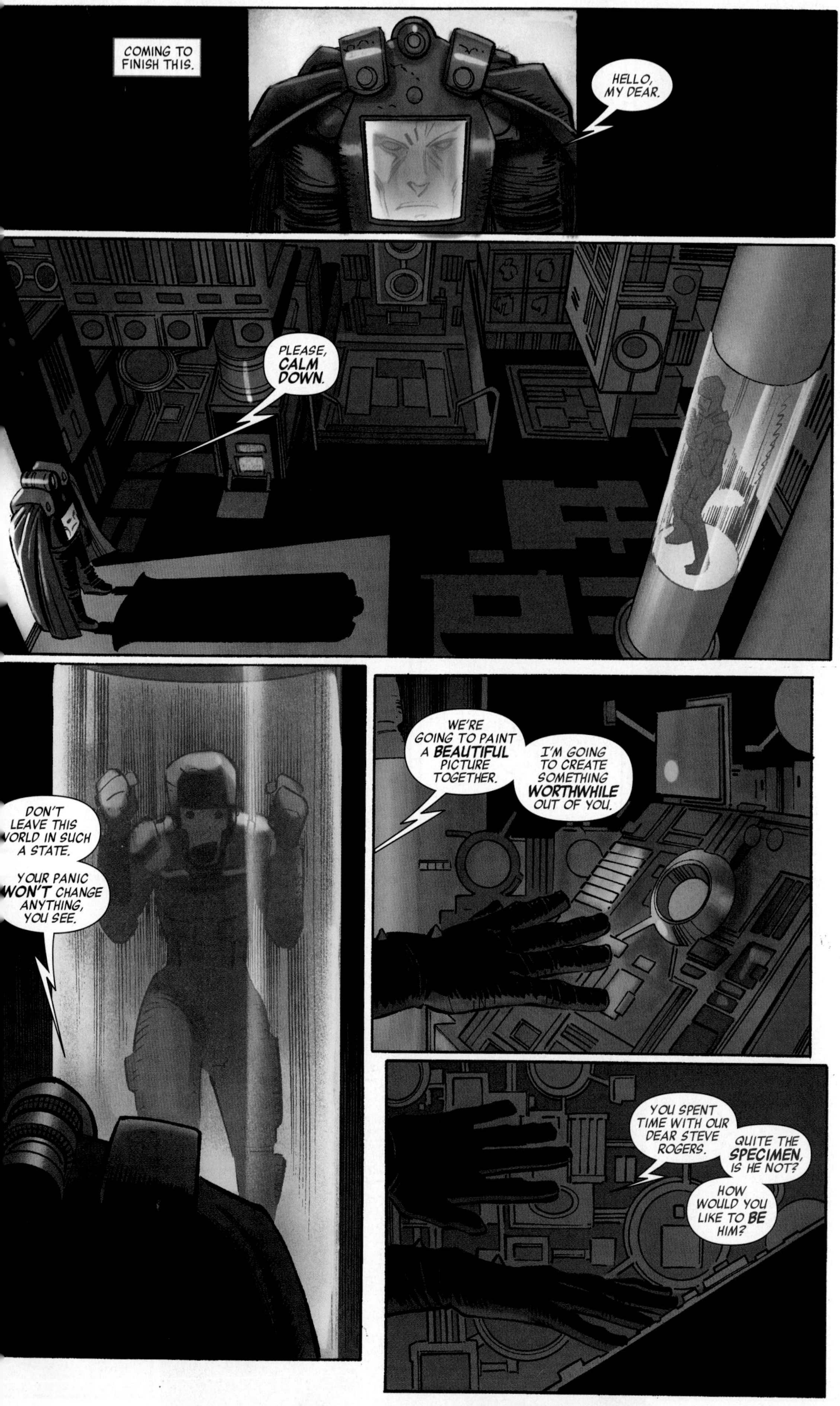
COMING TO FINISH THIS.
HELLO, MY DEAR.
PLEASE, CALM DOWN.
DON'T LEAVE THIS WORLD IN SUCH A STATE.
YOUR PANIC WON'T CHANGE ANYTHING, YOU SEE.
WE'RE GOING TO PAINT A BEAUTIFUL PICTURE TOGETHER.
I'M GOING TO CREATE SOMETHING WORTHWHILE OUT OF YOU.
YOU SPENT TIME WITH OUR DEAR STEVE ROGERS.
QUITE THE SPECIMEN, IS HE NOT?
HOW WOULD YOU LIKE TO BE HIM?

GHHAAAAKKK...

"THERE IS **MUCH** TO BE GRATEFUL FOR.

"MOST OF YOUR PHROX BRETHREN ARE SCARIFIED TO MERELY CREATE MUTATES.

"A **LOW** FATE, I ADMIT.

"**TRANSFORMING** ORGANIC MATERIAL IS SO MUCH FASTER THAN **GROWING** IT FRESH, YOU SEE.

"A PERFECT BIOLOGICAL CLAY.

SHLUKP

"YOUR PEOPLE HAVE SERVED ME WELL IN THIS CAPACITY."

YOU WILL SERVE ME IN AN EVEN **GREATER** ONE.

YOU WILL BECOME THE **PERFECT** SPY TO INFILTRATE EARTH.

A NECESSARY MEASURE BEFORE I CAN BEGIN THE **EXPANSION.**

"YOU WILL BECOME CAPTAIN AMERICA.

"WE MUST CONCENTRATE, BUILDING WITH GREAT CARE.

"HENCE FAR SOME COMPONENT, ALMOST LIVING WITHIN THE SUPER-SOLDIER SERUM, HAS MADE IT **NEARLY** IMPOSSIBLE TO CREATE A PERFECT CLONE."

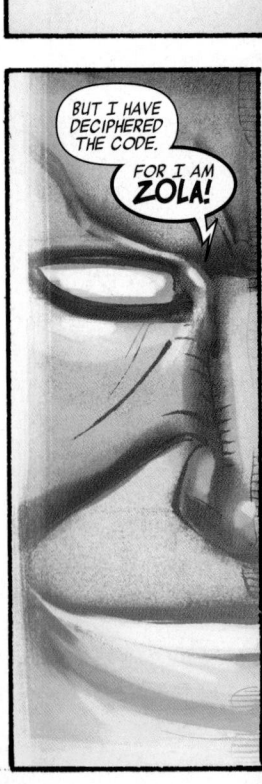

BUT I HAVE DECIPHERED THE CODE.

FOR I AM **ZOLA!**

COME NOW, ALMOST THERE...

BEND TO MY WILL!

HOLD YOUR FORM... YES--

YES! FINALLY, AFTER ALL THIS TIME...

MASTER ZOLA!

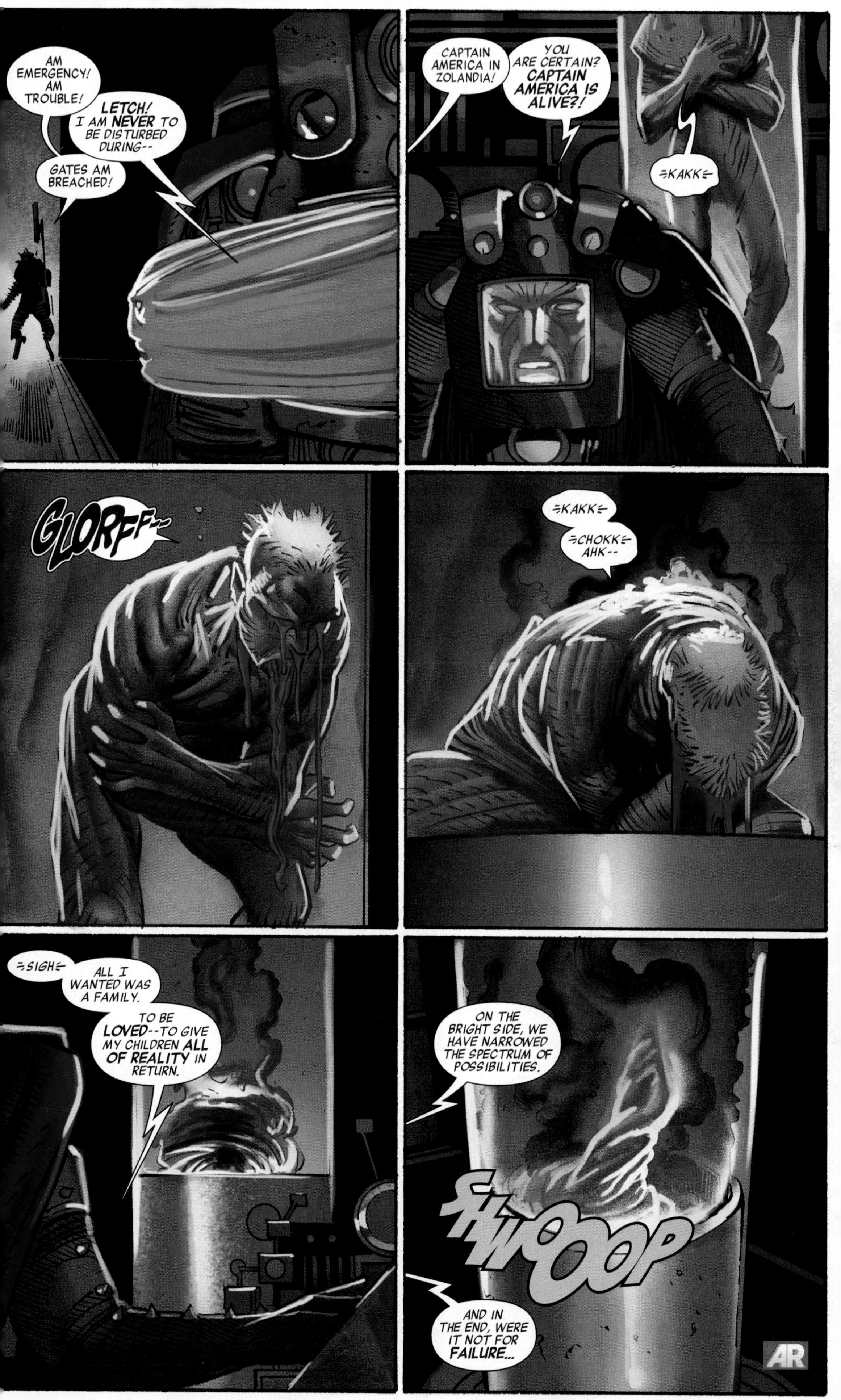
AM EMERGENCY! AM TROUBLE!
LETCH! I AM NEVER TO BE DISTURBED DURING--
GATES AM BREACHED!
CAPTAIN AMERICA IN ZOLANDIA!
YOU ARE CERTAIN? CAPTAIN AMERICA IS ALIVE?!
=KAKK=
GLORFF--
=KAKK=
=CHOKK= AHK--
=SIGH=
ALL I WANTED WAS A FAMILY.
TO BE LOVED--TO GIVE MY CHILDREN ALL OF REALITY IN RETURN.
ON THE BRIGHT SIDE, WE HAVE NARROWED THE SPECTRUM OF POSSIBILITIES.
SHWOOOP
AND IN THE END, WERE IT NOT FOR FAILURE...
AR

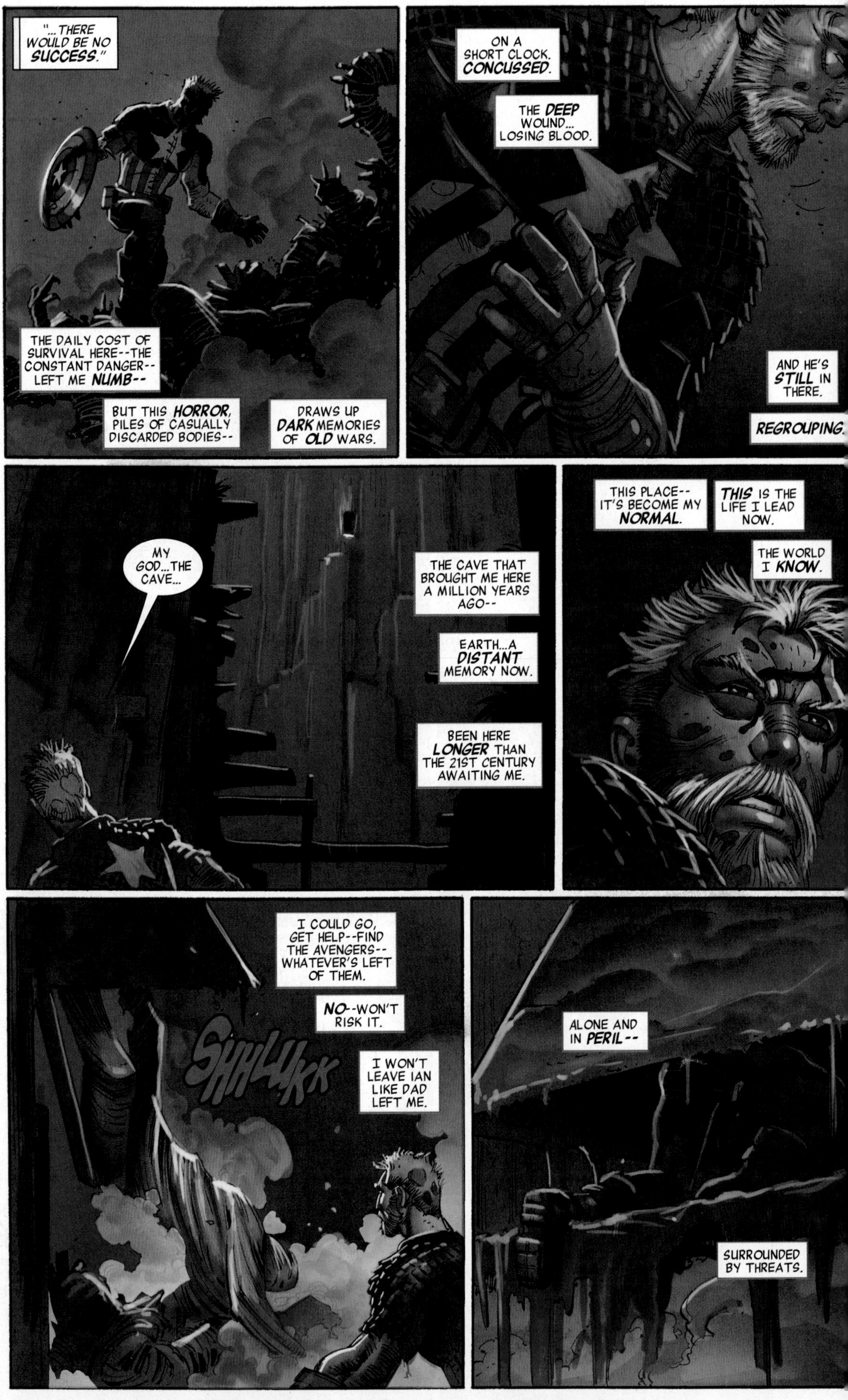
"...THERE WOULD BE NO SUCCESS."
THE DAILY COST OF SURVIVAL HERE--THE CONSTANT DANGER--LEFT ME NUMB--
BUT THIS HORROR, PILES OF CASUALLY DISCARDED BODIES--
DRAWS UP DARK MEMORIES OF OLD WARS.
ON A SHORT CLOCK. CONCUSSED.
THE DEEP WOUND... LOSING BLOOD.
AND HE'S STILL IN THERE.
REGROUPING.
MY GOD...THE CAVE...
THE CAVE THAT BROUGHT ME HERE A MILLION YEARS AGO--
EARTH...A DISTANT MEMORY NOW.
BEEN HERE LONGER THAN THE 21ST CENTURY AWAITING ME.
THIS PLACE--IT'S BECOME MY NORMAL.
THIS IS THE LIFE I LEAD NOW.
THE WORLD I KNOW.
I COULD GO, GET HELP--FIND THE AVENGERS--WHATEVER'S LEFT OF THEM.
NO--WON'T RISK IT.
SHHLUKK
I WON'T LEAVE IAN LIKE DAD LEFT ME.
ALONE AND IN PERIL--
SURROUNDED BY THREATS.

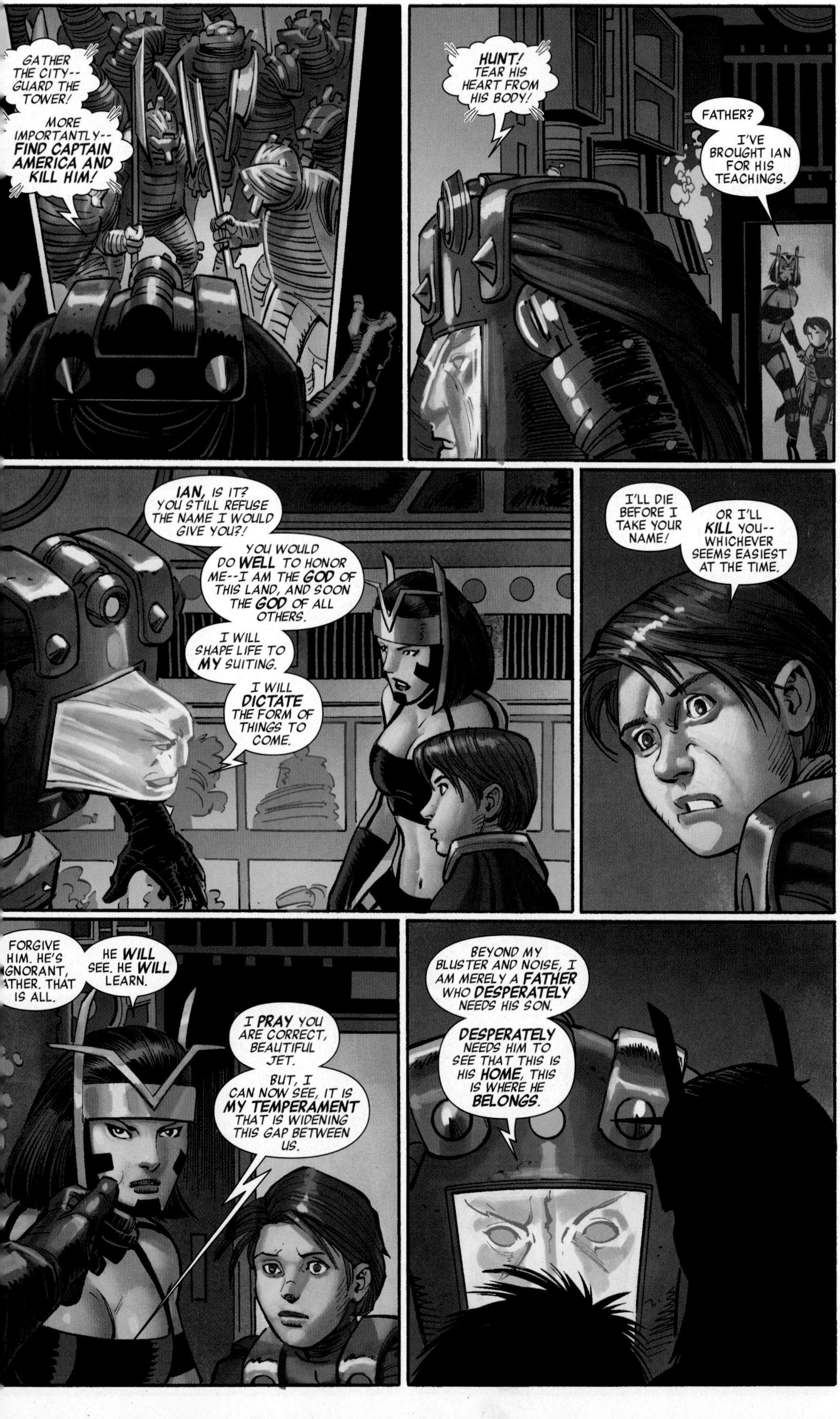
GATHER THE CITY-- GUARD THE TOWER!
MORE IMPORTANTLY-- FIND CAPTAIN AMERICA AND KILL HIM!
HUNT! TEAR HIS HEART FROM HIS BODY!
FATHER?
I'VE BROUGHT IAN FOR HIS TEACHINGS.
IAN, IS IT? YOU STILL REFUSE THE NAME I WOULD GIVE YOU?!
YOU WOULD DO WELL TO HONOR ME--I AM THE GOD OF THIS LAND, AND SOON THE GOD OF ALL OTHERS.
I WILL SHAPE LIFE TO MY SUITING.
I WILL DICTATE THE FORM OF THINGS TO COME.
I'LL DIE BEFORE I TAKE YOUR NAME!
OR I'LL KILL YOU-- WHICHEVER SEEMS EASIEST AT THE TIME.
FORGIVE HIM. HE'S IGNORANT, FATHER. THAT IS ALL.
HE WILL SEE. HE WILL LEARN.
I PRAY YOU ARE CORRECT, BEAUTIFUL JET.
BUT, I CAN NOW SEE, IT IS MY TEMPERAMENT THAT IS WIDENING THIS GAP BETWEEN US.
BEYOND MY BLUSTER AND NOISE, I AM MERELY A FATHER WHO DESPERATELY NEEDS HIS SON.
DESPERATELY NEEDS HIM TO SEE THAT THIS IS HIS HOME, THIS IS WHERE HE BELONGS.

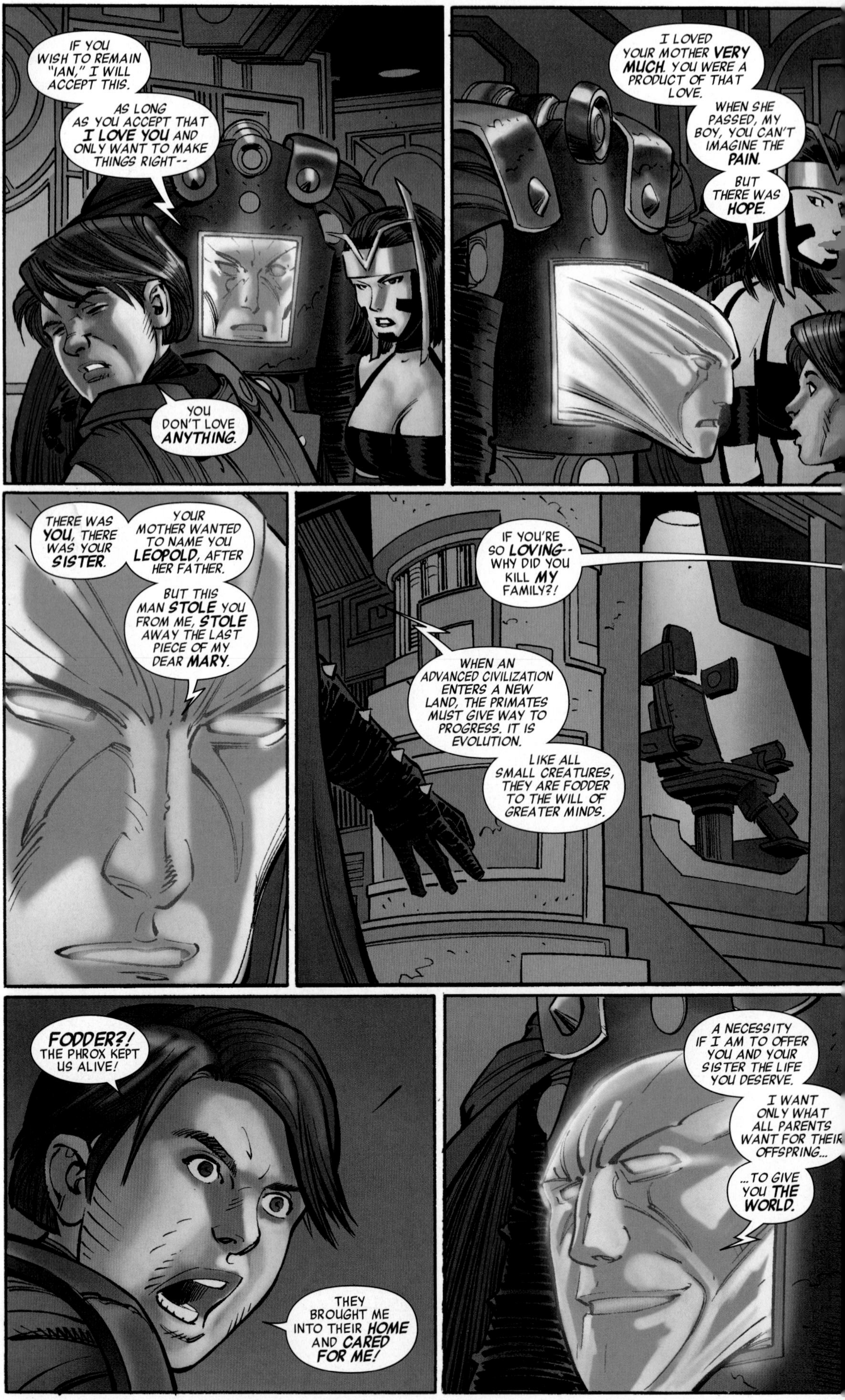

IF YOU WISH TO REMAIN "IAN," I WILL ACCEPT THIS.
AS LONG AS YOU ACCEPT THAT I LOVE YOU AND ONLY WANT TO MAKE THINGS RIGHT--
YOU DON'T LOVE ANYTHING.
I LOVED YOUR MOTHER VERY MUCH. YOU WERE A PRODUCT OF THAT LOVE.
WHEN SHE PASSED, MY BOY, YOU CAN'T IMAGINE THE PAIN.
BUT THERE WAS HOPE.
THERE WAS YOU, THERE WAS YOUR SISTER.
YOUR MOTHER WANTED TO NAME YOU LEOPOLD, AFTER HER FATHER.
BUT THIS MAN STOLE YOU FROM ME, STOLE AWAY THE LAST PIECE OF MY DEAR MARY.
IF YOU'RE SO LOVING-- WHY DID YOU KILL MY FAMILY?!
WHEN AN ADVANCED CIVILIZATION ENTERS A NEW LAND, THE PRIMATES MUST GIVE WAY TO PROGRESS. IT IS EVOLUTION.
LIKE ALL SMALL CREATURES, THEY ARE FODDER TO THE WILL OF GREATER MINDS.
FODDER?! THE PHROX KEPT US ALIVE!
THEY BROUGHT ME INTO THEIR HOME AND CARED FOR ME!
A NECESSITY IF I AM TO OFFER YOU AND YOUR SISTER THE LIFE YOU DESERVE.
I WANT ONLY WHAT ALL PARENTS WANT FOR THEIR OFFSPRING...
...TO GIVE YOU THE WORLD.

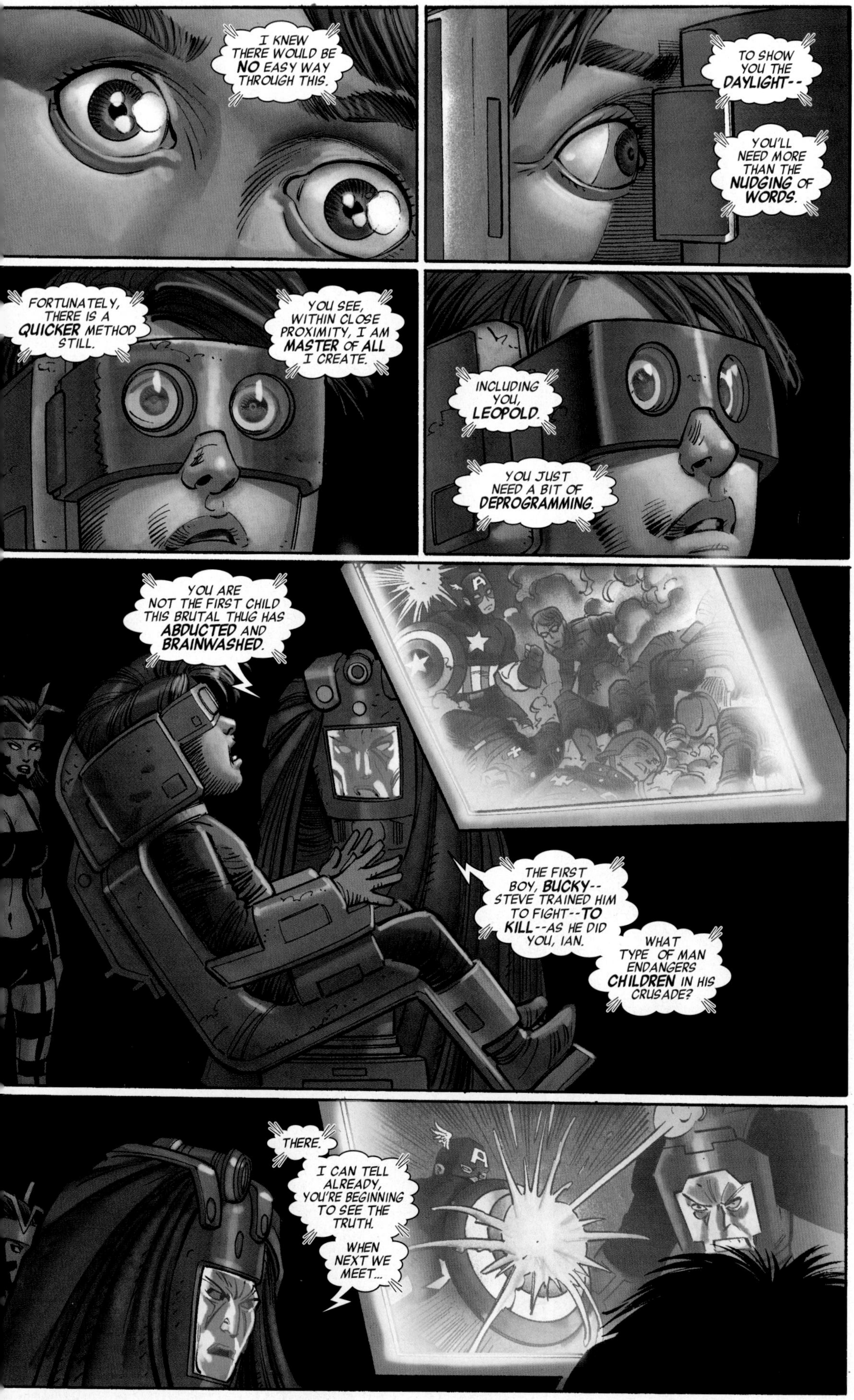
I KNEW THERE WOULD BE NO EASY WAY THROUGH THIS.
TO SHOW YOU THE DAYLIGHT--
YOU'LL NEED MORE THAN THE NUDGING OF WORDS.
FORTUNATELY, THERE IS A QUICKER METHOD STILL.
YOU SEE, WITHIN CLOSE PROXIMITY, I AM MASTER OF ALL I CREATE.
INCLUDING YOU, LEOPOLD.
YOU JUST NEED A BIT OF DEPROGRAMMING.
YOU ARE NOT THE FIRST CHILD THIS BRUTAL THUG HAS ABDUCTED AND BRAINWASHED.
THE FIRST BOY, BUCKY--STEVE TRAINED HIM TO FIGHT--TO KILL--AS HE DID YOU, IAN.
WHAT TYPE OF MAN ENDANGERS CHILDREN IN HIS CRUSADE?
THERE.
I CAN TELL ALREADY, YOU'RE BEGINNING TO SEE THE TRUTH.
WHEN NEXT WE MEET...

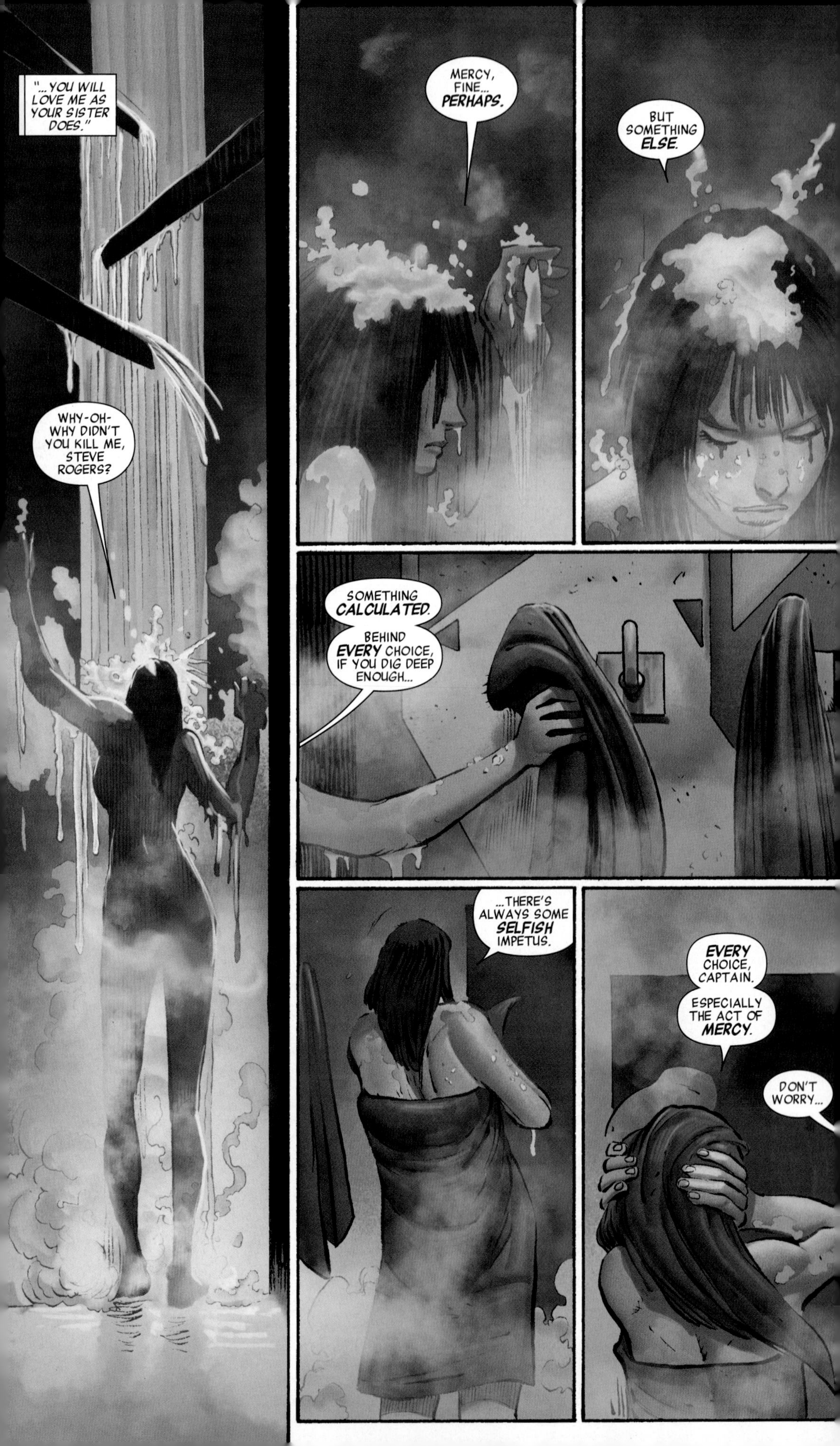
"...YOU WILL LOVE ME AS YOUR SISTER DOES."
WHY-OH-WHY DIDN'T YOU KILL ME, STEVE ROGERS?
MERCY, FINE... PERHAPS.
BUT SOMETHING ELSE.
SOMETHING CALCULATED.
BEHIND EVERY CHOICE, IF YOU DIG DEEP ENOUGH...
...THERE'S ALWAYS SOME SELFISH IMPETUS.
EVERY CHOICE, CAPTAIN.
ESPECIALLY THE ACT OF MERCY.
DON'T WORRY...

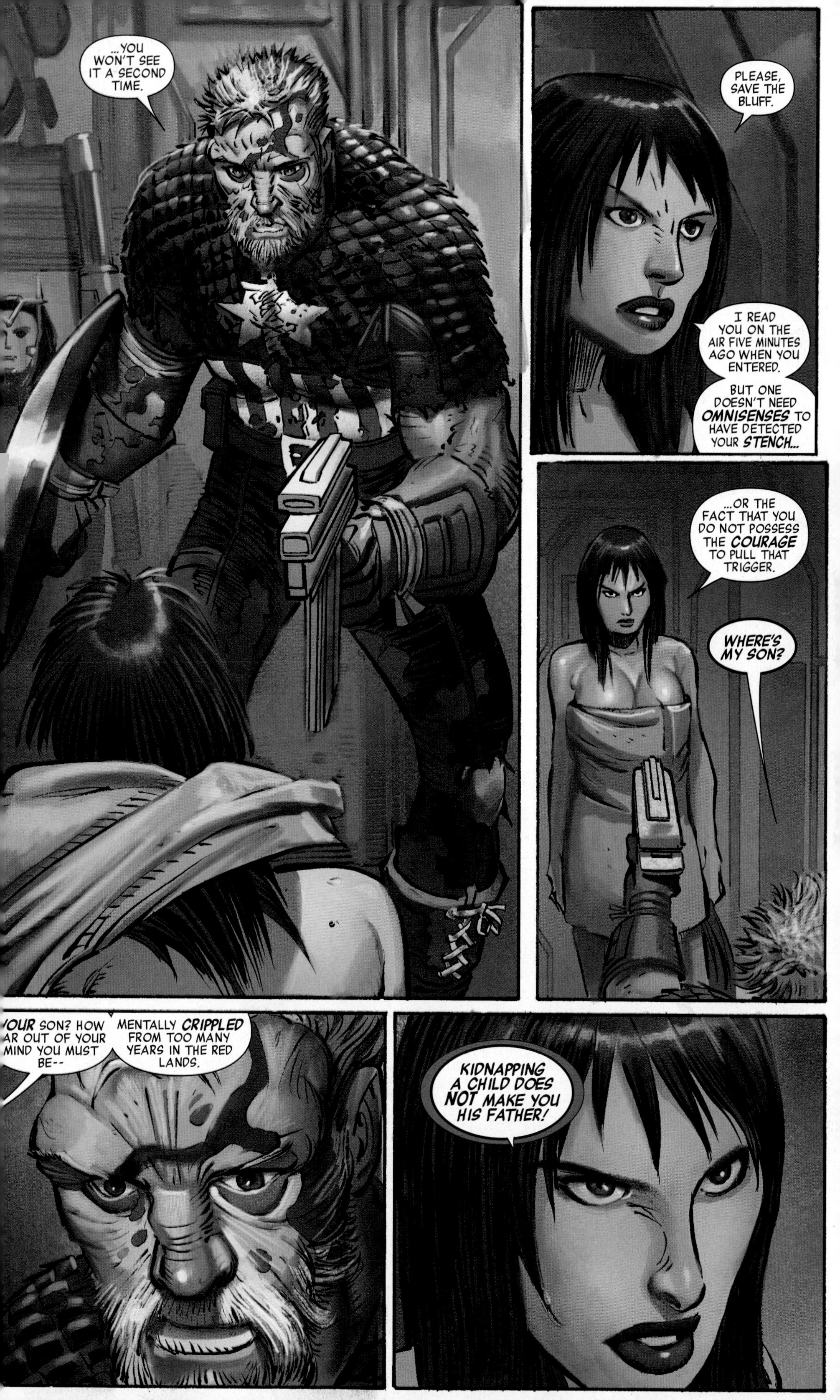

...YOU WON'T SEE IT A SECOND TIME.
PLEASE, SAVE THE BLUFF.
I READ YOU ON THE AIR FIVE MINUTES AGO WHEN YOU ENTERED.
BUT ONE DOESN'T NEED OMNISENSES TO HAVE DETECTED YOUR STENCH...
...OR THE FACT THAT YOU DO NOT POSSESS THE COURAGE TO PULL THAT TRIGGER.
WHERE'S MY SON?
YOUR SON? HOW AR OUT OF YOUR MIND YOU MUST BE--
MENTALLY CRIPPLED FROM TOO MANY YEARS IN THE RED LANDS.
KIDNAPPING A CHILD DOES NOT MAKE YOU HIS FATHER!

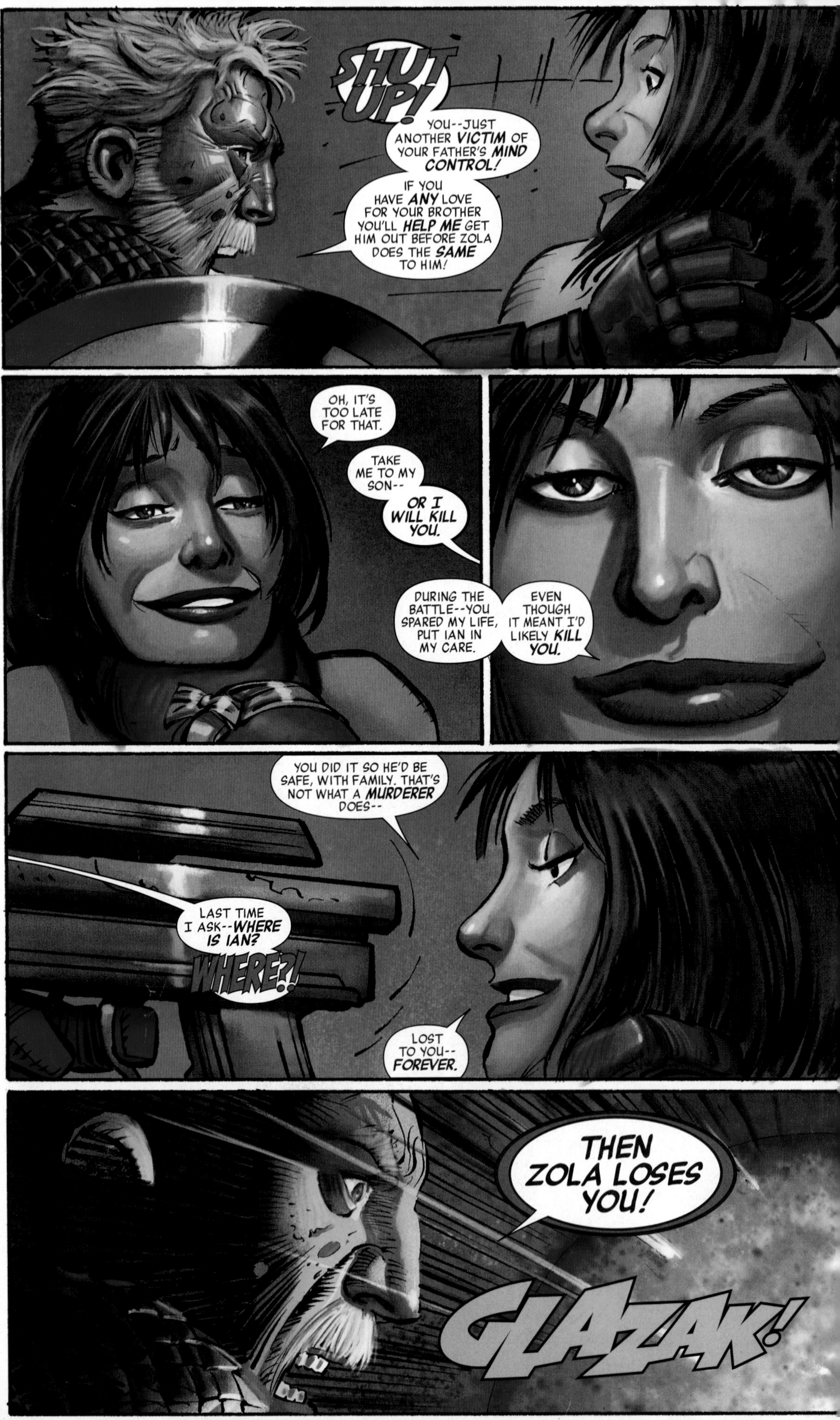
SHUT UP!
YOU--JUST ANOTHER VICTIM OF YOUR FATHER'S MIND CONTROL!
IF YOU HAVE ANY LOVE FOR YOUR BROTHER YOU'LL HELP ME GET HIM OUT BEFORE ZOLA DOES THE SAME TO HIM!
OH, IT'S TOO LATE FOR THAT.
TAKE ME TO MY SON-- OR I WILL KILL YOU.
DURING THE BATTLE--YOU SPARED MY LIFE, PUT IAN IN MY CARE.
EVEN THOUGH IT MEANT I'D LIKELY KILL YOU.
YOU DID IT SO HE'D BE SAFE, WITH FAMILY. THAT'S NOT WHAT A MURDERER DOES--
LAST TIME I ASK--WHERE IS IAN?
WHERE?!
LOST TO YOU-- FOREVER.
THEN ZOLA LOSES YOU!
CLAZAK!

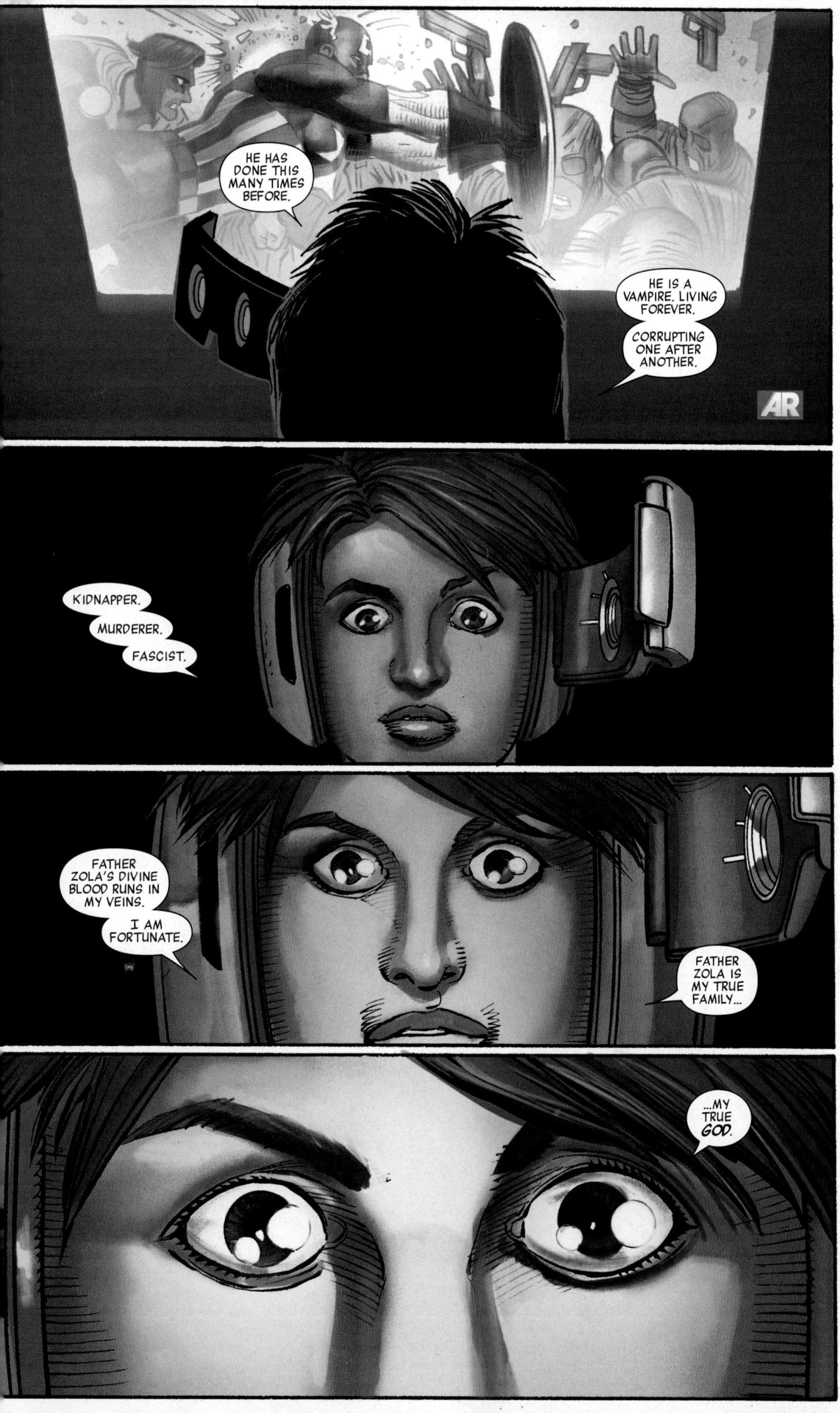
HE HAS DONE THIS MANY TIMES BEFORE.
HE IS A VAMPIRE. LIVING FOREVER.
CORRUPTING ONE AFTER ANOTHER.
AR
KIDNAPPER.
MURDERER.
FASCIST.
FATHER ZOLA'S DIVINE BLOOD RUNS IN MY VEINS.
I AM FORTUNATE.
FATHER ZOLA IS MY TRUE FAMILY...
...MY TRUE *GOD*.

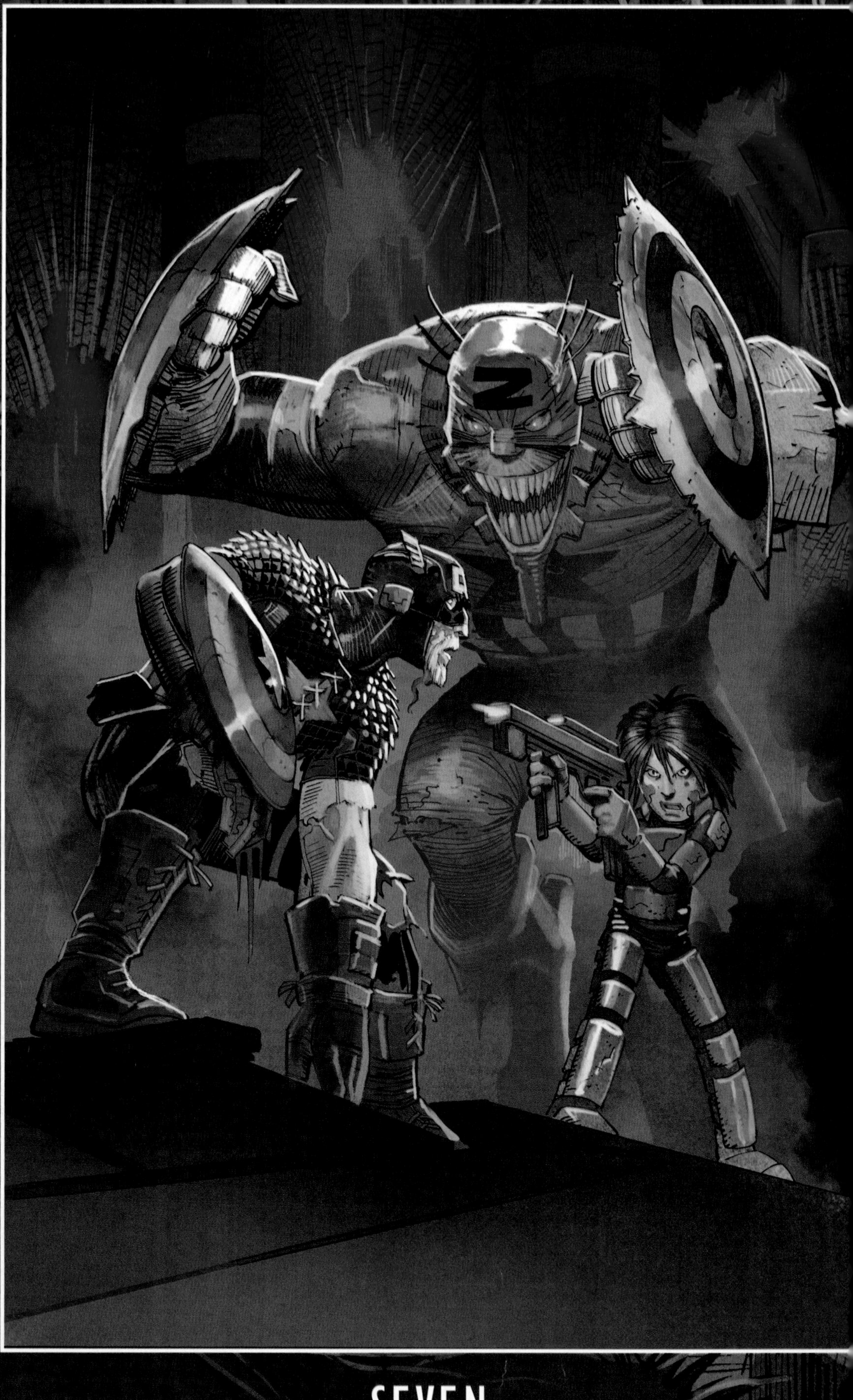

SEVEN

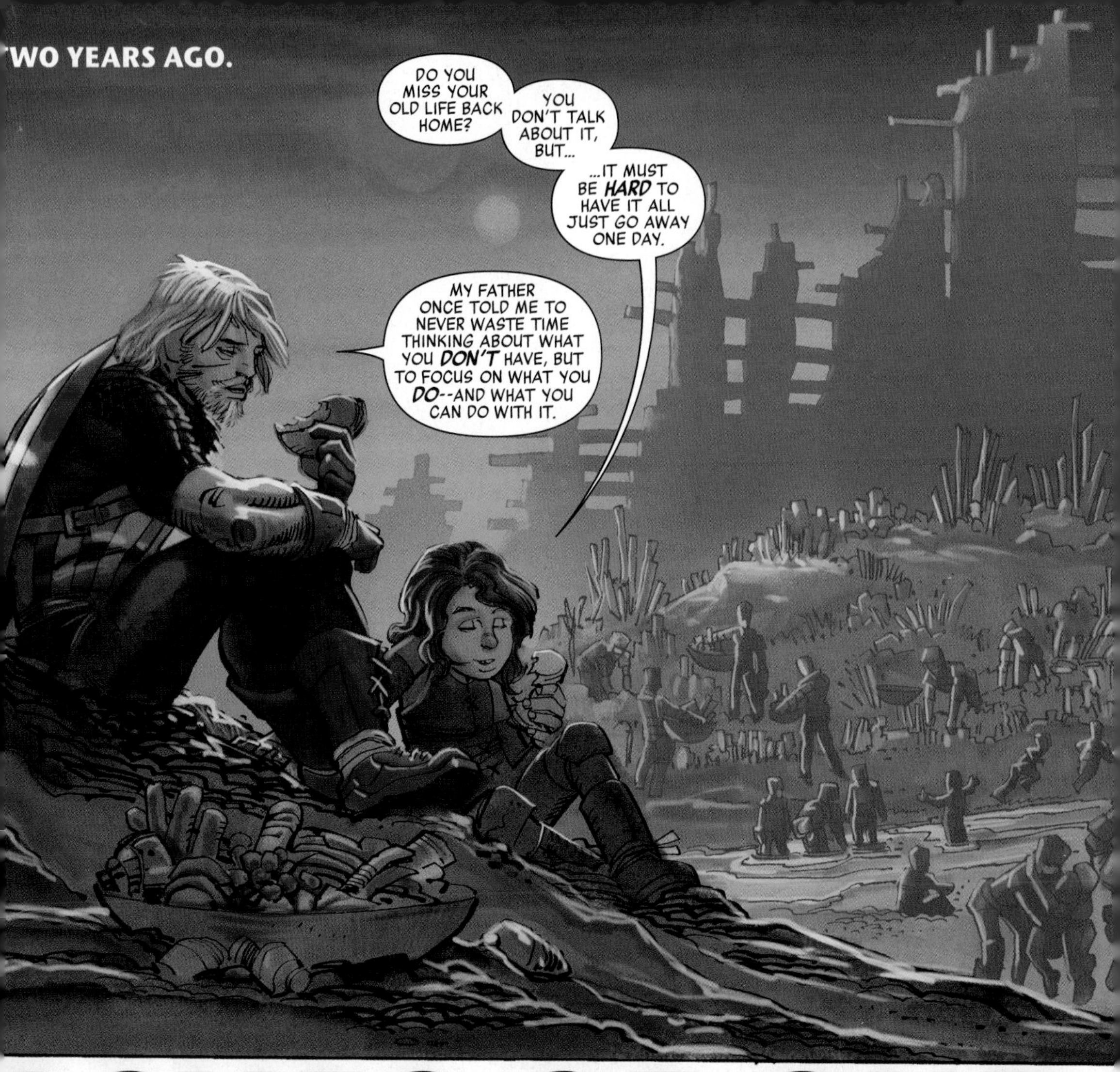

WO YEARS AGO.
DO YOU MISS YOUR OLD LIFE BACK HOME?
YOU DON'T TALK ABOUT IT, BUT...
...IT MUST BE HARD TO HAVE IT ALL JUST GO AWAY ONE DAY.
MY FATHER ONCE TOLD ME TO NEVER WASTE TIME THINKING ABOUT WHAT YOU DON'T HAVE, BUT TO FOCUS ON WHAT YOU DO--AND WHAT YOU CAN DO WITH IT.

ASHES OF OUR FATHERS

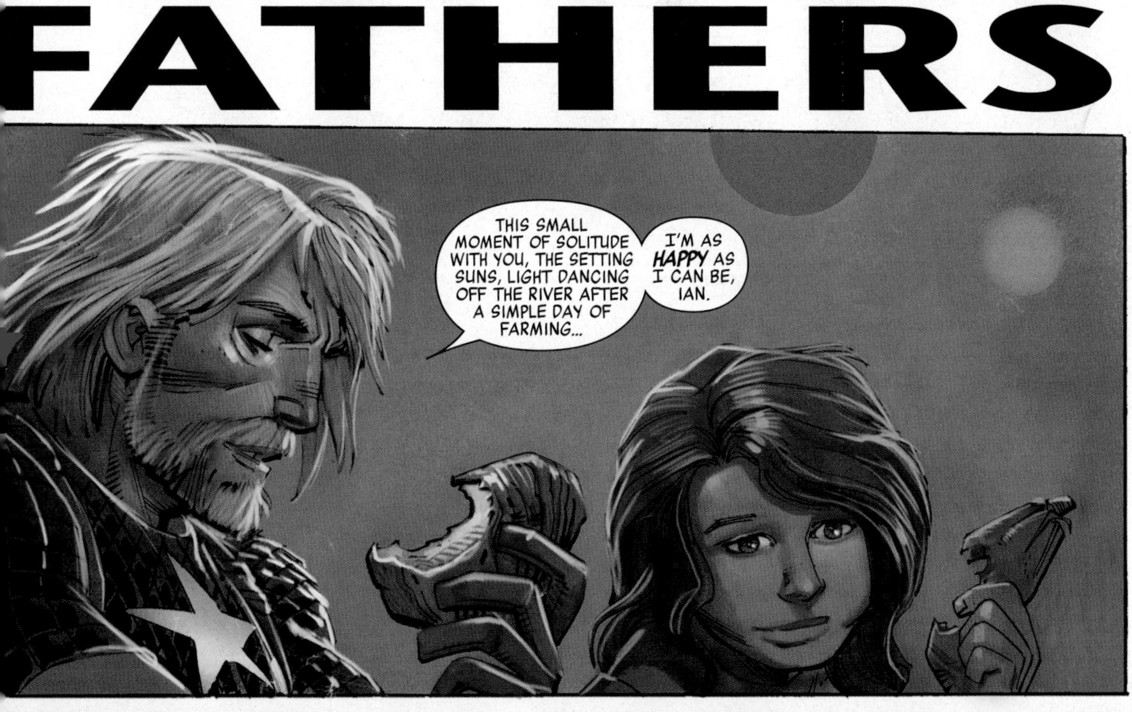

THIS SMALL MOMENT OF SOLITUDE WITH YOU, THE SETTING SUNS, LIGHT DANCING OFF THE RIVER AFTER A SIMPLE DAY OF FARMING...
I'M AS HAPPY AS I CAN BE, IAN.

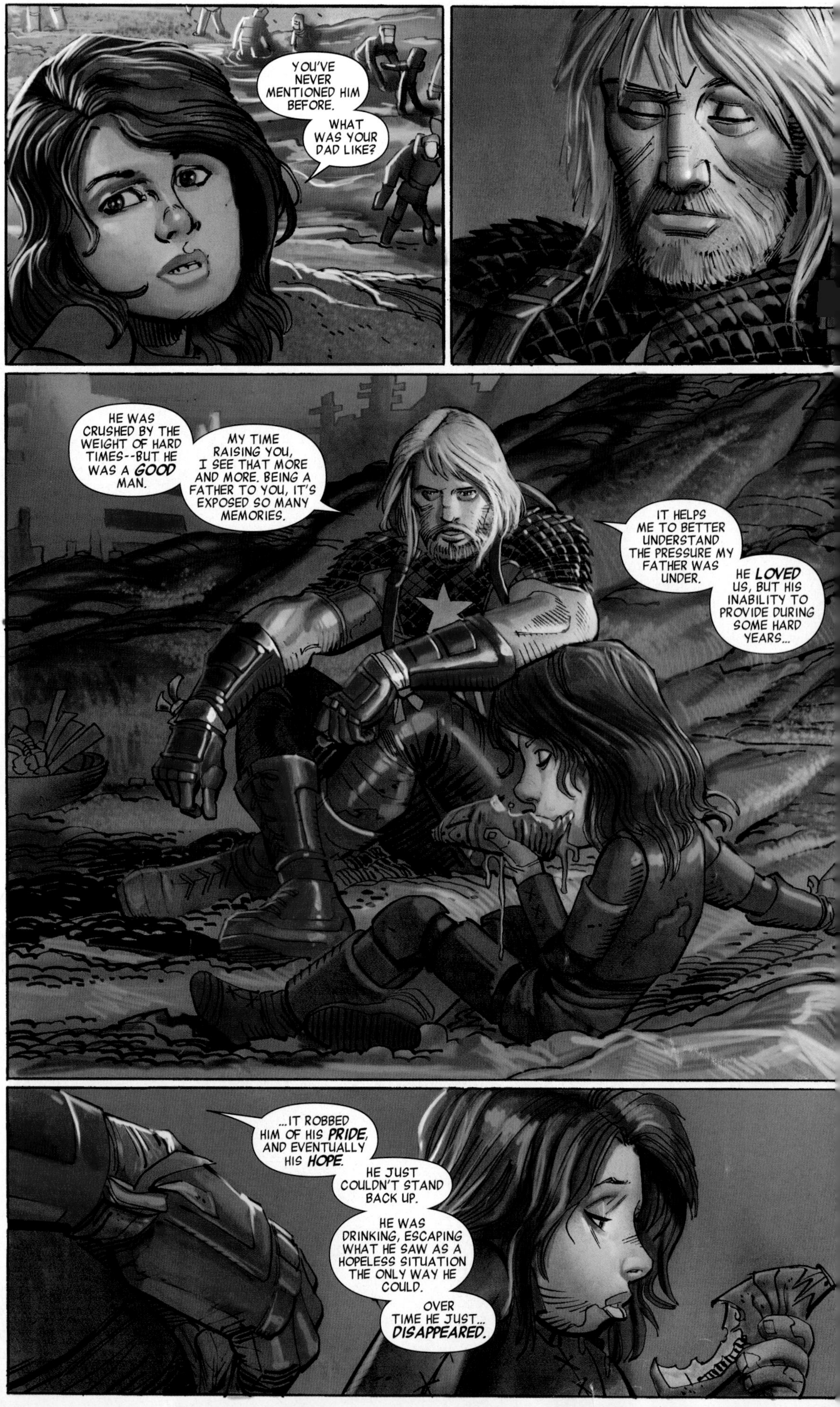
YOU'VE NEVER MENTIONED HIM BEFORE.
WHAT WAS YOUR DAD LIKE?
HE WAS CRUSHED BY THE WEIGHT OF HARD TIMES--BUT HE WAS A GOOD MAN.
MY TIME RAISING YOU, I SEE THAT MORE AND MORE. BEING A FATHER TO YOU, IT'S EXPOSED SO MANY MEMORIES.
IT HELPS ME TO BETTER UNDERSTAND THE PRESSURE MY FATHER WAS UNDER.
HE LOVED US, BUT HIS INABILITY TO PROVIDE DURING SOME HARD YEARS...
...IT ROBBED HIM OF HIS PRIDE, AND EVENTUALLY HIS HOPE.
HE JUST COULDN'T STAND BACK UP.
HE WAS DRINKING, ESCAPING WHAT HE SAW AS A HOPELESS SITUATION THE ONLY WAY HE COULD.
OVER TIME HE JUST... DISAPPEARED.

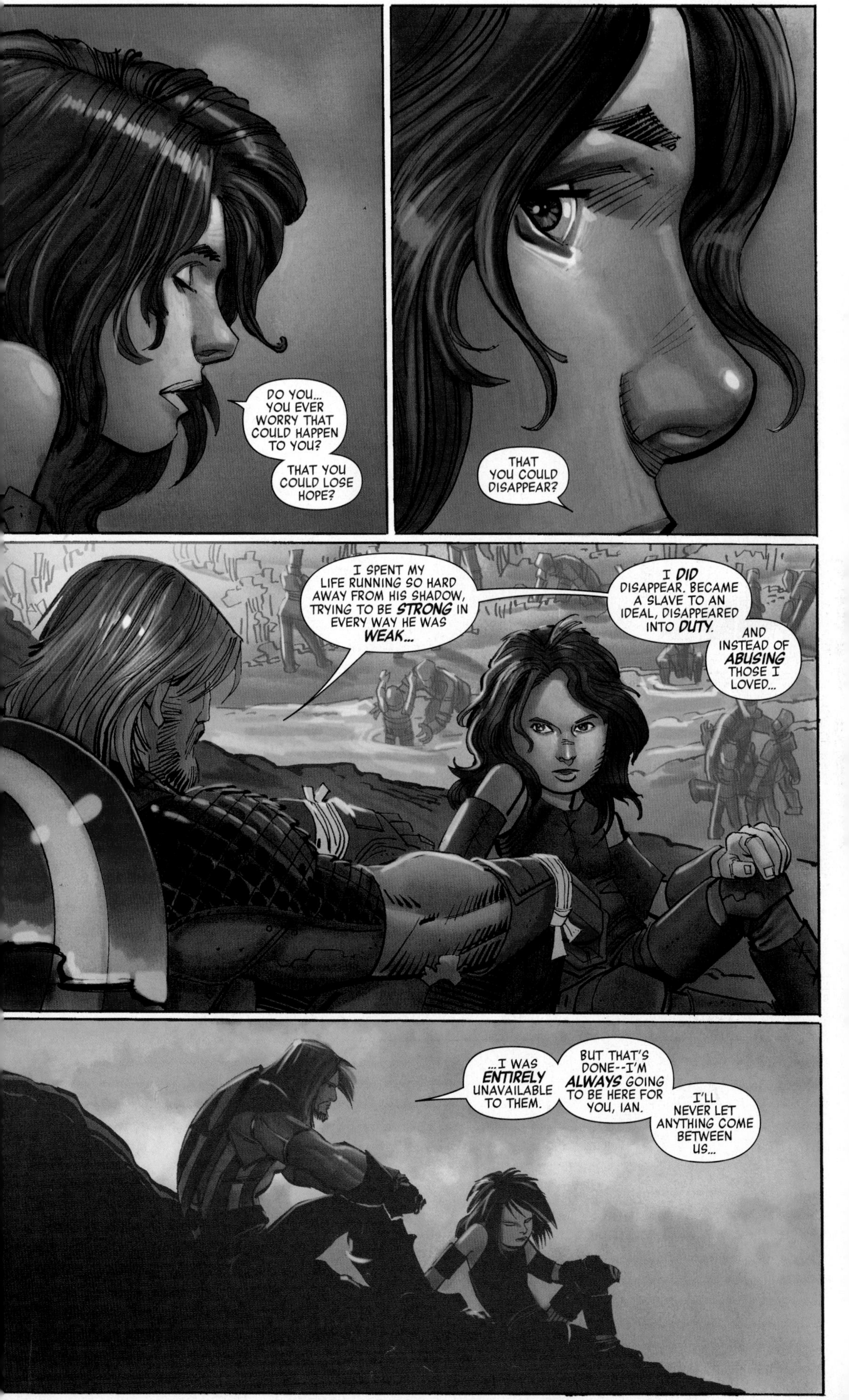
DO YOU... YOU EVER WORRY THAT COULD HAPPEN TO YOU?
THAT YOU COULD LOSE HOPE?
THAT YOU COULD DISAPPEAR?
I SPENT MY LIFE RUNNING SO HARD AWAY FROM HIS SHADOW, TRYING TO BE STRONG IN EVERY WAY HE WAS WEAK...
I DID DISAPPEAR. BECAME A SLAVE TO AN IDEAL, DISAPPEARED INTO DUTY.
AND INSTEAD OF ABUSING THOSE I LOVED...
...I WAS ENTIRELY UNAVAILABLE TO THEM.
BUT THAT'S DONE--I'M ALWAYS GOING TO BE HERE FOR YOU, IAN.
I'LL NEVER LET ANYTHING COME BETWEEN US...

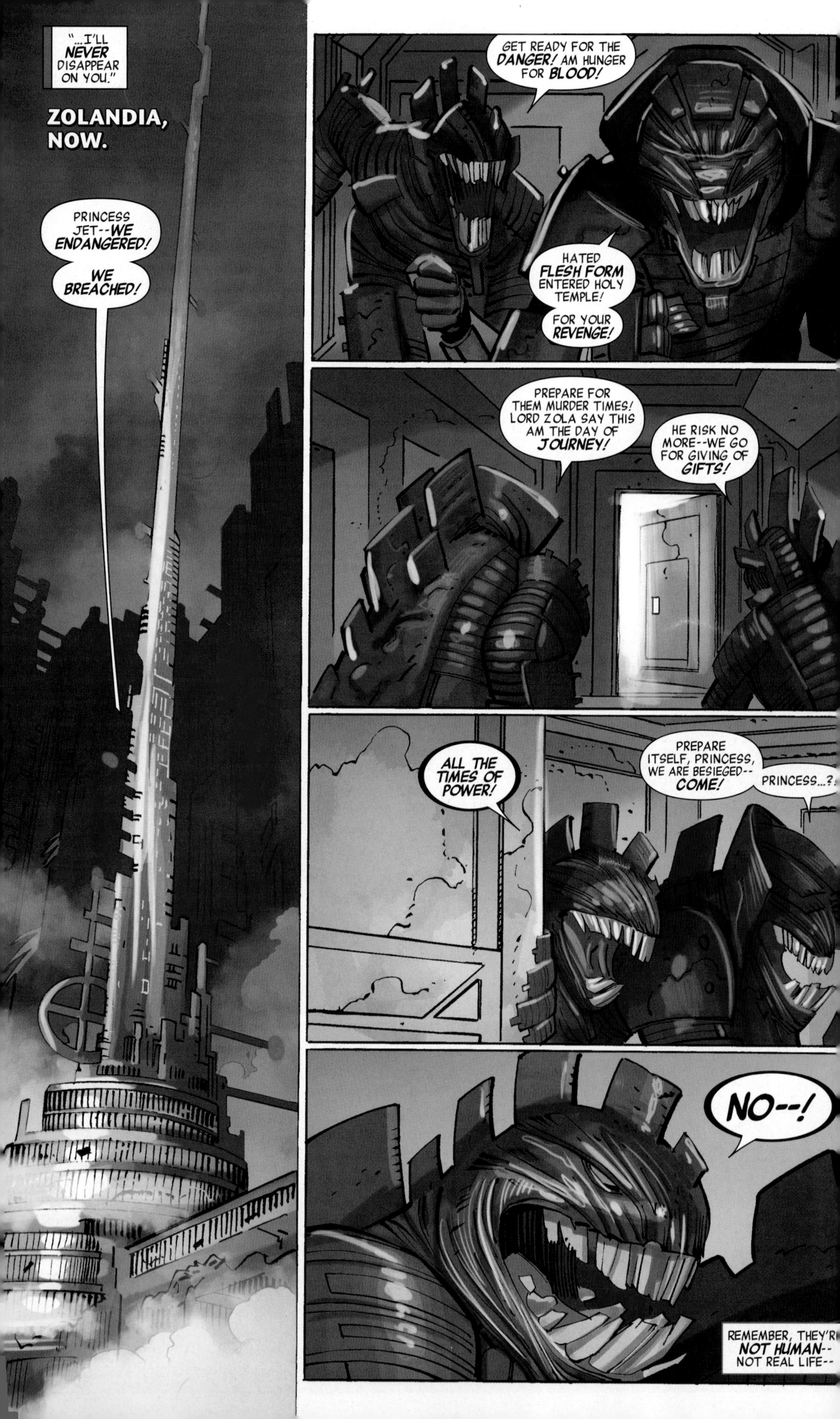
"...I'LL NEVER DISAPPEAR ON YOU."
ZOLANDIA, NOW.
PRINCESS JET--WE ENDANGERED!
WE BREACHED!
GET READY FOR THE DANGER! AM HUNGER FOR BLOOD!
HATED FLESH FORM ENTERED HOLY TEMPLE!
FOR YOUR REVENGE!
PREPARE FOR THEM MURDER TIMES! LORD ZOLA SAY THIS AM THE DAY OF JOURNEY!
HE RISK NO MORE--WE GO FOR GIVING OF GIFTS!
ALL THE TIMES OF POWER!
PREPARE ITSELF, PRINCESS, WE ARE BESIEGED--COME!
PRINCESS...?
NO--!
REMEMBER, THEY'RE NOT HUMAN--NOT REAL LIFE--

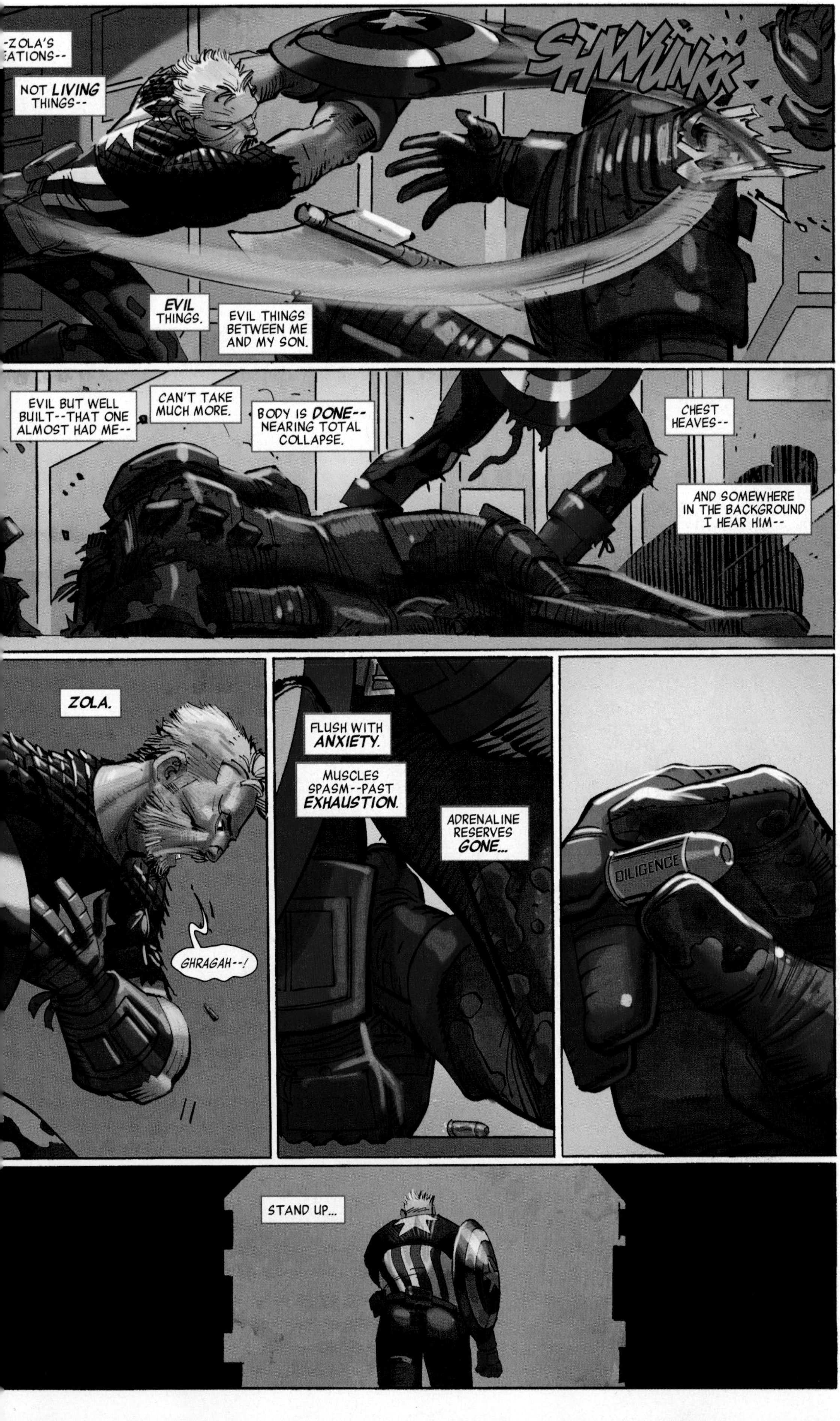

-ZOLA'S
EATIONS--
NOT LIVING THINGS--
SHWUNKK
EVIL THINGS.
EVIL THINGS BETWEEN ME AND MY SON.
EVIL BUT WELL BUILT--THAT ONE ALMOST HAD ME--
CAN'T TAKE MUCH MORE.
BODY IS DONE-- NEARING TOTAL COLLAPSE.
CHEST HEAVES--
AND SOMEWHERE IN THE BACKGROUND I HEAR HIM--
ZOLA.
GHRAGAH--!
FLUSH WITH ANXIETY.
MUSCLES SPASM--PAST EXHAUSTION.
ADRENALINE RESERVES GONE...
DILIGENCE
STAND UP...

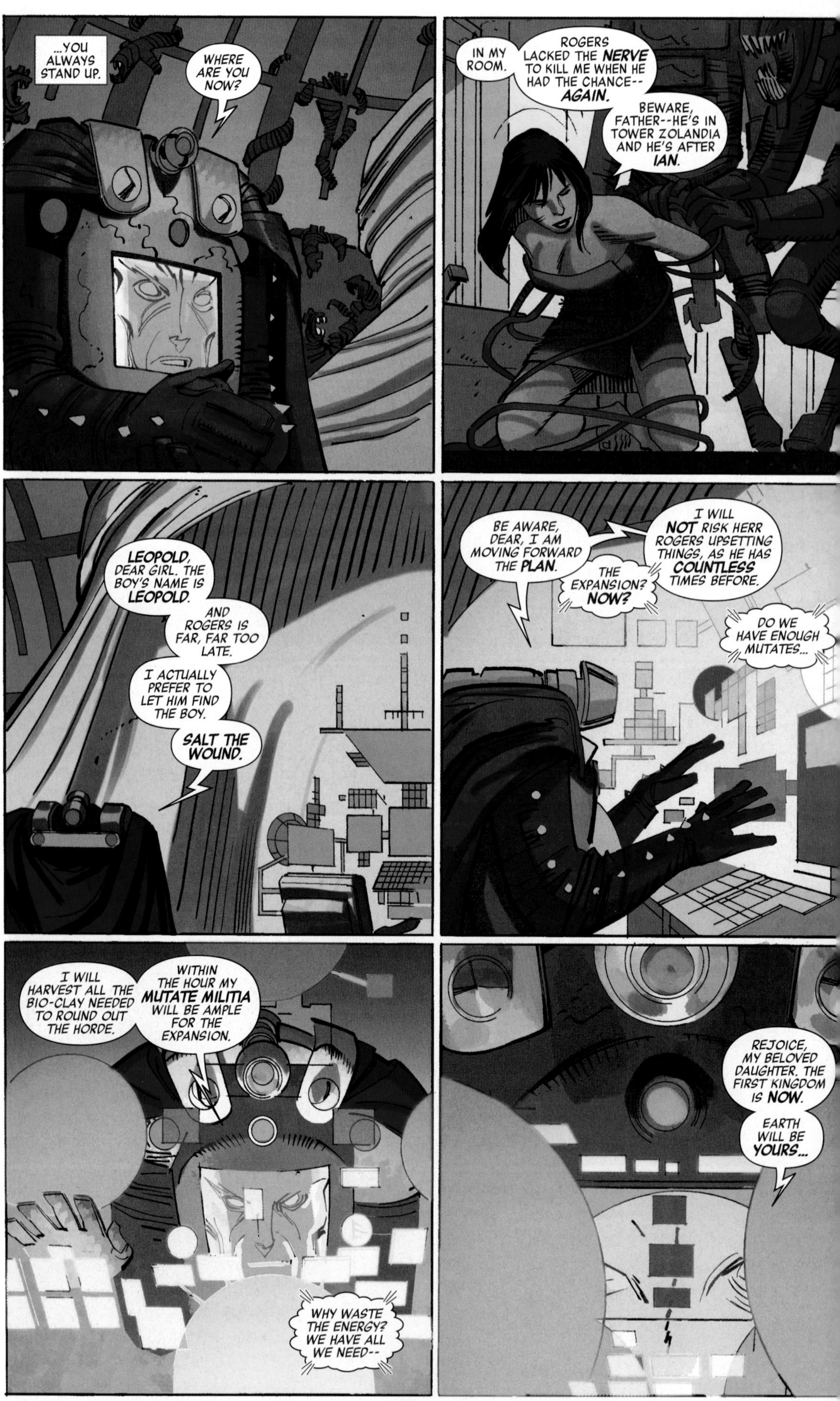
...YOU ALWAYS STAND UP.
WHERE ARE YOU NOW?
IN MY ROOM.
ROGERS LACKED THE NERVE TO KILL ME WHEN HE HAD THE CHANCE-- AGAIN.
BEWARE, FATHER--HE'S IN TOWER ZOLANDIA AND HE'S AFTER IAN.
LEOPOLD, DEAR GIRL. THE BOY'S NAME IS LEOPOLD.
AND ROGERS IS FAR, FAR TOO LATE.
I ACTUALLY PREFER TO LET HIM FIND THE BOY.
SALT THE WOUND.
BE AWARE, DEAR, I AM MOVING FORWARD THE PLAN.
THE EXPANSION? NOW?
I WILL NOT RISK HERR ROGERS UPSETTING THINGS, AS HE HAS COUNTLESS TIMES BEFORE.
DO WE HAVE ENOUGH MUTATES...
I WILL HARVEST ALL THE BIO-CLAY NEEDED TO ROUND OUT THE HORDE.
WITHIN THE HOUR MY MUTATE MILITIA WILL BE AMPLE FOR THE EXPANSION.
WHY WASTE THE ENERGY? WE HAVE ALL WE NEED--
REJOICE, MY BELOVED DAUGHTER. THE FIRST KINGDOM IS NOW.
EARTH WILL BE YOURS...

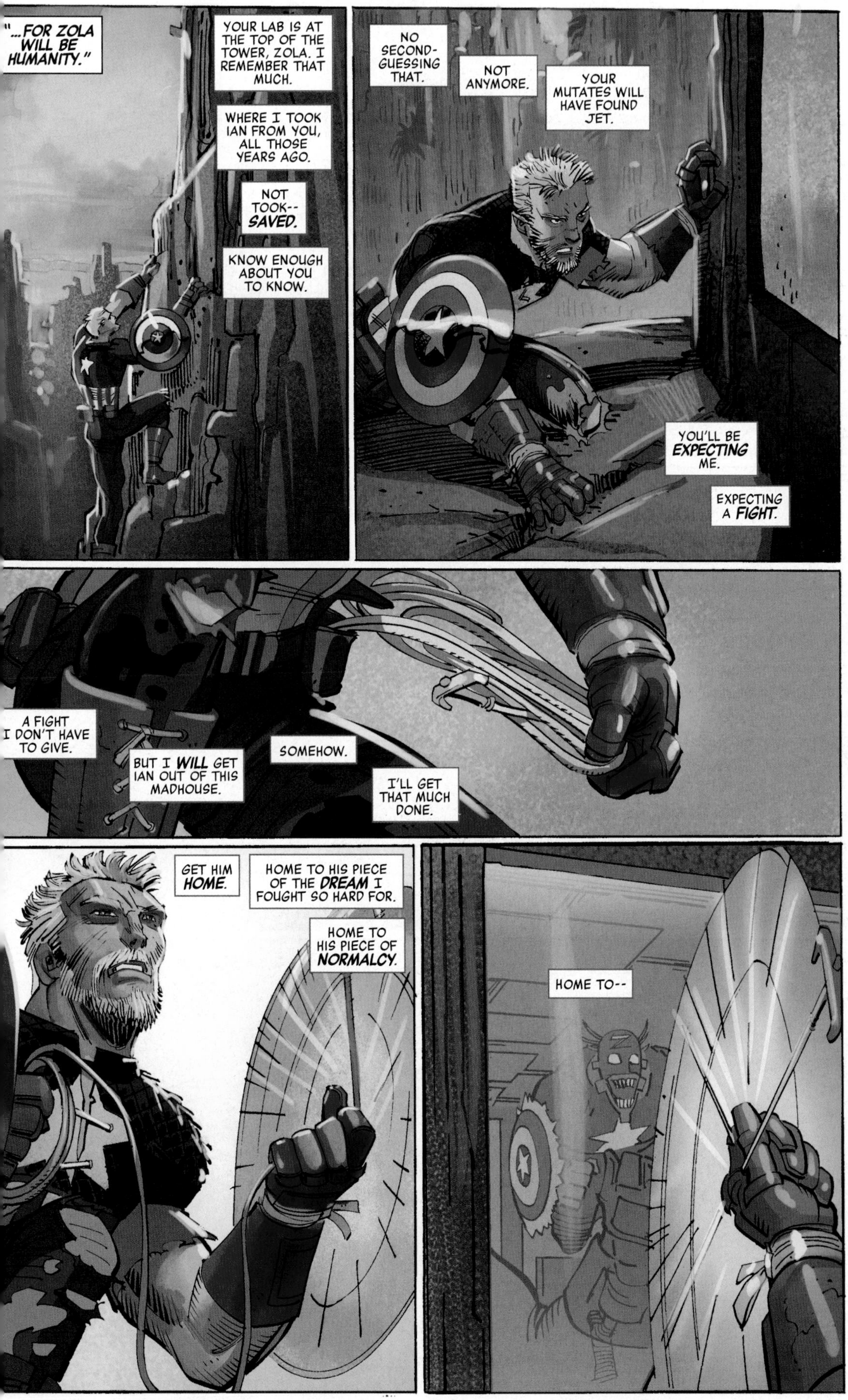
"...FOR ZOLA WILL BE HUMANITY."
YOUR LAB IS AT THE TOP OF THE TOWER, ZOLA. I REMEMBER THAT MUCH.
WHERE I TOOK IAN FROM YOU, ALL THOSE YEARS AGO.
NOT TOOK--SAVED.
KNOW ENOUGH ABOUT YOU TO KNOW.
NO SECOND-GUESSING THAT.
NOT ANYMORE.
YOUR MUTATES WILL HAVE FOUND JET.
YOU'LL BE EXPECTING ME.
EXPECTING A FIGHT.
A FIGHT I DON'T HAVE TO GIVE.
BUT I WILL GET IAN OUT OF THIS MADHOUSE.
SOMEHOW.
I'LL GET THAT MUCH DONE.
GET HIM HOME.
HOME TO HIS PIECE OF THE DREAM I FOUGHT SO HARD FOR.
HOME TO HIS PIECE OF NORMALCY.
HOME TO--

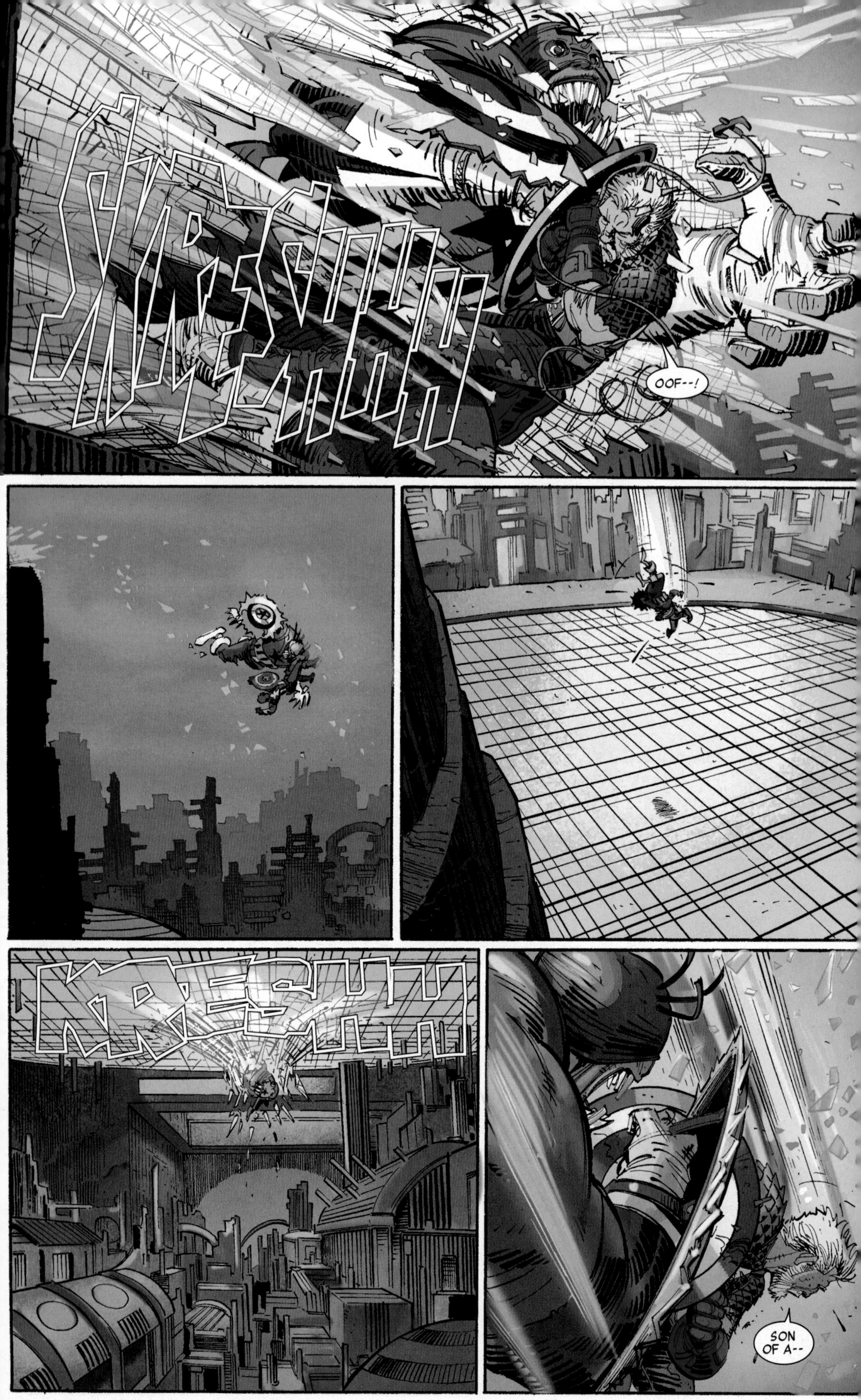
OOF--!
SON OF A--

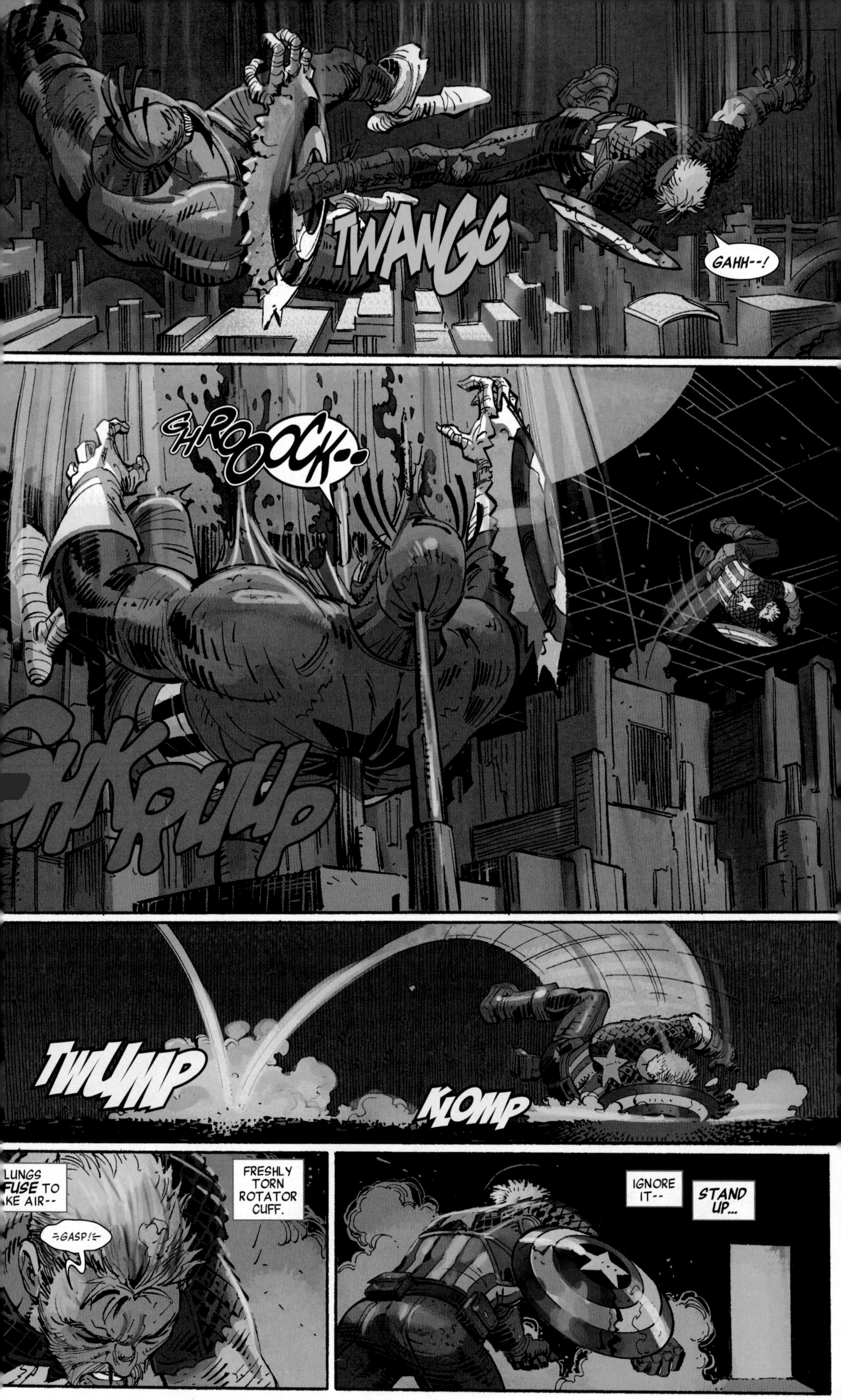
TWANGG
GAHH--!
CHROOOCK--
SHKRUMP
TWUMP
KLOMP
LUNGS
FUSE TO
KE AIR--
=GASP!=
FRESHLY TORN ROTATOR CUFF.
IGNORE IT--
STAND UP...

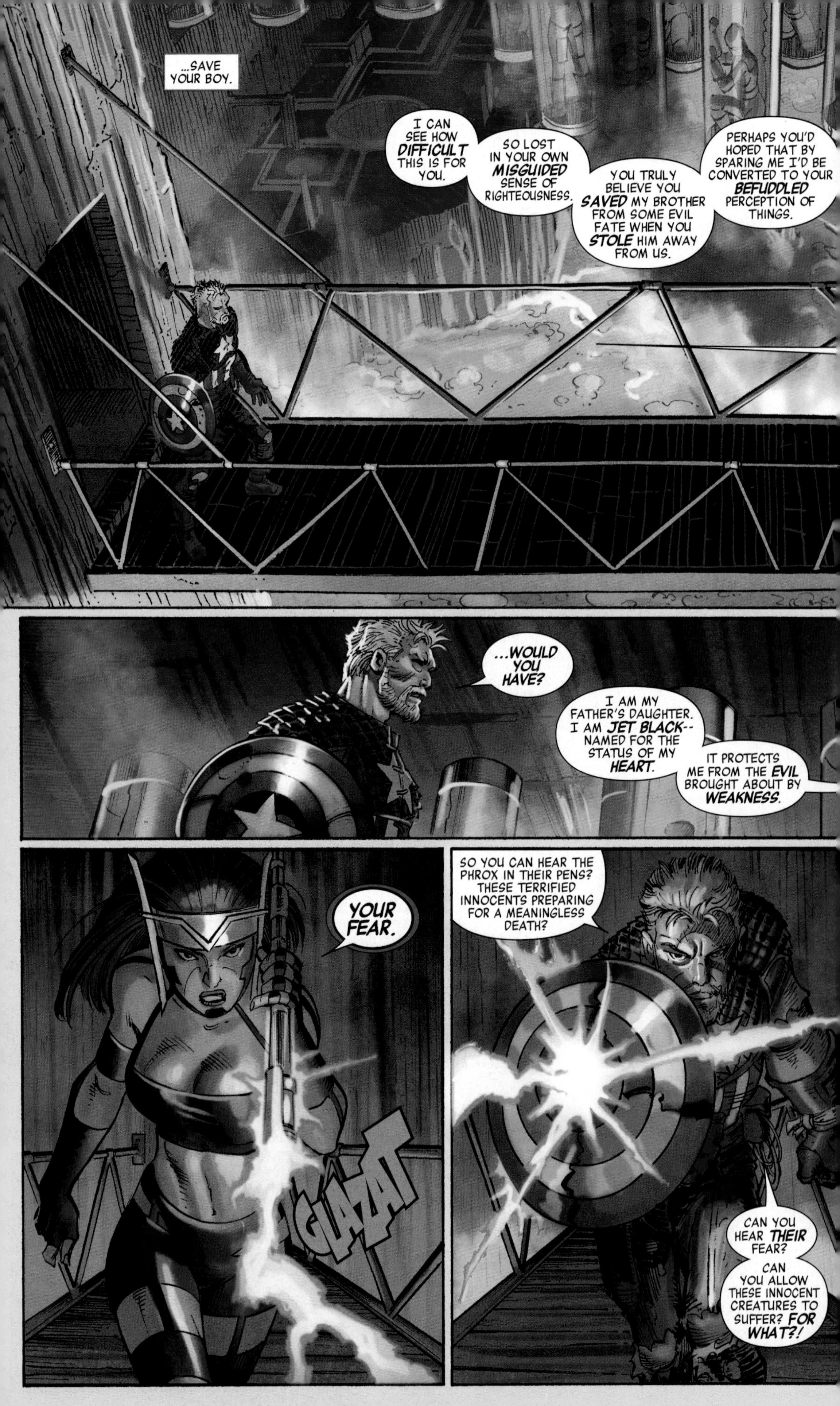

...SAVE YOUR BOY.
I CAN SEE HOW DIFFICULT THIS IS FOR YOU.
SO LOST IN YOUR OWN MISGUIDED SENSE OF RIGHTEOUSNESS.
YOU TRULY BELIEVE YOU SAVED MY BROTHER FROM SOME EVIL FATE WHEN YOU STOLE HIM AWAY FROM US.
PERHAPS YOU'D HOPED THAT BY SPARING ME I'D BE CONVERTED TO YOUR BEFUDDLED PERCEPTION OF THINGS.
...WOULD YOU HAVE?
I AM MY FATHER'S DAUGHTER. I AM JET BLACK--NAMED FOR THE STATUS OF MY HEART.
IT PROTECTS ME FROM THE EVIL BROUGHT ABOUT BY WEAKNESS.
YOUR FEAR.
GLAZAT
SO YOU CAN HEAR THE PHROX IN THEIR PENS? THESE TERRIFIED INNOCENTS PREPARING FOR A MEANINGLESS DEATH?
CAN YOU HEAR THEIR FEAR?
CAN YOU ALLOW THESE INNOCENT CREATURES TO SUFFER? FOR WHAT?!

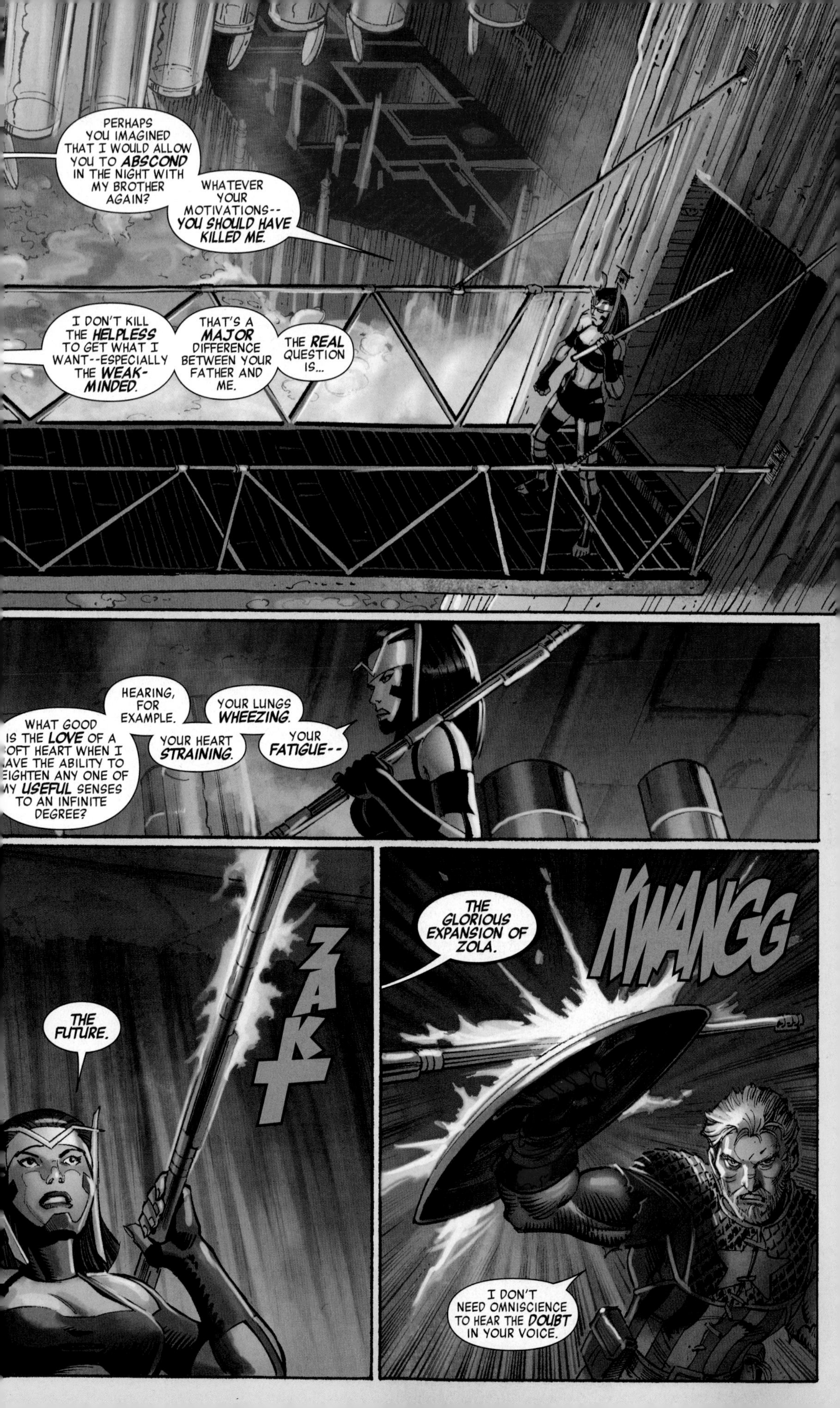
PERHAPS YOU IMAGINED THAT I WOULD ALLOW YOU TO ABSCOND IN THE NIGHT WITH MY BROTHER AGAIN?
WHATEVER YOUR MOTIVATIONS-- YOU SHOULD HAVE KILLED ME.
I DON'T KILL THE HELPLESS TO GET WHAT I WANT--ESPECIALLY THE WEAK-MINDED.
THAT'S A MAJOR DIFFERENCE BETWEEN YOUR FATHER AND ME.
THE REAL QUESTION IS...
WHAT GOOD IS THE LOVE OF A SOFT HEART WHEN I HAVE THE ABILITY TO HEIGHTEN ANY ONE OF MY USEFUL SENSES TO AN INFINITE DEGREE?
HEARING, FOR EXAMPLE.
YOUR HEART STRAINING.
YOUR LUNGS WHEEZING.
YOUR FATIGUE--
THE FUTURE.
ZAKT
THE GLORIOUS EXPANSION OF ZOLA.
KWANGG
I DON'T NEED OMNISCIENCE TO HEAR THE DOUBT IN YOUR VOICE.

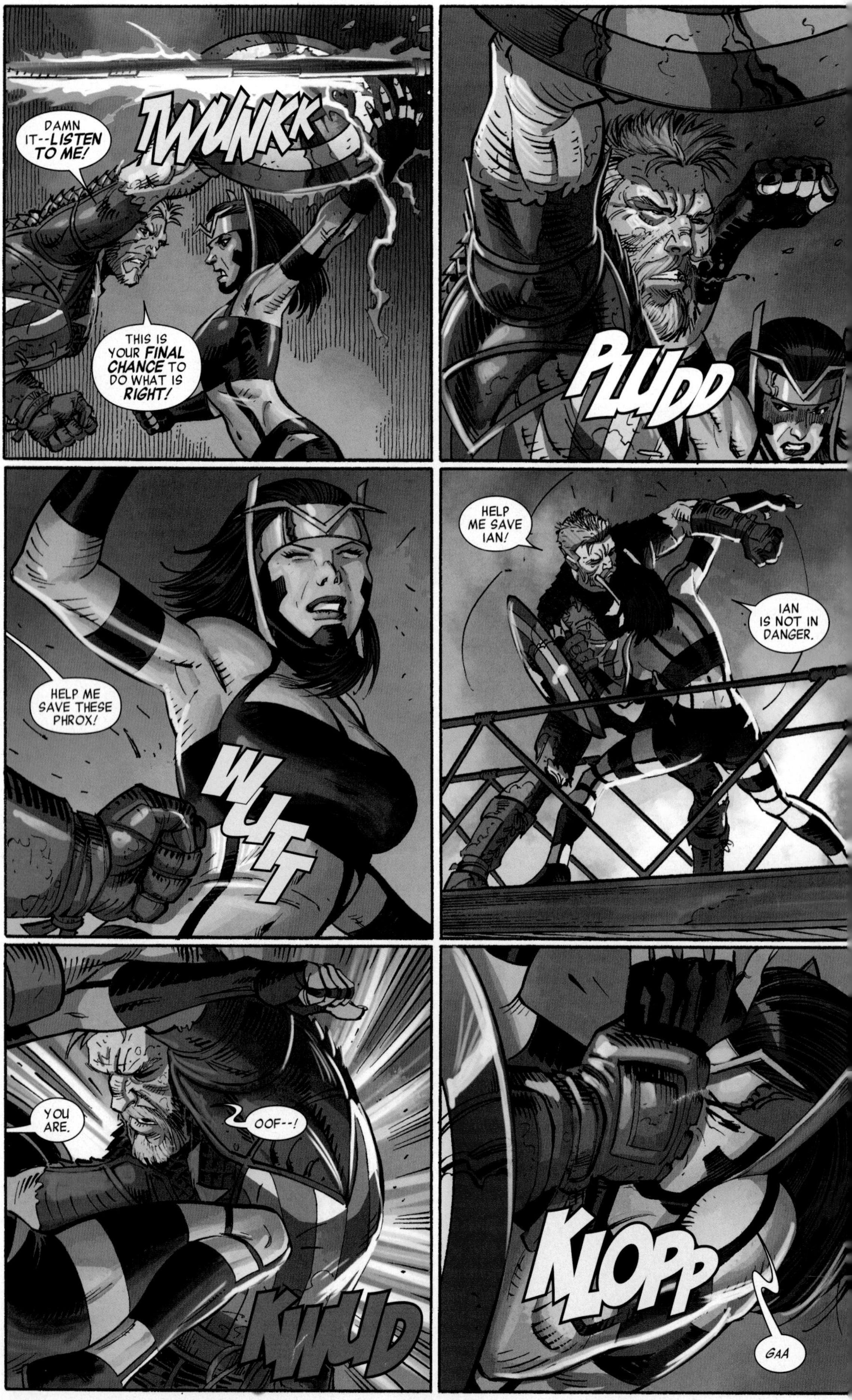
TWUNKK
DAMN IT--LISTEN TO ME!
THIS IS YOUR FINAL CHANCE TO DO WHAT IS RIGHT!
PLUDD
HELP ME SAVE THESE PHROX!
WUTT
HELP ME SAVE IAN!
IAN IS NOT IN DANGER.
YOU ARE.
OOF--!
KNUD
KLOPP
GAA

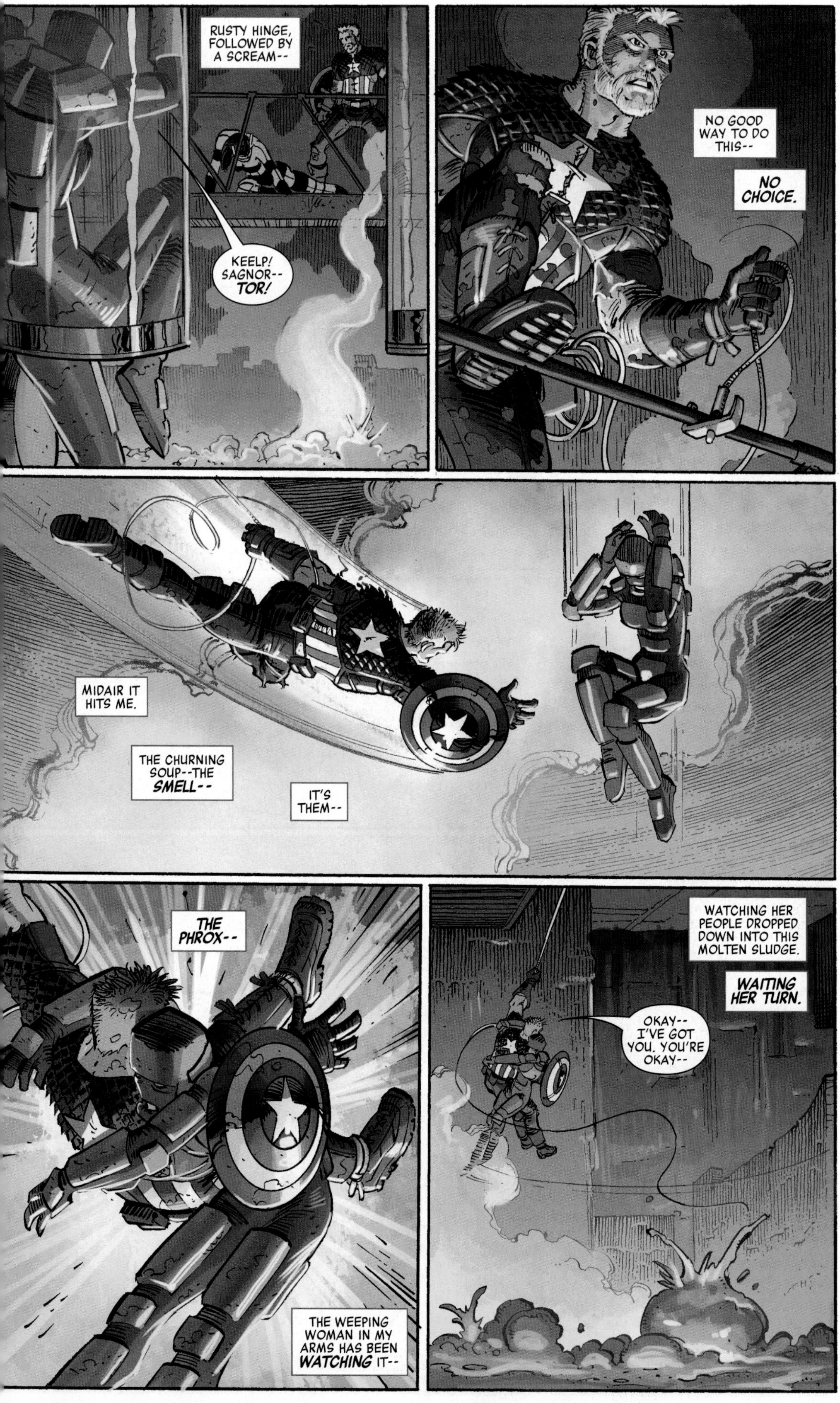

RUSTY HINGE, FOLLOWED BY A SCREAM--
KEELP! SAGNOR-- TOR!
NO GOOD WAY TO DO THIS--
NO CHOICE.
MIDAIR IT HITS ME.
THE CHURNING SOUP--THE SMELL--
IT'S THEM--
THE PHROX--
THE WEEPING WOMAN IN MY ARMS HAS BEEN WATCHING IT--
WATCHING HER PEOPLE DROPPED DOWN INTO THIS MOLTEN SLUDGE.
WAITING HER TURN.
OKAY-- I'VE GOT YOU. YOU'RE OKAY--

PULL US UP! BEFORE ANOTHER ONE IS DROPPED IN--*BEFORE ANOTHER DIES!*

FOOL, WHY SHOULD I LISTEN FOR A SINGLE MOMENT?

YOUR FATHER KEPT YOU HERE SO YOU NEVER HAD A CHANCE TO SEE *COMPASSION*--

IT'S *NOT* YOUR FAULT WHAT HE'S DONE--*NONE OF IT!*

THE NAUSEA, THE TIGHTNESS IN YOUR CHEST, THE SLEEPLESS NIGHTS-- *YOU KNOW THIS IS WRONG!*

IF YOU STAND BY AND DO NOTHING--YOU *SHARE THE GUILT!*

YOU'VE SEEN BOTH OPTIONS, JET, SO PICK--

WHAT SIDE DO YOU CHOOSE?

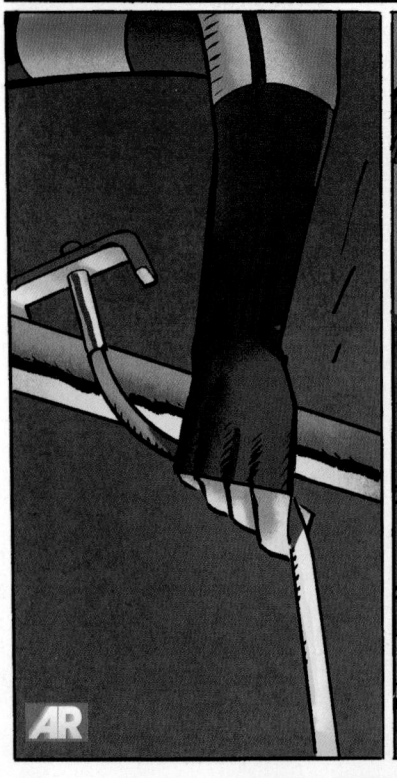

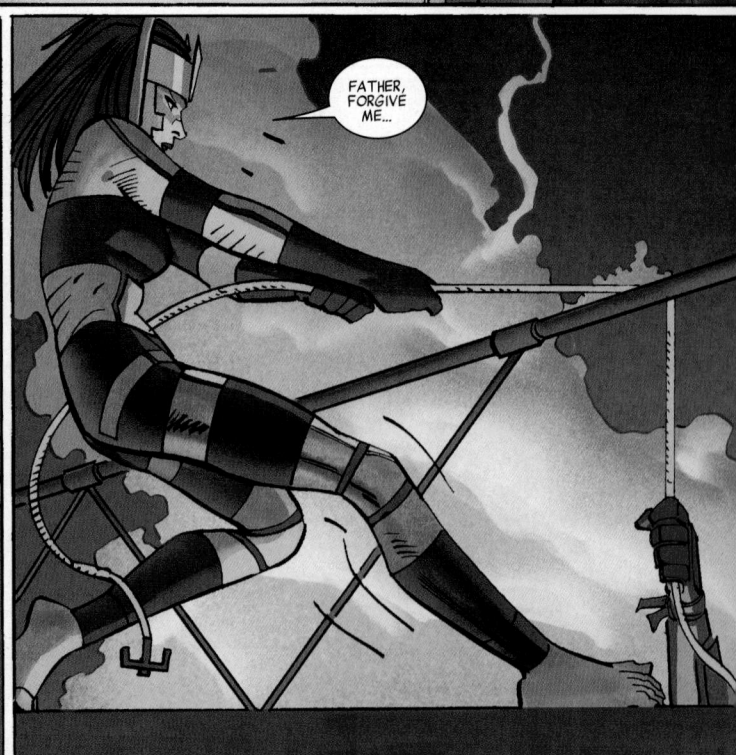

FATHER, FORGIVE ME...

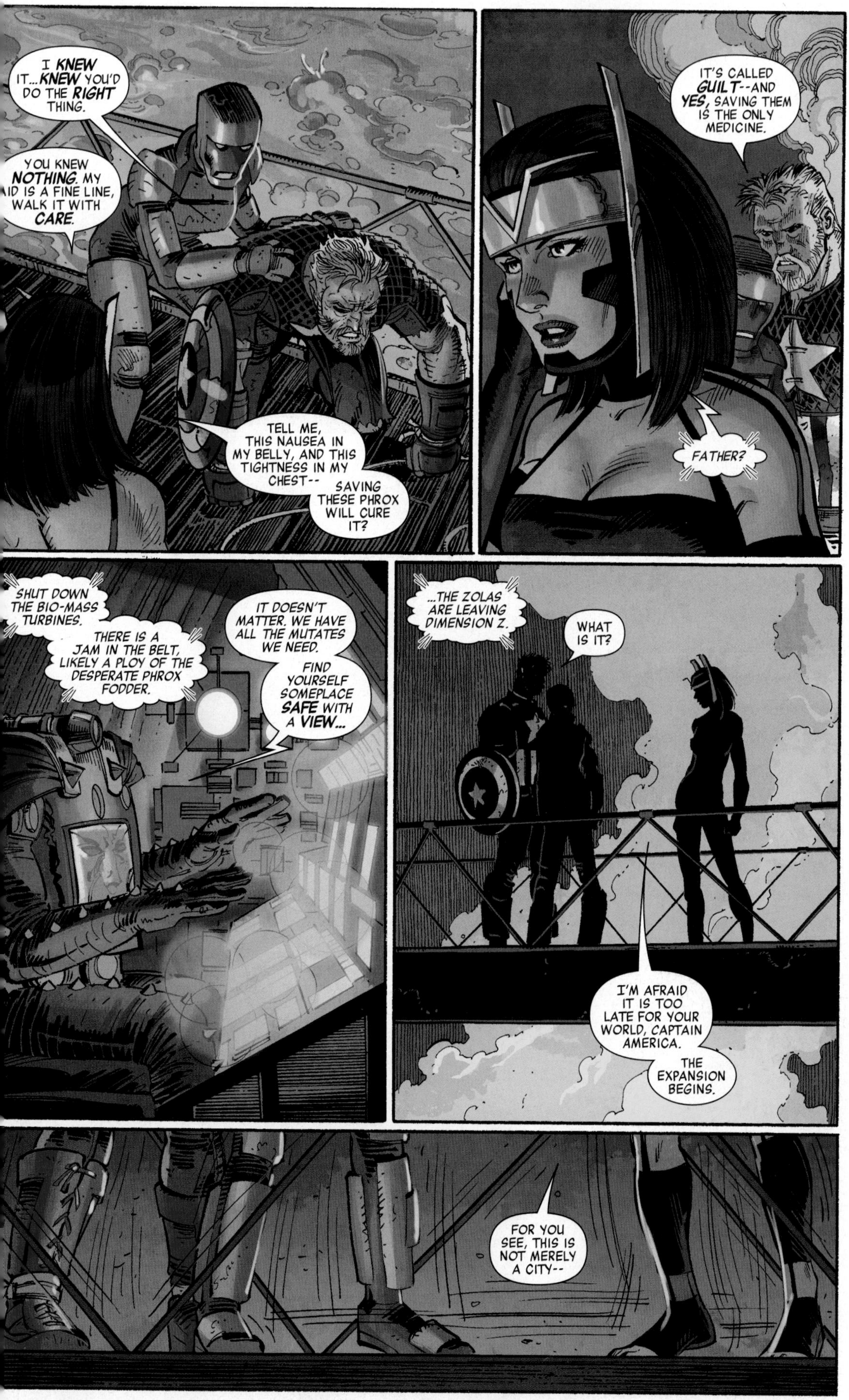
I KNEW IT...KNEW YOU'D DO THE RIGHT THING.
YOU KNEW NOTHING. MY AID IS A FINE LINE, WALK IT WITH CARE.
TELL ME, THIS NAUSEA IN MY BELLY, AND THIS TIGHTNESS IN MY CHEST--
SAVING THESE PHROX WILL CURE IT?
IT'S CALLED GUILT--AND YES, SAVING THEM IS THE ONLY MEDICINE.
FATHER?
SHUT DOWN THE BIO-MASS TURBINES.
THERE IS A JAM IN THE BELT, LIKELY A PLOY OF THE DESPERATE PHROX FODDER.
IT DOESN'T MATTER. WE HAVE ALL THE MUTATES WE NEED.
FIND YOURSELF SOMEPLACE SAFE WITH A VIEW...
...THE ZOLAS ARE LEAVING DIMENSION Z.
WHAT IS IT?
I'M AFRAID IT IS TOO LATE FOR YOUR WORLD, CAPTAIN AMERICA.
THE EXPANSION BEGINS.
FOR YOU SEE, THIS IS NOT MERELY A CITY--

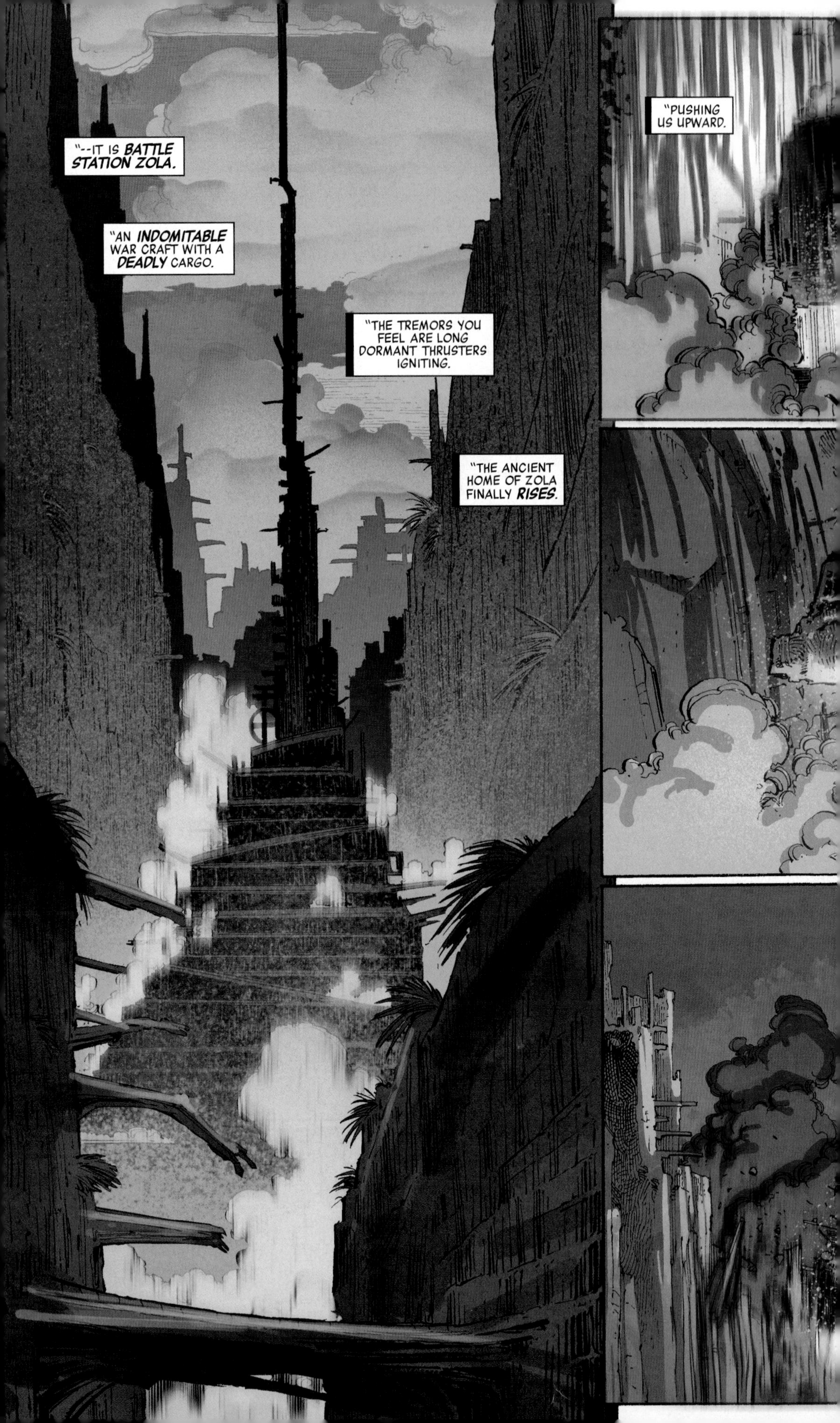
"--IT IS BATTLE STATION ZOLA.
"AN INDOMITABLE WAR CRAFT WITH A DEADLY CARGO.
"THE TREMORS YOU FEEL ARE LONG DORMANT THRUSTERS IGNITING.
"THE ANCIENT HOME OF ZOLA FINALLY RISES.
"PUSHING US UPWARD.

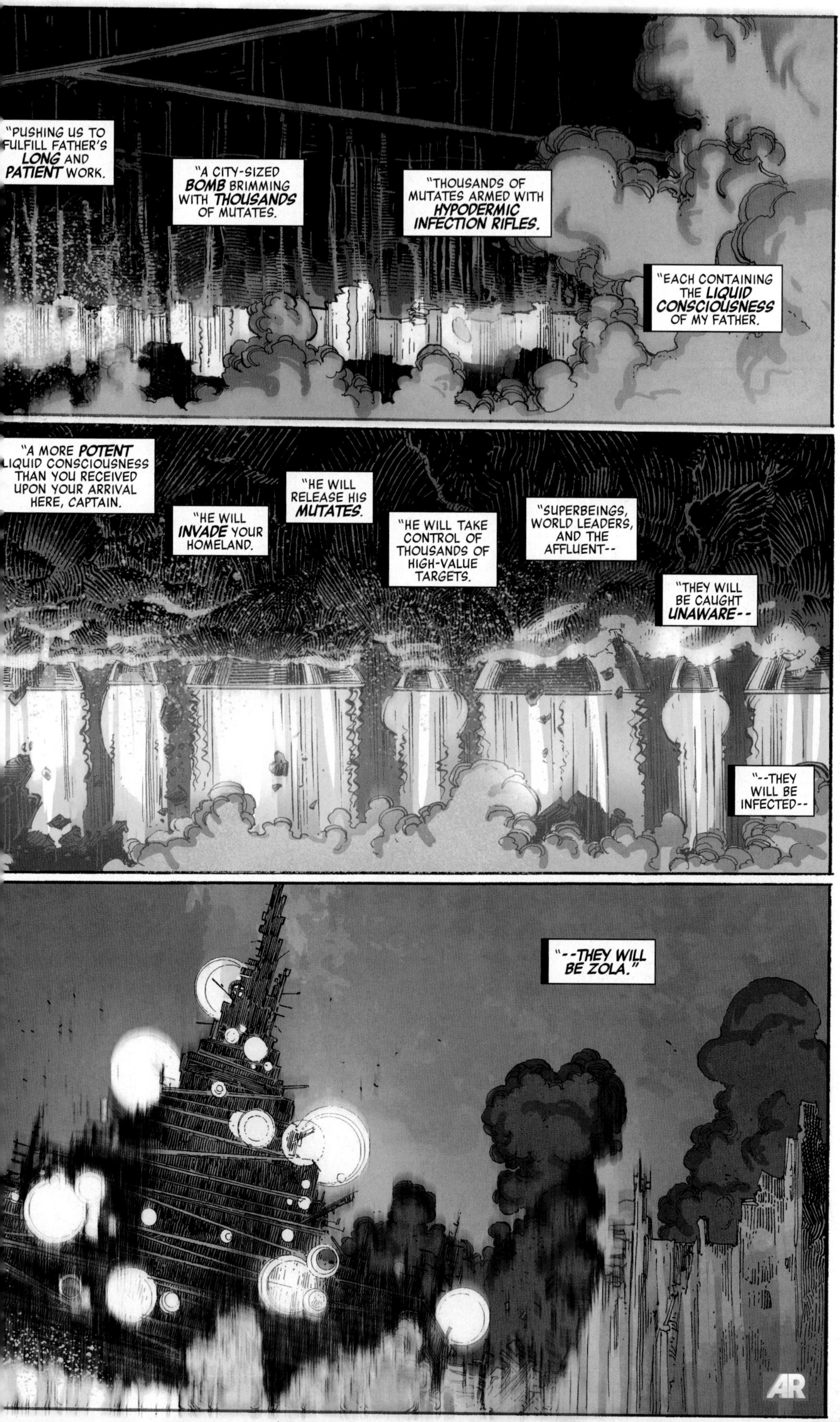
"PUSHING US TO FULFILL FATHER'S LONG AND PATIENT WORK.
"A CITY-SIZED BOMB BRIMMING WITH THOUSANDS OF MUTATES.
"THOUSANDS OF MUTATES ARMED WITH HYPODERMIC INFECTION RIFLES.
"EACH CONTAINING THE LIQUID CONSCIOUSNESS OF MY FATHER.
"A MORE POTENT LIQUID CONSCIOUSNESS THAN YOU RECEIVED UPON YOUR ARRIVAL HERE, CAPTAIN.
"HE WILL INVADE YOUR HOMELAND.
"HE WILL RELEASE HIS MUTATES.
"HE WILL TAKE CONTROL OF THOUSANDS OF HIGH-VALUE TARGETS.
"SUPERBEINGS, WORLD LEADERS, AND THE AFFLUENT--
"THEY WILL BE CAUGHT UNAWARE--
"--THEY WILL BE INFECTED--
"--THEY WILL BE ZOLA."

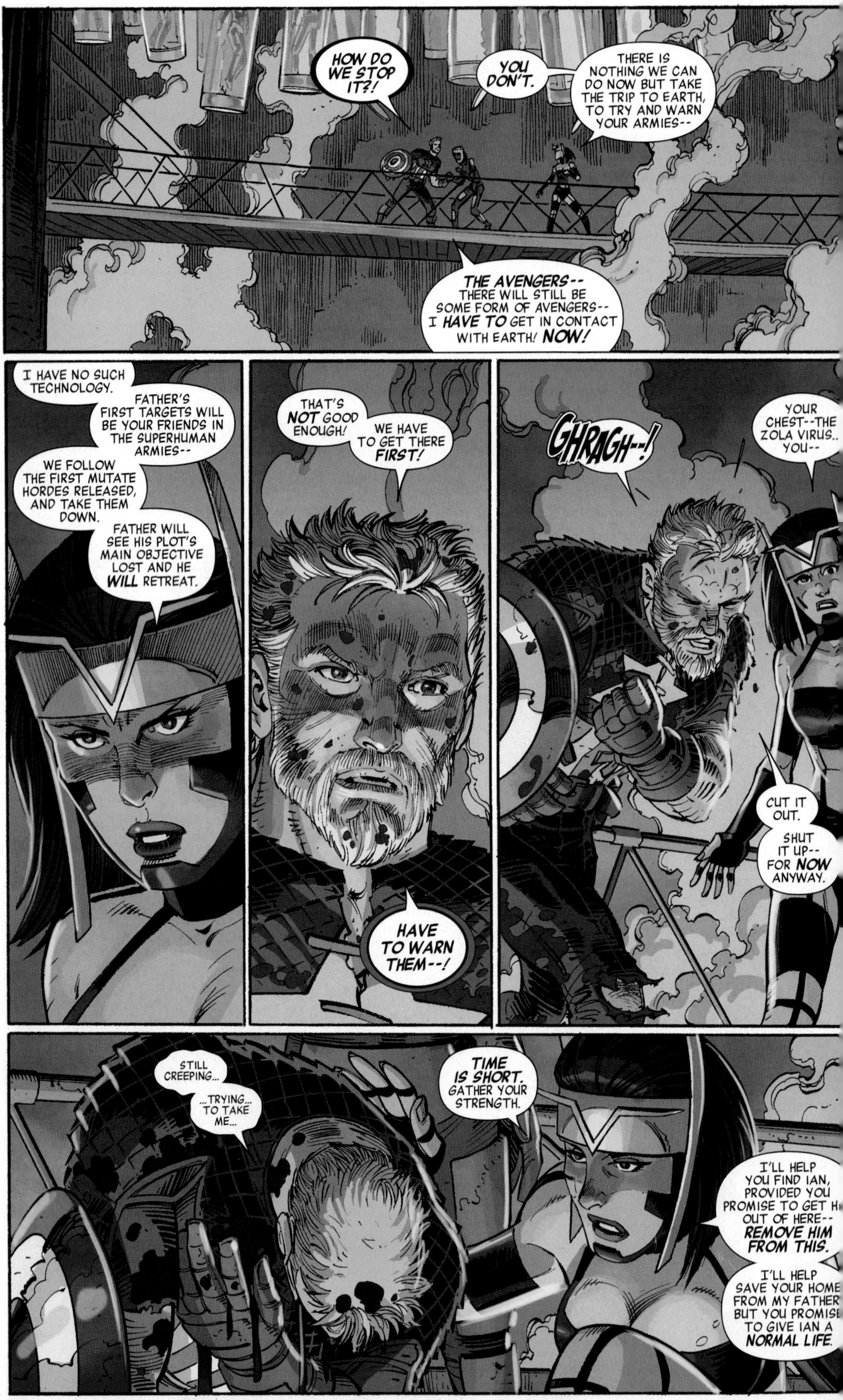

HOW DO WE STOP IT?!
YOU DON'T.
THERE IS NOTHING WE CAN DO NOW BUT TAKE THE TRIP TO EARTH, TO TRY AND WARN YOUR ARMIES--
THE AVENGERS-- THERE WILL STILL BE SOME FORM OF AVENGERS-- I HAVE TO GET IN CONTACT WITH EARTH! NOW!
I HAVE NO SUCH TECHNOLOGY.
FATHER'S FIRST TARGETS WILL BE YOUR FRIENDS IN THE SUPERHUMAN ARMIES--
WE FOLLOW THE FIRST MUTATE HORDES RELEASED, AND TAKE THEM DOWN.
FATHER WILL SEE HIS PLOT'S MAIN OBJECTIVE LOST AND HE WILL RETREAT.
THAT'S NOT GOOD ENOUGH!
WE HAVE TO GET THERE FIRST!
HAVE TO WARN THEM--!
GHRAGH--!
YOUR CHEST--THE ZOLA VIRUS.. YOU--
CUT IT OUT.
SHUT IT UP-- FOR NOW ANYWAY.
STILL CREEPING...
...TRYING... TO TAKE ME...
TIME IS SHORT. GATHER YOUR STRENGTH.
I'LL HELP YOU FIND IAN, PROVIDED YOU PROMISE TO GET H OUT OF HERE-- REMOVE HIM FROM THIS.
I'LL HELP SAVE YOUR HOME FROM MY FATHER BUT YOU PROMISE TO GIVE IAN A NORMAL LIFE.

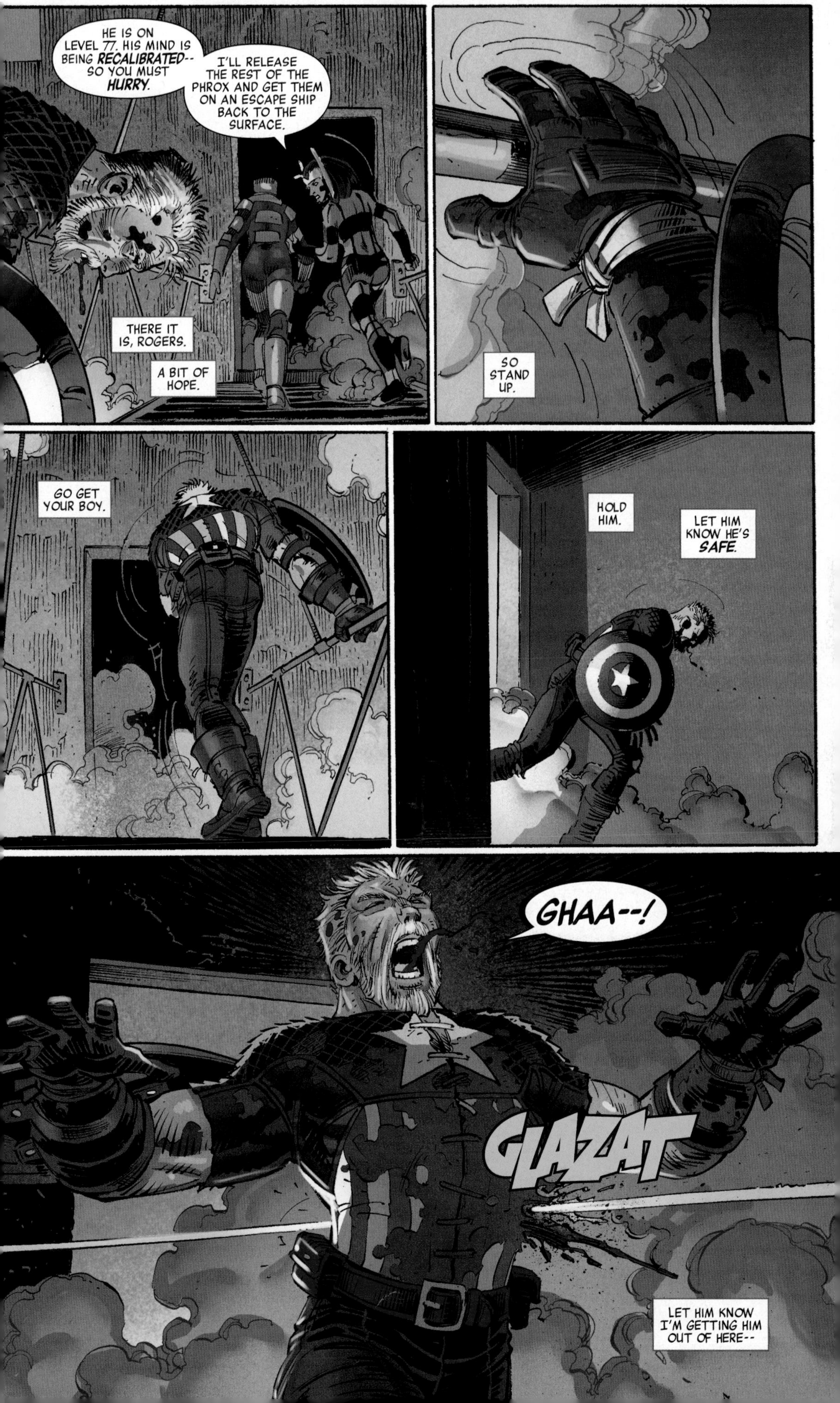

HE IS ON LEVEL 77. HIS MIND IS BEING RECALIBRATED-- SO YOU MUST HURRY.
I'LL RELEASE THE REST OF THE PHROX AND GET THEM ON AN ESCAPE SHIP BACK TO THE SURFACE.
THERE IT IS, ROGERS.
A BIT OF HOPE.
SO STAND UP.
GO GET YOUR BOY.
HOLD HIM.
LET HIM KNOW HE'S SAFE.
GHAA--!
GLAZAT
LET HIM KNOW I'M GETTING HIM OUT OF HERE--

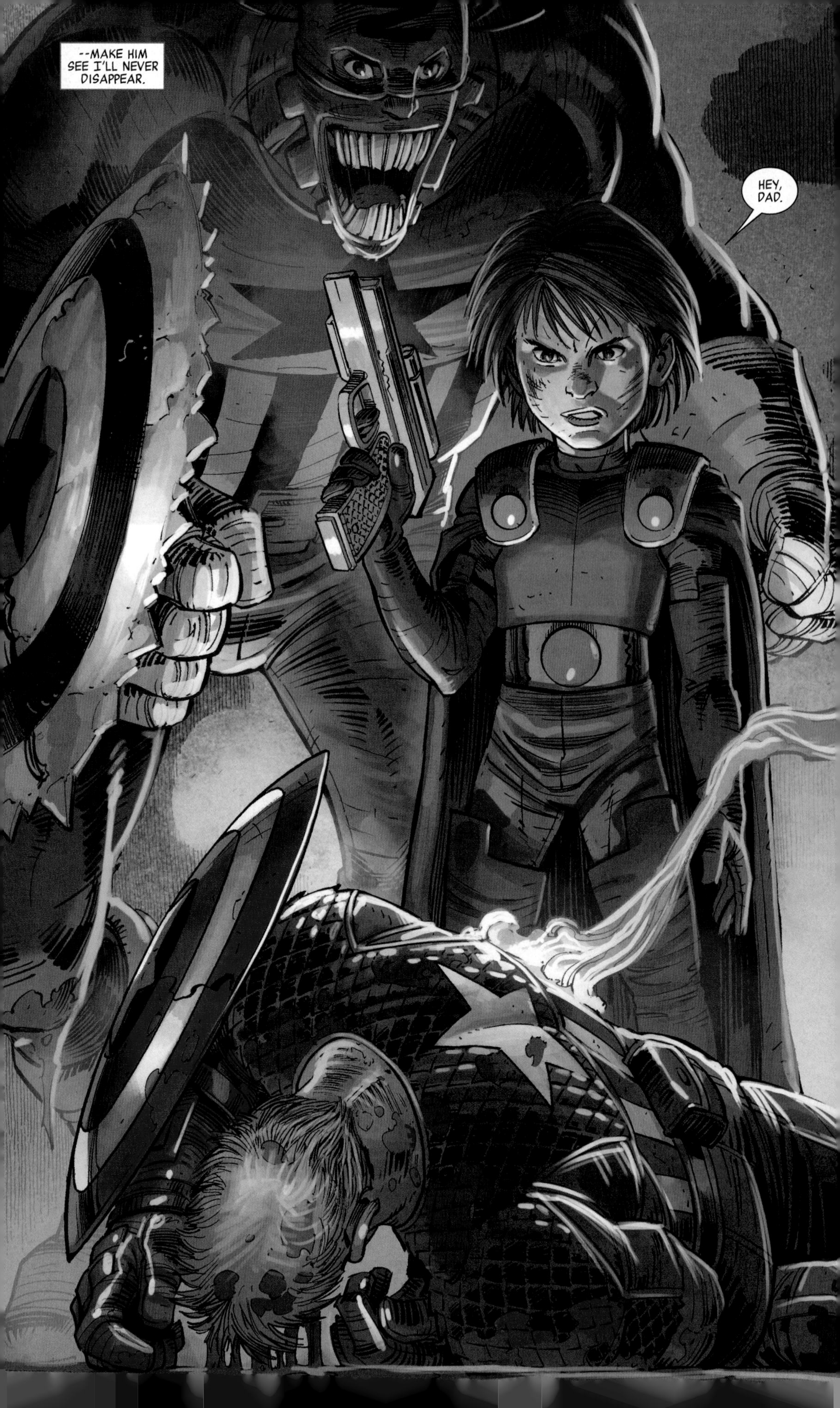
--MAKE HIM SEE I'LL NEVER DISAPPEAR.
HEY, DAD.

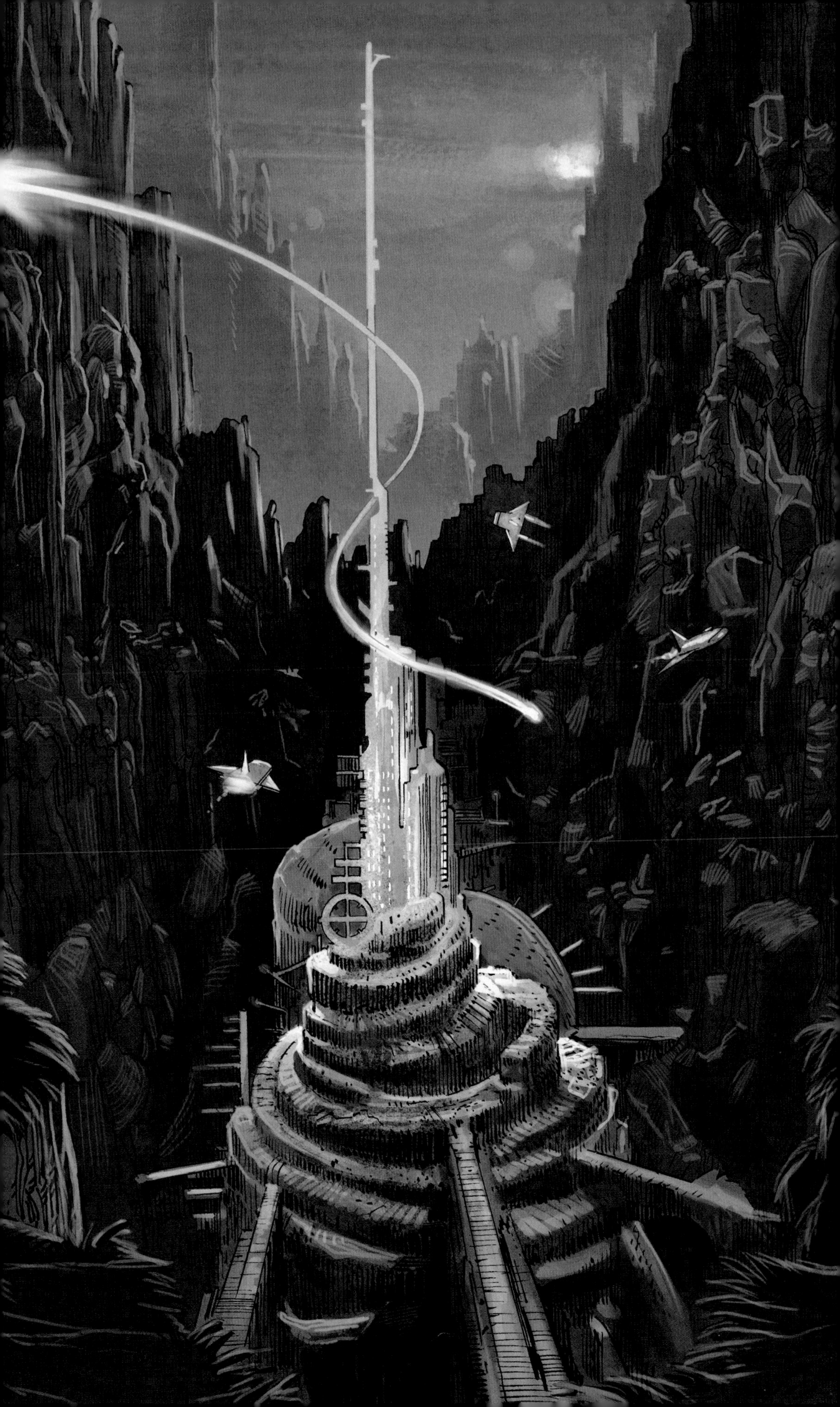

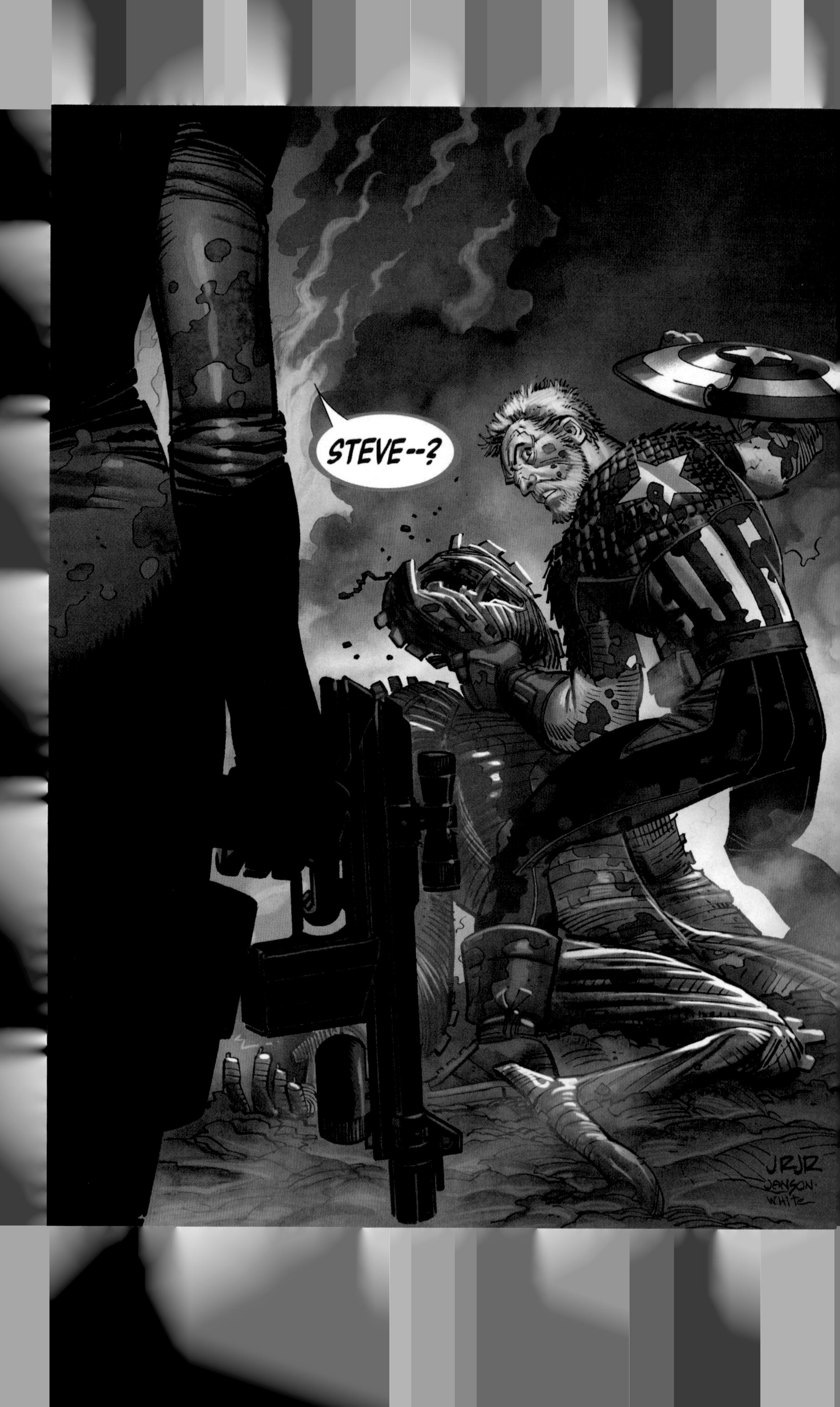
STEVE--?
JRJR
JANSON
WHITE

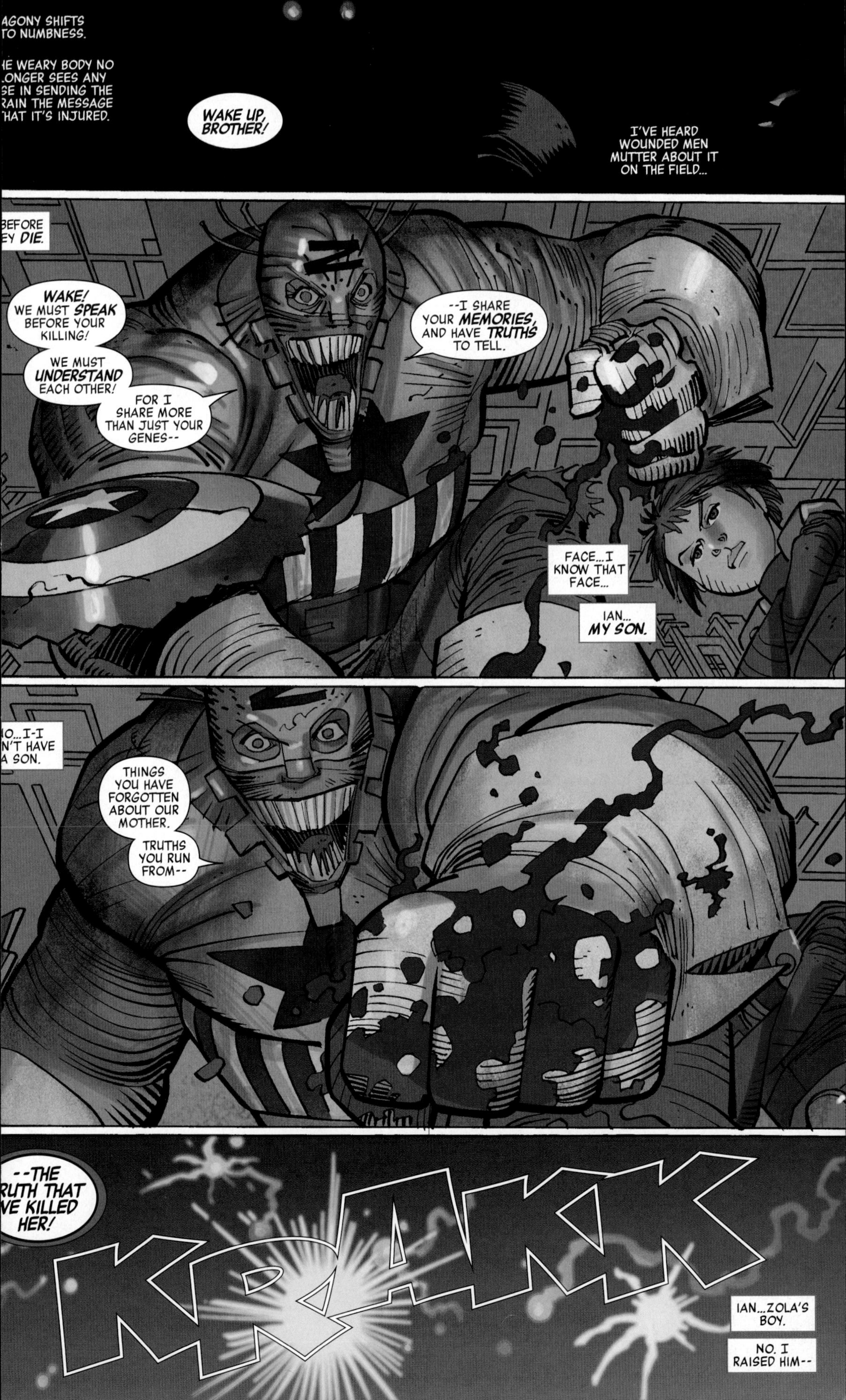
AGONY SHIFTS TO NUMBNESS.
HE WEARY BODY NO LONGER SEES ANY SE IN SENDING THE RAIN THE MESSAGE HAT IT'S INJURED.
WAKE UP, BROTHER!
I'VE HEARD WOUNDED MEN MUTTER ABOUT IT ON THE FIELD...
BEFORE EY DIE.
WAKE! WE MUST SPEAK BEFORE YOUR KILLING!
WE MUST UNDERSTAND EACH OTHER!
FOR I SHARE MORE THAN JUST YOUR GENES--
--I SHARE YOUR MEMORIES, AND HAVE TRUTHS TO TELL.
FACE...I KNOW THAT FACE...
IAN... MY SON.
O...I-I N'T HAVE A SON.
THINGS YOU HAVE FORGOTTEN ABOUT OUR MOTHER.
TRUTHS YOU RUN FROM--
--THE RUTH THAT E KILLED HER!
KRAKK
IAN...ZOLA'S BOY.
NO. I RAISED HIM--

--AND HE *KILLED ME.*

POOR, SAD MOTHER. BURIED A DRUNKEN HUSBAND.

WORKED TO THE GRAVE FEEDING A SICKLY, NINETY-EIGHT POUND *PARASITE.*

CAPTAIN ZOLANDIA TELLS ME YOU WERE A *LEECH* ON THAT POOR, *DYING* WOMAN'S NECK. IT'S *WHY* YOU WENT TO FIGHT IN THE WAR--

--TO *DIE.* TO *FORGET!*

GAWAK--!

NO. SHE WAS THE REASON I BECAME A SOLDIER--

REASON I FOUGHT FOR AMERICA--

SHONKK

IAN'S VOICE--

--DISTORTED-- *CONFUSED*--

ZOLA'S TAMPERING.

DEAR GOD, GIVE ME *STRENGTH*--

--HELP ME--

HELP ME GET HIM *HOME*--SOMEPLACE *SAFE*--

JUST A FE MORE STEP

--JUST A LITTLE MORE *FIGHT.*

GWUNKK

ARROGANT *PIG!* YOU DESERVE TO *DIE* JUST LIKE YOUR SAD MOTHER DID--

--IN A *GUTTER!*

IGNORE THE TERRIBLE WORDS--

TWUPP

BOY KNOWS BETTER--

--TAUGHT HIM *RIGHT*--

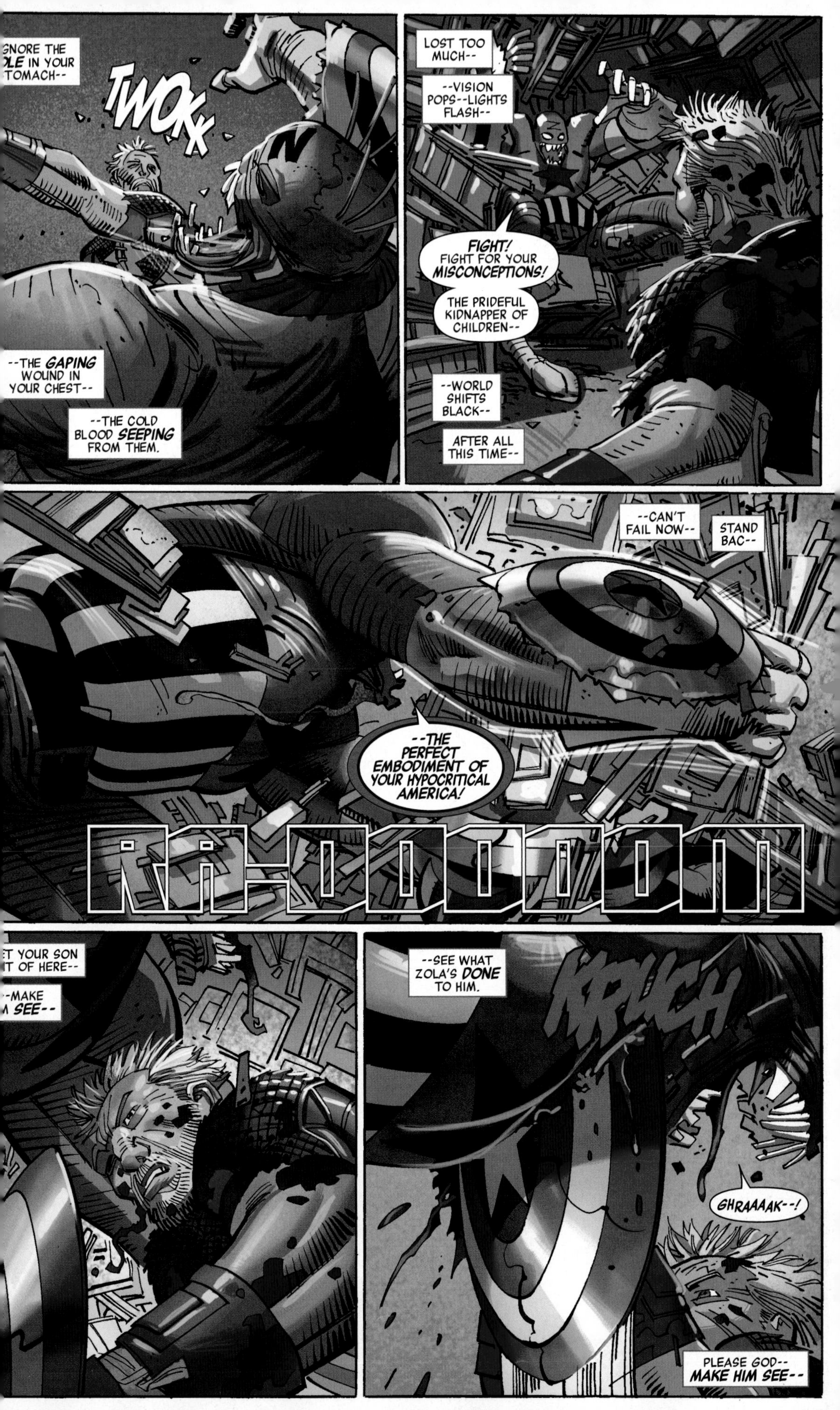

GNORE THE
OLE IN YOUR
TOMACH--
TWOKK
--THE GAPING WOUND IN YOUR CHEST--
--THE COLD BLOOD SEEPING FROM THEM.
LOST TOO MUCH--
--VISION POPS--LIGHTS FLASH--
FIGHT! FIGHT FOR YOUR MISCONCEPTIONS!
THE PRIDEFUL KIDNAPPER OF CHILDREN--
--WORLD SHIFTS BLACK--
AFTER ALL THIS TIME--
--CAN'T FAIL NOW--
STAND BAC--
--THE PERFECT EMBODIMENT OF YOUR HYPOCRITICAL AMERICA!
RA-DOOOOM
T YOUR SON
T OF HERE--
-MAKE
M SEE--
--SEE WHAT ZOLA'S DONE TO HIM.
KRUCH
GHRAAAAK--!
PLEASE GOD-- MAKE HIM SEE--

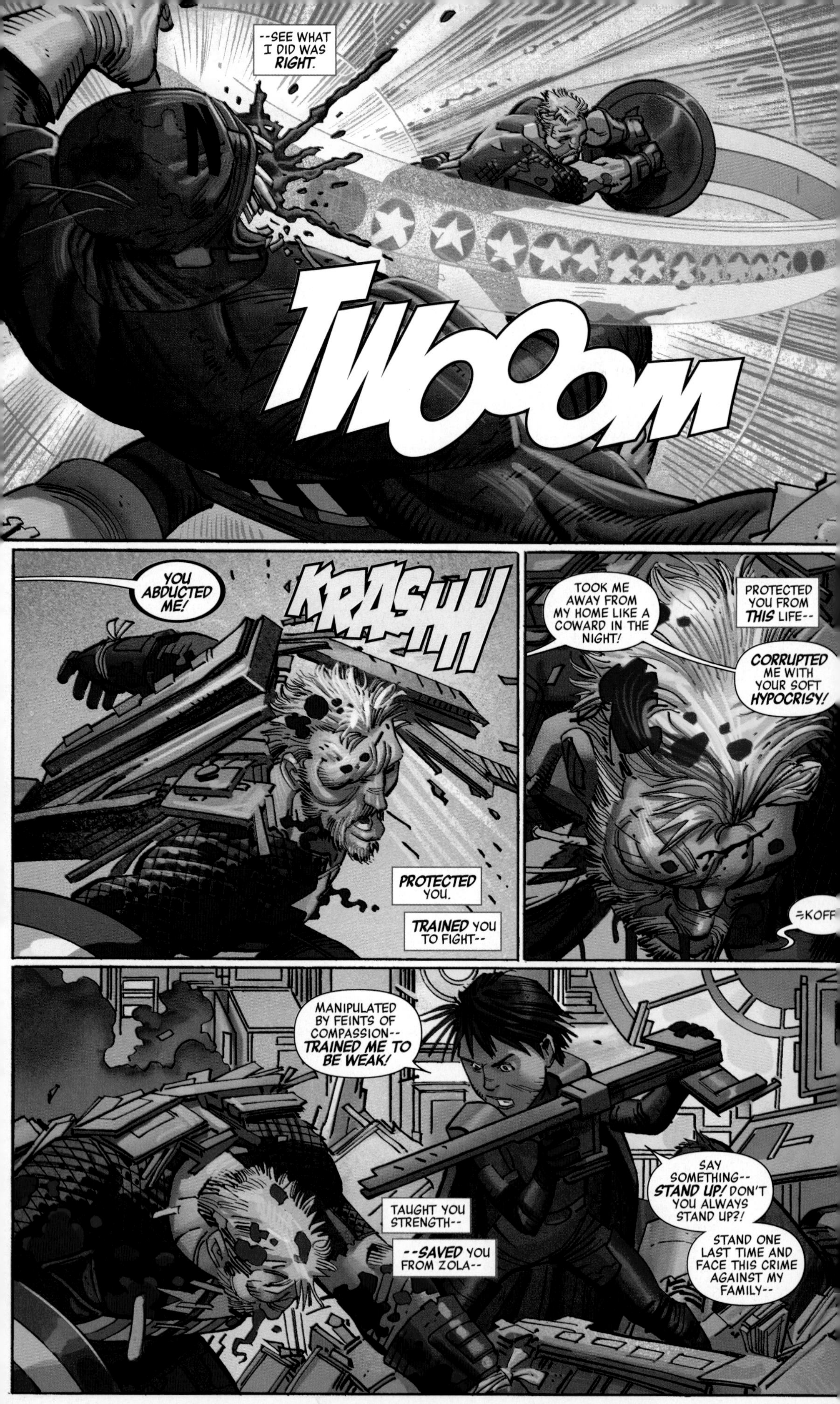
--SEE WHAT I DID WAS RIGHT.
THOOOM
YOU ABDUCTED ME!
KRASHH
PROTECTED YOU.
TRAINED YOU TO FIGHT--
TOOK ME AWAY FROM MY HOME LIKE A COWARD IN THE NIGHT!
PROTECTED YOU FROM THIS LIFE--
CORRUPTED ME WITH YOUR SOFT HYPOCRISY!
KOFF
MANIPULATED BY FEINTS OF COMPASSION--TRAINED ME TO BE WEAK!
TAUGHT YOU STRENGTH--
--SAVED YOU FROM ZOLA--
SAY SOMETHING--STAND UP! DON'T YOU ALWAYS STAND UP?!
STAND ONE LAST TIME AND FACE THIS CRIME AGAINST MY FAMILY--

"HE LAST TIME
EVER MEDDLE
HE AFFAIRS OF
A ZOLA."
WE HAVE REACHED THE ALTITUDE.
WE ARE PREPARED, ALL-GOD.
ZOLANDIA
ND ITS FURIOUS
HABITANTS STAND
READY TO INFECT
EARTH.
LEOPOLD?
RELEASED, SENT TO ERADICATE CAPTAIN AMERICA.
THE BATTLE IS BEING RECORDED?
AS INSTRUCTED.
LEOPOLD WILL KILL THE GOOD CAPTAIN.
ROGERS LACKS THE VERVE TO KILL THE BOY. LEOPOLD WILL TASTE HIS FIRST VICTORY.
THE REST OF THE MUTATES?
GATHERED FOR THE GLORIOUS EXPANSION.
THE GENERATORS?
PRIMED FOR THE GREAT JOURNEY.
THE GATE OF THE GALE AWAITS MY KEY.
MY CENTURIES HERE COME TO AN END, AT LONG LAST.
IT INSPIRES MISTY RECOLLECTIONS.
LANDMARKS PUNCTUATING THE PASSAGE OF TIME OFTEN DO.
BUT THERE IS NO TIME FOR NOSTALGIA OR REFLECTION.
THE WORLD OF MY FATHER, AND THE MEN LIKE HIM, THOSE WHO SAW ME AS A WEAK AND FRAIL THING...

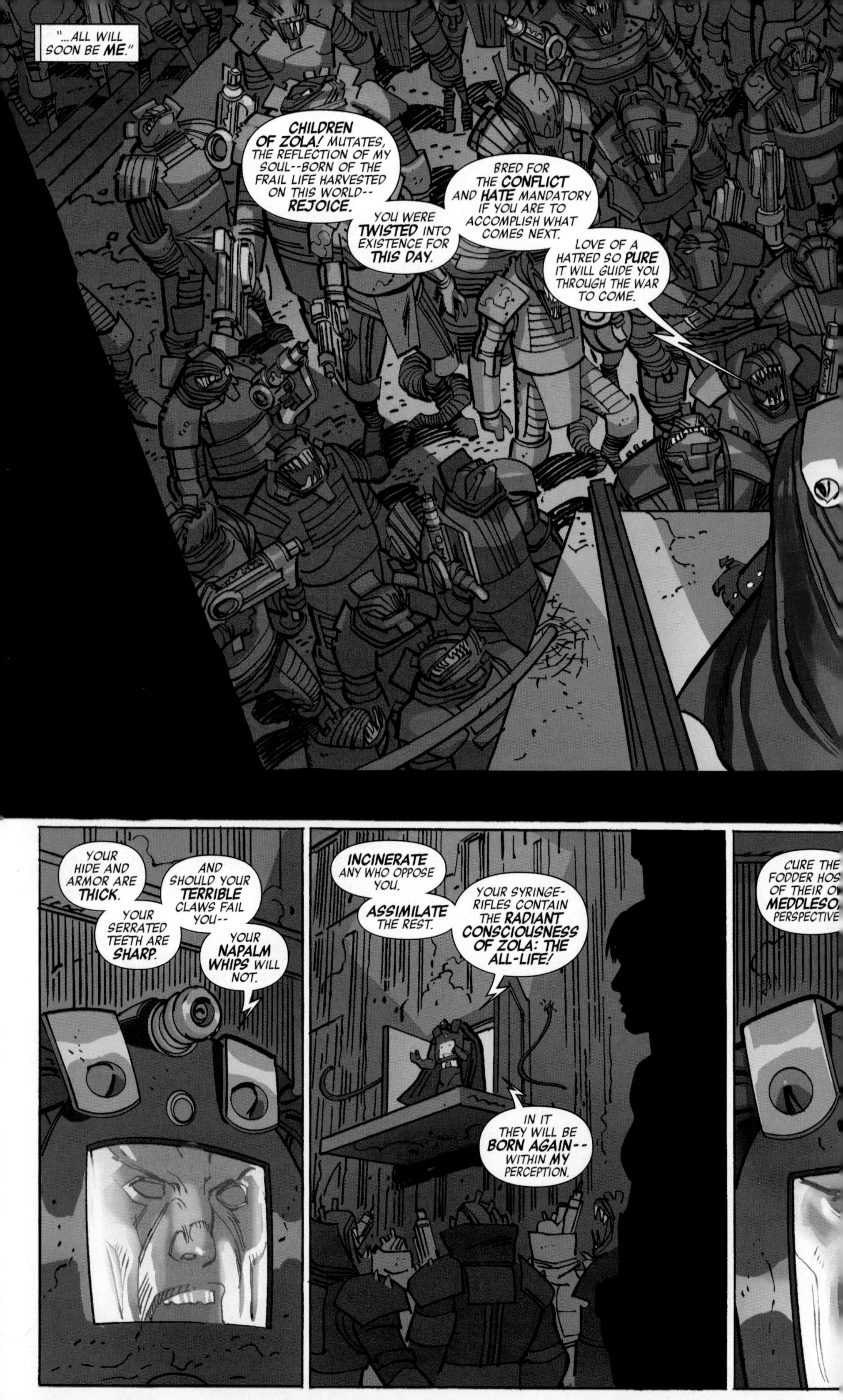

"...ALL WILL SOON BE ME."
CHILDREN OF ZOLA! MUTATES, THE REFLECTION OF MY SOUL--BORN OF THE FRAIL LIFE HARVESTED ON THIS WORLD-- REJOICE.
YOU WERE TWISTED INTO EXISTENCE FOR THIS DAY.
BRED FOR THE CONFLICT AND HATE MANDATORY IF YOU ARE TO ACCOMPLISH WHAT COMES NEXT.
LOVE OF A HATRED SO PURE IT WILL GUIDE YOU THROUGH THE WAR TO COME.
YOUR HIDE AND ARMOR ARE THICK.
YOUR SERRATED TEETH ARE SHARP.
AND SHOULD YOUR TERRIBLE CLAWS FAIL YOU--
YOUR NAPALM WHIPS WILL NOT.
INCINERATE ANY WHO OPPOSE YOU.
ASSIMILATE THE REST.
YOUR SYRINGE-RIFLES CONTAIN THE RADIANT CONSCIOUSNESS OF ZOLA: THE ALL-LIFE!
IN IT THEY WILL BE BORN AGAIN-- WITHIN MY PERCEPTION.
CURE THE FODDER HOS OF THEIR O MEDDLESO PERSPECTIVE

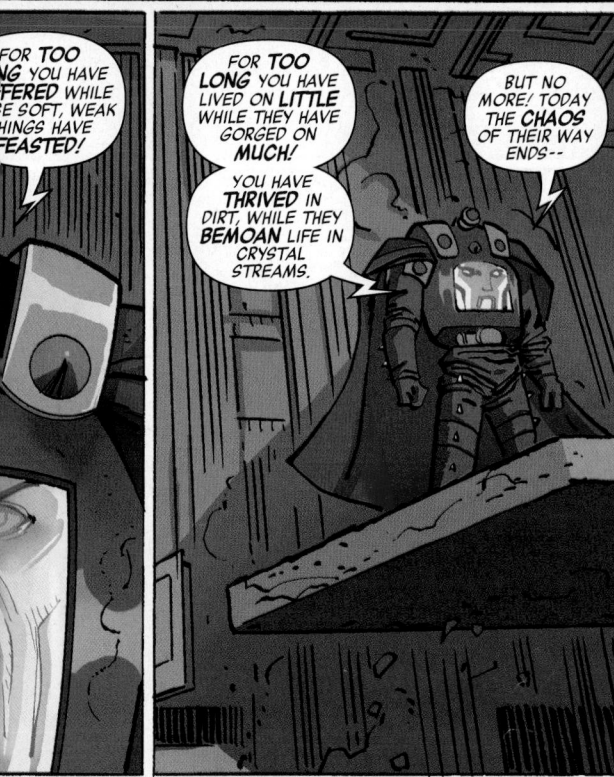

YOU, MY AVATARS, ARE **INCAPABLE** OF FAILING.

FOR YOU SERVE MY CHILDREN-- THE **RIGHTFUL** INHERITORS OF THE WORLD YOU MARCH ON. THEY ARE **YOUR CHILDREN** AS WELL.

GENETICALLY ENGINEERED TO CHERISH THEM AS MUCH AS I.

THE RIGHTFUL **KING** AND **QUEEN** OF THE **MIRACULOUS** BLUE GEM YOU SET OUT TO CLEANSE.

FOR **TOO** ~~NG~~ YOU HAVE ~~FERED~~ WHILE ~~E~~ SOFT, WEAK ~~HINGS~~ HAVE ~~FEASTED!~~

FOR **TOO LONG** YOU HAVE LIVED ON **LITTLE** WHILE THEY HAVE GORGED ON **MUCH!**

YOU HAVE **THRIVED** IN DIRT, WHILE THEY **BEMOAN** LIFE IN CRYSTAL STREAMS.

BUT NO **MORE!** TODAY THE **CHAOS** OF THEIR WAY ENDS--

TODAY, THE ERA OF ZOLA BEGINS!

"YOU **STOLE** ME AWAY FROM MY FAMILY-- **BRAINWASHED ME!**"

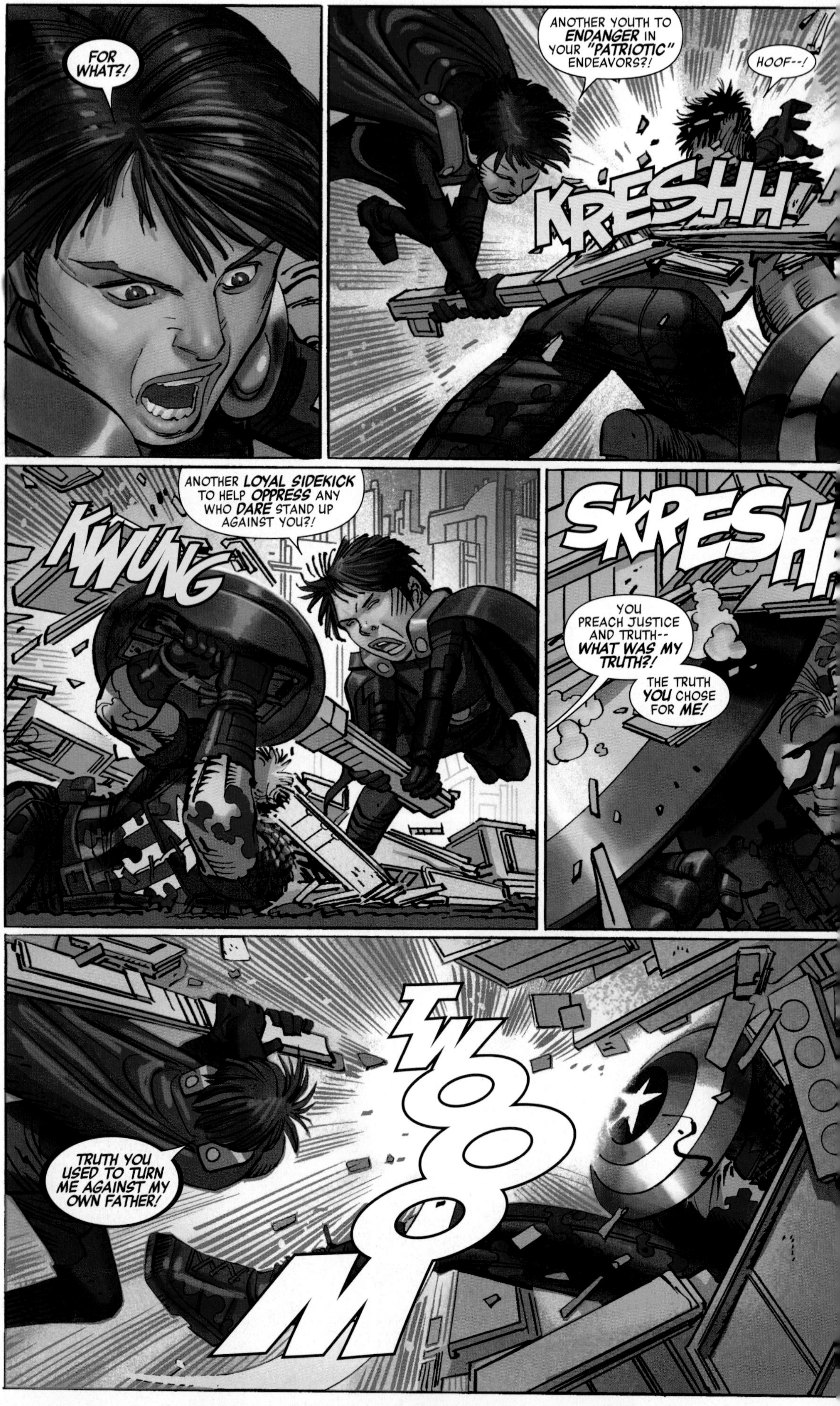
FOR WHAT?!
ANOTHER YOUTH TO ENDANGER IN YOUR "PATRIOTIC" ENDEAVORS?!
HOOF--!
KRESHH
KWUNG
ANOTHER LOYAL SIDEKICK TO HELP OPPRESS ANY WHO DARE STAND UP AGAINST YOU?!
SKRESH
YOU PREACH JUSTICE AND TRUTH-- WHAT WAS MY TRUTH?!
THE TRUTH YOU CHOSE FOR ME!
TRUTH YOU USED TO TURN ME AGAINST MY OWN FATHER!

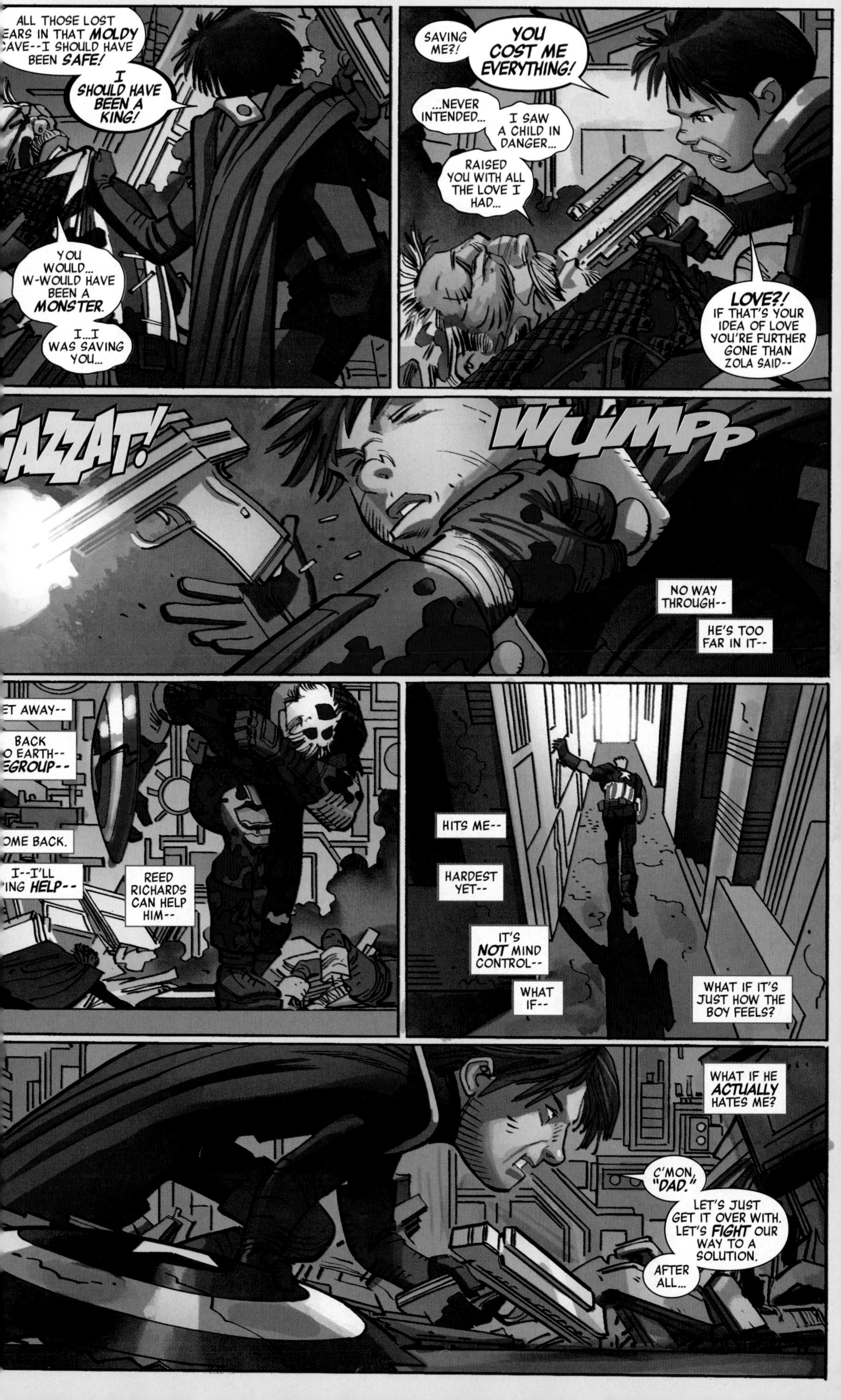
ALL THOSE LOST EARS IN THAT MOLDY CAVE--I SHOULD HAVE BEEN SAFE!
I SHOULD HAVE BEEN A KING!
YOU WOULD... W-WOULD HAVE BEEN A MONSTER.
I...I WAS SAVING YOU...
SAVING ME?!
YOU COST ME EVERYTHING!
...NEVER INTENDED...
I SAW A CHILD IN DANGER...
RAISED YOU WITH ALL THE LOVE I HAD...
LOVE?! IF THAT'S YOUR IDEA OF LOVE YOU'RE FURTHER GONE THAN ZOLA SAID--
ZAZZAT!
WUMPP
NO WAY THROUGH--
HE'S TOO FAR IN IT--
ET AWAY--
BACK O EARTH--
EGROUP--
OME BACK.
I--I'LL PING HELP--
REED RICHARDS CAN HELP HIM--
HITS ME--
HARDEST YET--
IT'S NOT MIND CONTROL--
WHAT IF--
WHAT IF IT'S JUST HOW THE BOY FEELS?
WHAT IF HE ACTUALLY HATES ME?
C'MON, "DAD."
LET'S JUST GET IT OVER WITH. LET'S FIGHT OUR WAY TO A SOLUTION.
AFTER ALL...

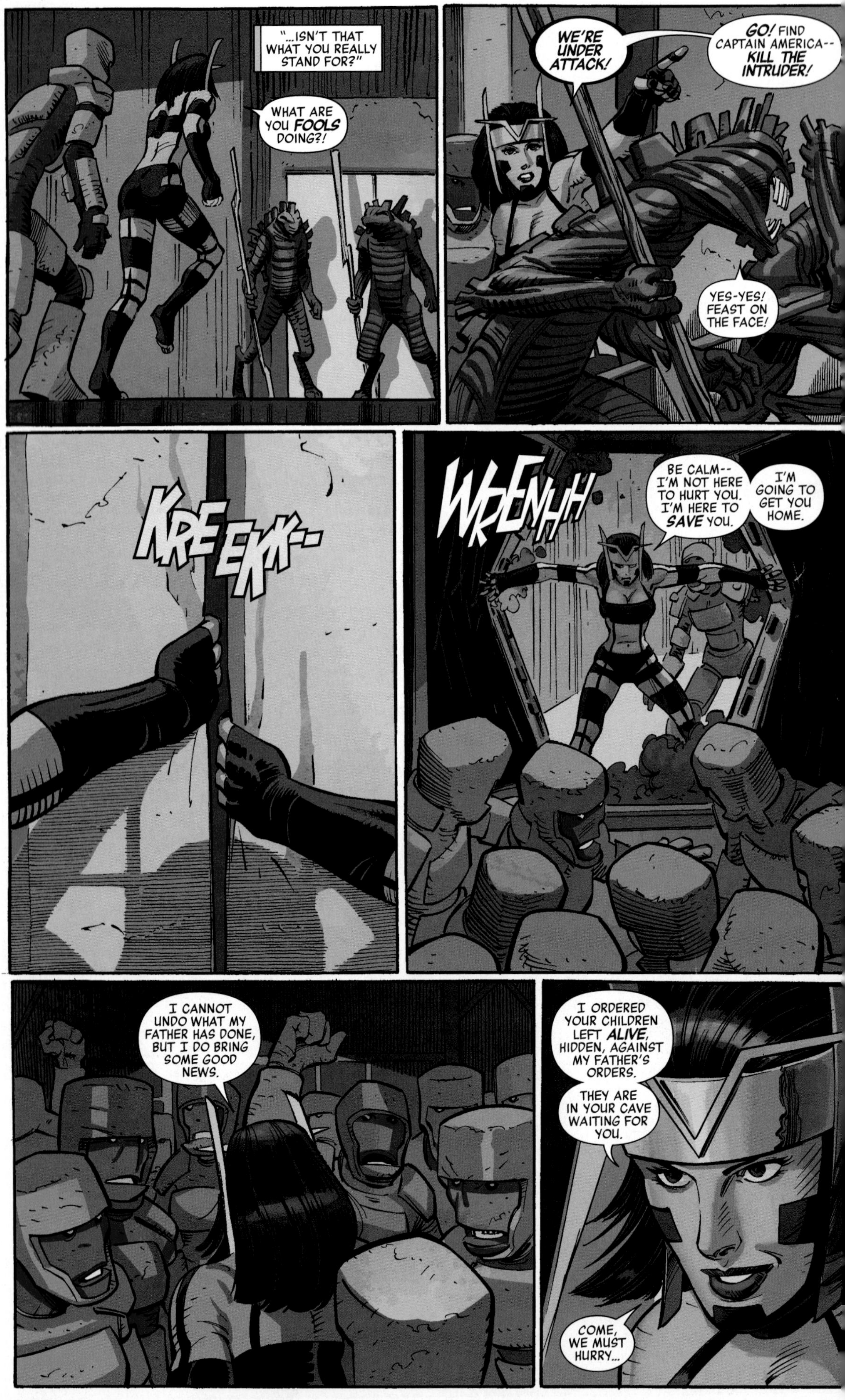
"...ISN'T THAT WHAT YOU REALLY STAND FOR?"
WHAT ARE YOU FOOLS DOING?!
WE'RE UNDER ATTACK!
GO! FIND CAPTAIN AMERICA-- KILL THE INTRUDER!
YES-YES! FEAST ON THE FACE!
KREEKK--
WRENHH
BE CALM-- I'M NOT HERE TO HURT YOU. I'M HERE TO SAVE YOU.
I'M GOING TO GET YOU HOME.
I CANNOT UNDO WHAT MY FATHER HAS DONE, BUT I DO BRING SOME GOOD NEWS.
I ORDERED YOUR CHILDREN LEFT ALIVE, HIDDEN, AGAINST MY FATHER'S ORDERS.
THEY ARE IN YOUR CAVE WAITING FOR YOU.
COME, WE MUST HURRY...

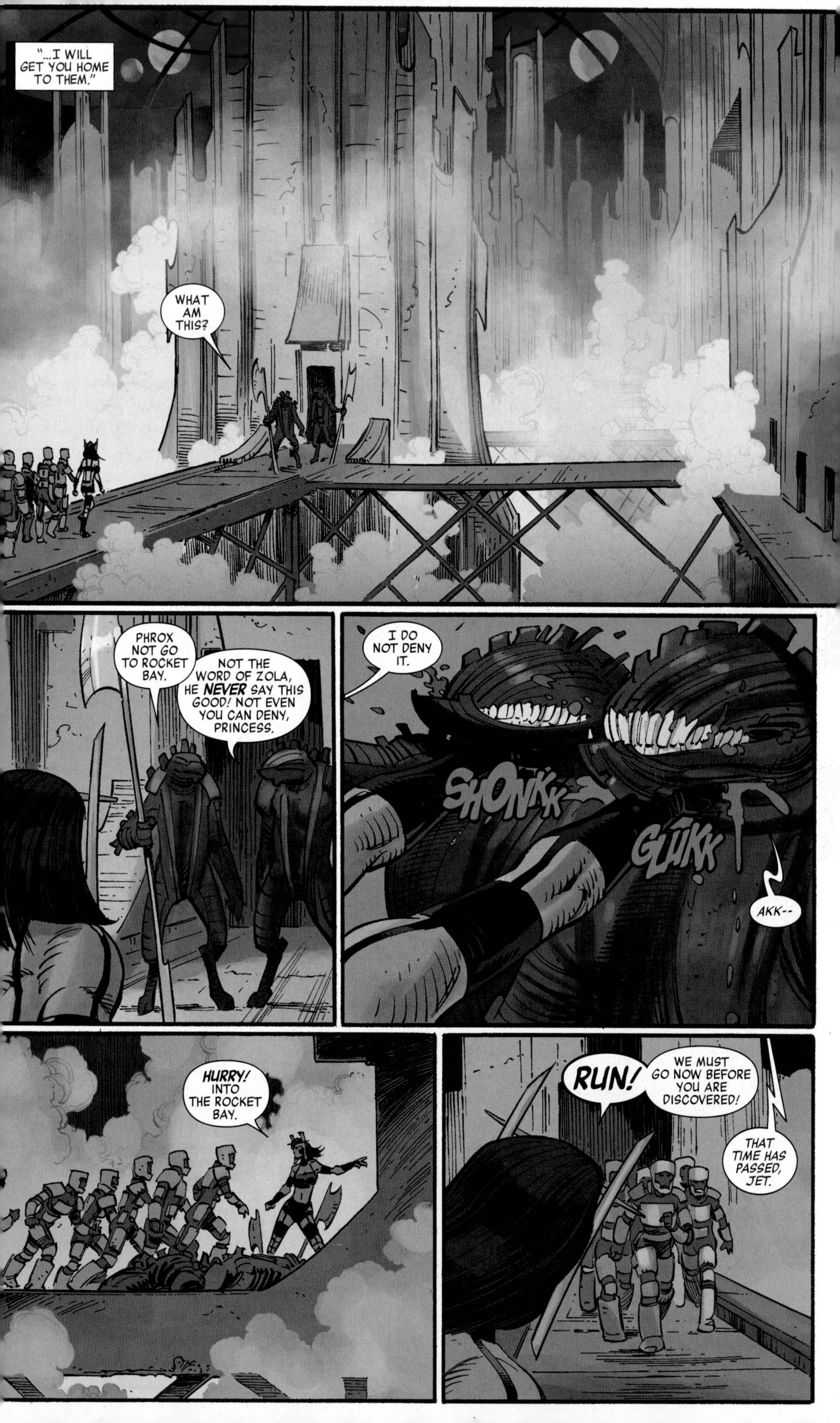
"...I WILL GET YOU HOME TO THEM."
WHAT AM THIS?
PHROX NOT GO TO ROCKET BAY.
NOT THE WORD OF ZOLA, HE NEVER SAY THIS GOOD! NOT EVEN YOU CAN DENY, PRINCESS.
I DO NOT DENY IT.
SHONKK
GLUKK
AKK--
HURRY! INTO THE ROCKET BAY.
RUN!
WE MUST GO NOW BEFORE YOU ARE DISCOVERED!
THAT TIME HAS PASSED, JET.

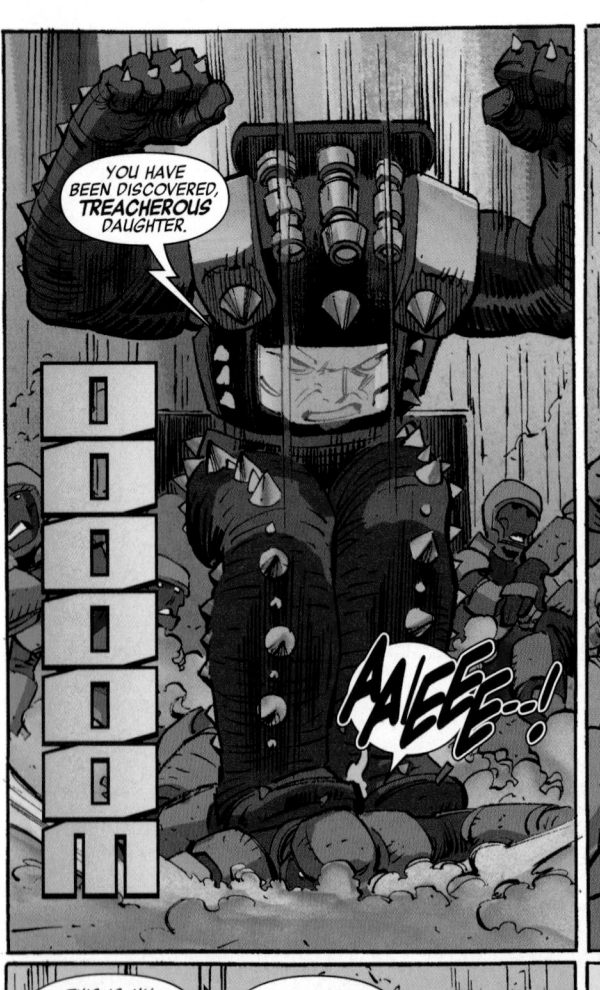

YOU HAVE BEEN DISCOVERED, *TREACHEROUS* DAUGHTER.

OOOOOM

AAIEE...!

STOP THIS! YOU HAVE AN ARMY OF MUTATES! YOU DON'T *NEED THEM*-- YOU SAID SO *YOURSELF!*

NEED? NEED HAS NOTHING TO *DO* WITH IT!

THIS IS MY *DISGUST* AT YOUR SUDDEN DESCENT INTO *COMPASSION* FOR THIS *FODDER!*

TO RISK YOUR STANDING, WHEN WE ARE SO CLOSE, FOR THESE...THINGS-- *IT IS BENEATH A ZOLA!*

I RAISED YOU BETTER THAN THIS *WEAKNESS!*

WHAT IS *WEAK* IS THAT I DIDN'T STAND AGAINST YOUR *ATROCITIES* SOONER.

"I'M CURIOUS, 'FATHER'..."

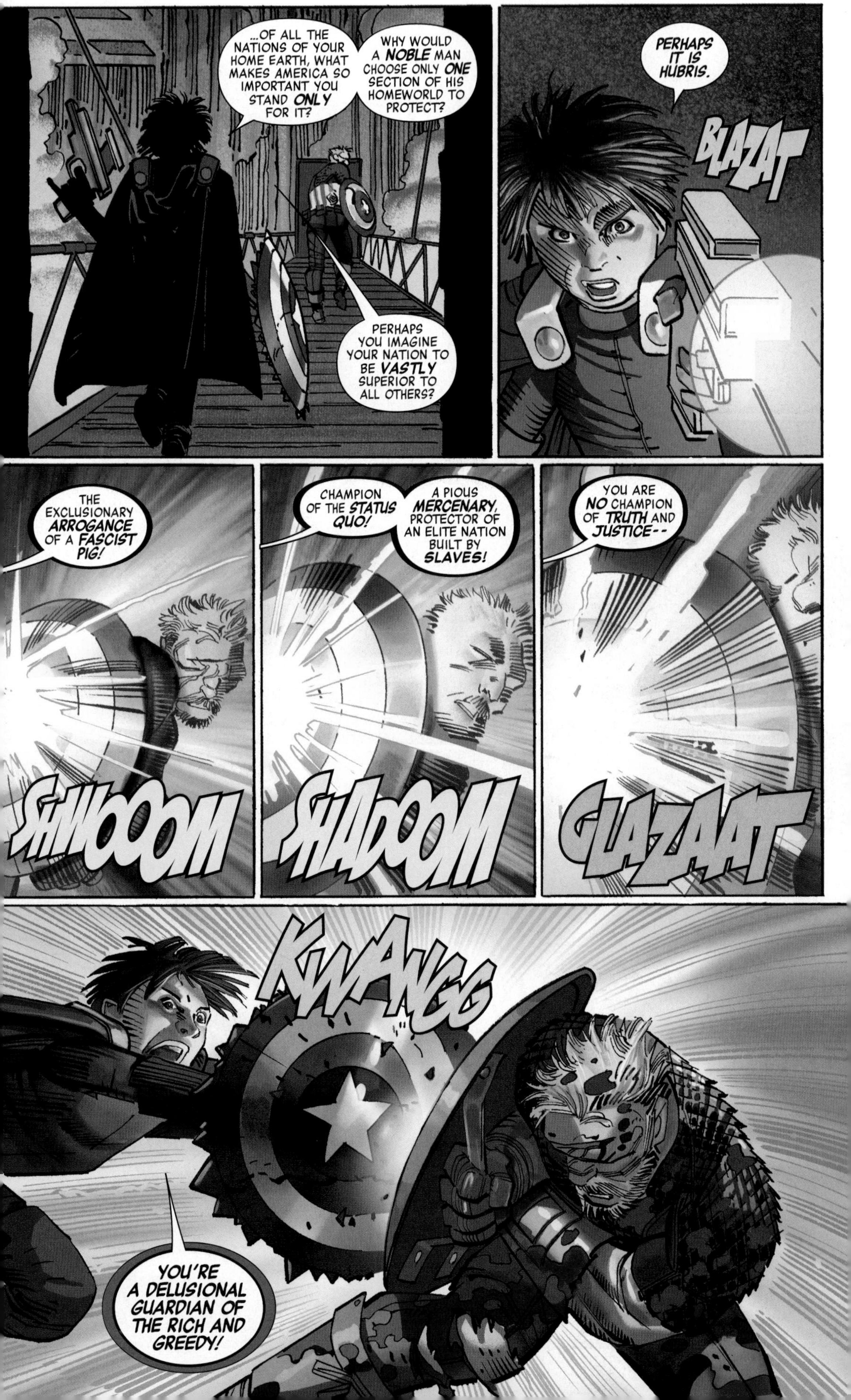
...OF ALL THE NATIONS OF YOUR HOME EARTH, WHAT MAKES AMERICA SO IMPORTANT YOU STAND ONLY FOR IT?
WHY WOULD A NOBLE MAN CHOOSE ONLY ONE SECTION OF HIS HOMEWORLD TO PROTECT?
PERHAPS YOU IMAGINE YOUR NATION TO BE VASTLY SUPERIOR TO ALL OTHERS?
PERHAPS IT IS HUBRIS.
BLAZAT
THE EXCLUSIONARY ARROGANCE OF A FASCIST PIG!
SHWOOOM
CHAMPION OF THE STATUS QUO!
A PIOUS MERCENARY, PROTECTOR OF AN ELITE NATION BUILT BY SLAVES!
SHADOOM
YOU ARE NO CHAMPION OF TRUTH AND JUSTICE--
GLAZAAT
KWANGG
YOU'RE A DELUSIONAL GUARDIAN OF THE RICH AND GREEDY!

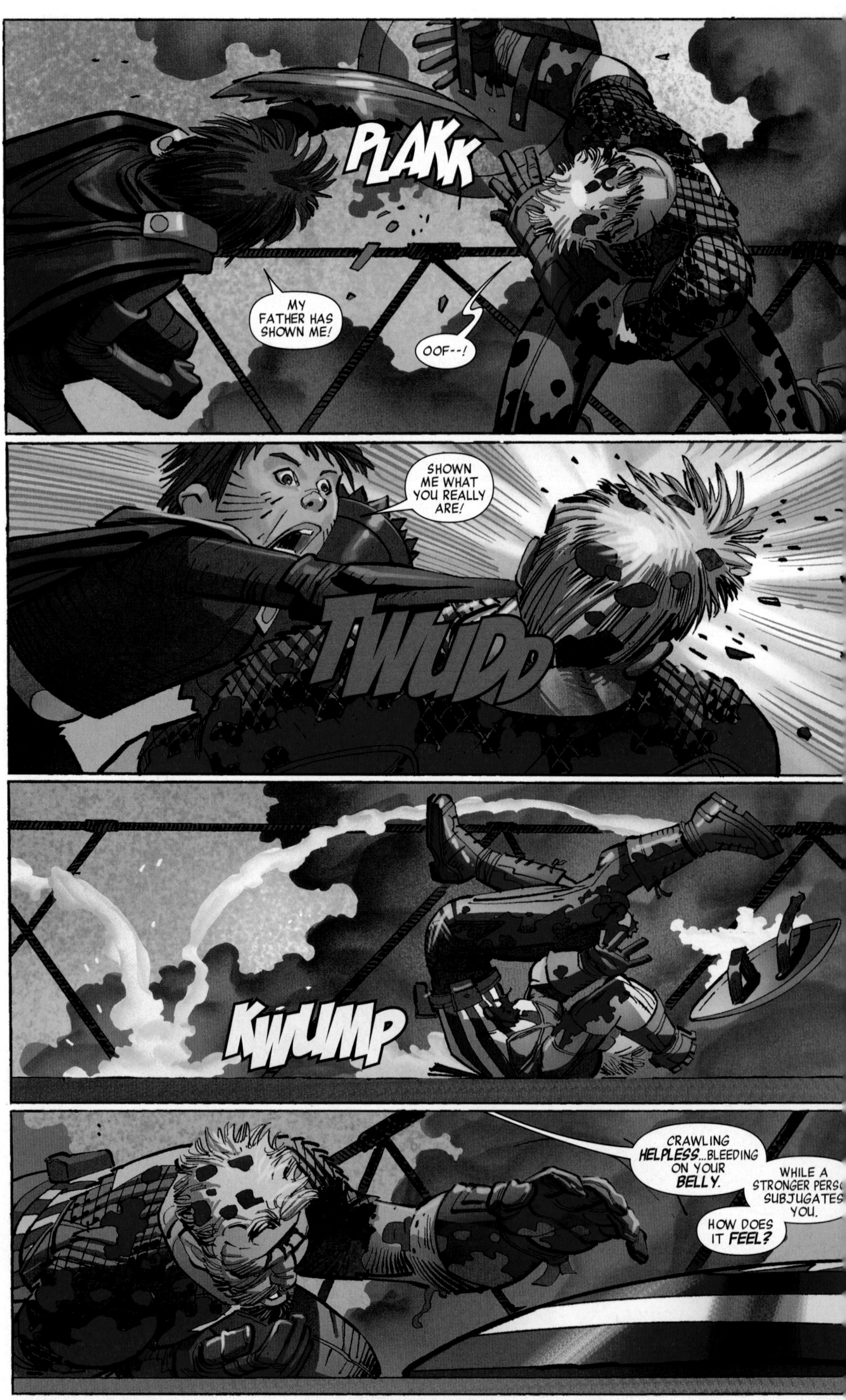
PLAKK
MY FATHER HAS SHOWN ME!
OOF--!
SHOWN ME WHAT YOU REALLY ARE!
TWUDD
KWUMP
CRAWLING HELPLESS...BLEEDING ON YOUR BELLY.
WHILE A STRONGER PERS SUBJUGATES YOU.
HOW DOES IT FEEL?

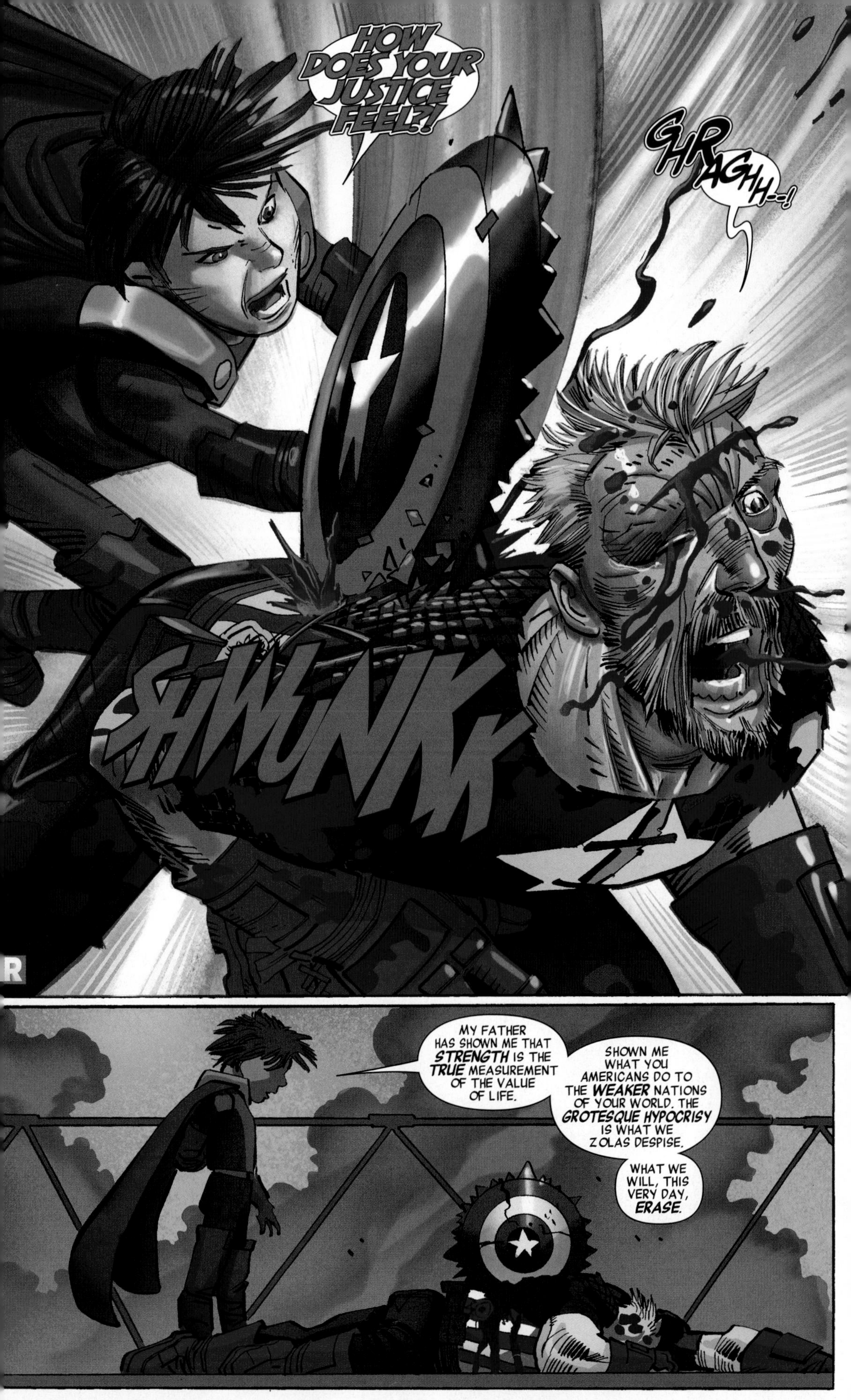

HOW DOES YOUR JUSTICE FEEL?!
GHRAGHH--!
SHWUNKK
MY FATHER HAS SHOWN ME THAT STRENGTH IS THE TRUE MEASUREMENT OF THE VALUE OF LIFE.
SHOWN ME WHAT YOU AMERICANS DO TO THE WEAKER NATIONS OF YOUR WORLD. THE GROTESQUE HYPOCRISY IS WHAT WE ZOLAS DESPISE.
WHAT WE WILL, THIS VERY DAY, ERASE.

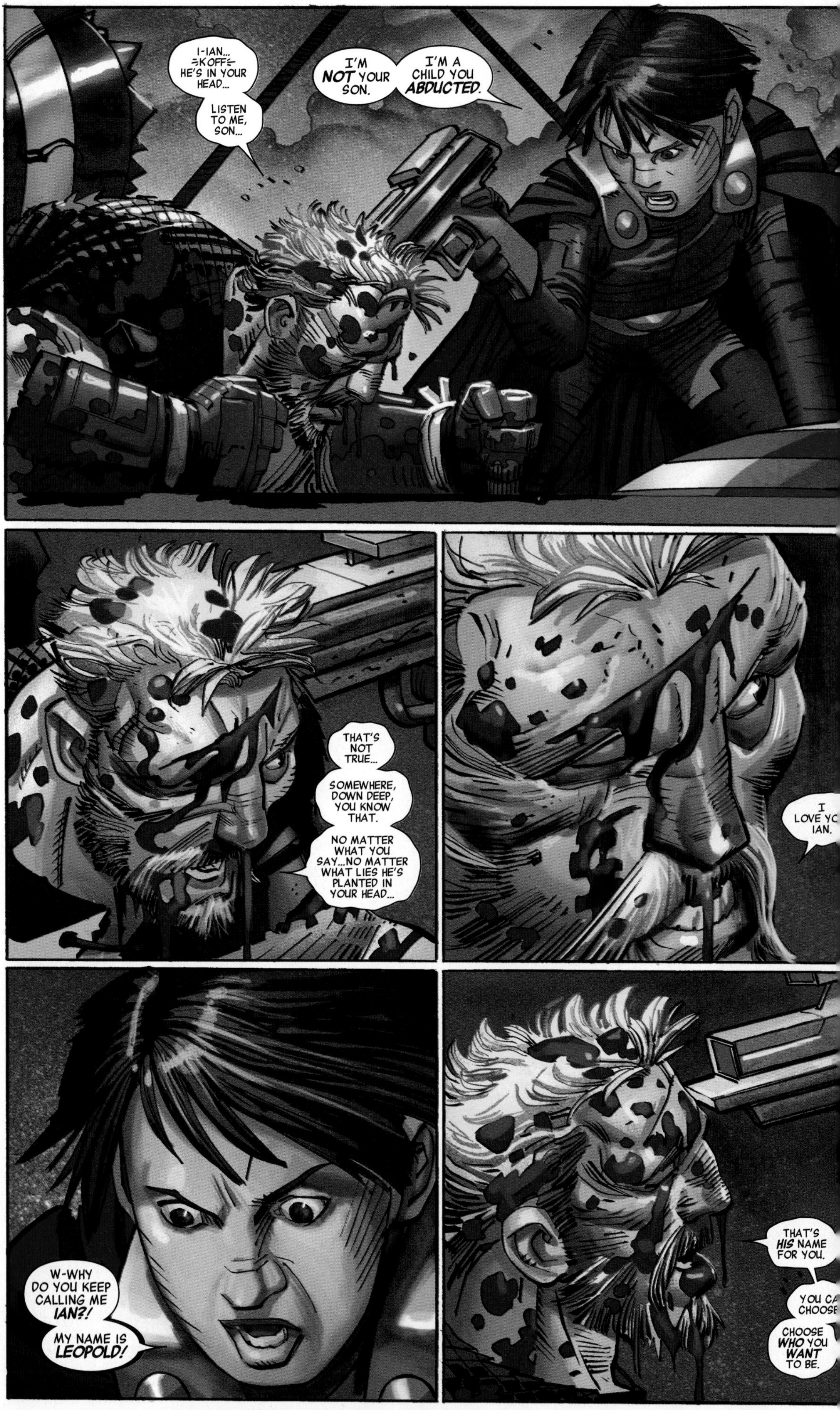

I-IAN... =KOFF= HE'S IN YOUR HEAD...
LISTEN TO ME, SON...
I'M NOT YOUR SON.
I'M A CHILD YOU ABDUCTED.
THAT'S NOT TRUE...
SOMEWHERE, DOWN DEEP, YOU KNOW THAT.
NO MATTER WHAT YOU SAY...NO MATTER WHAT LIES HE'S PLANTED IN YOUR HEAD...
I LOVE YO
IAN.
W-WHY DO YOU KEEP CALLING ME IAN?!
MY NAME IS LEOPOLD!
THAT'S HIS NAME FOR YOU.
YOU CA
CHOOSE
CHOOSE WHO YOU WANT TO BE.

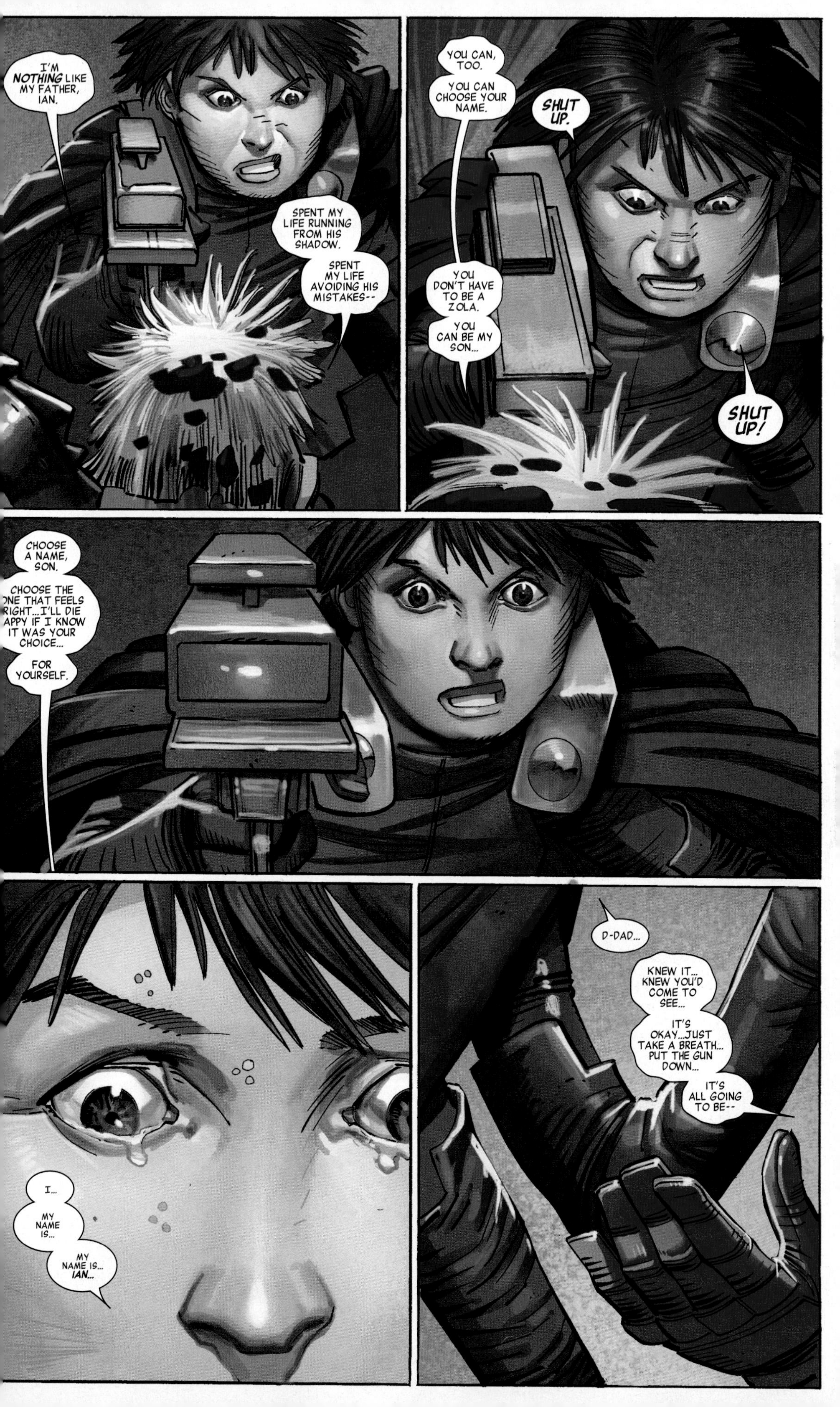

I'M NOTHING LIKE MY FATHER, IAN.
SPENT MY LIFE RUNNING FROM HIS SHADOW.
SPENT MY LIFE AVOIDING HIS MISTAKES--
YOU CAN, TOO.
YOU CAN CHOOSE YOUR NAME.
SHUT UP.
YOU DON'T HAVE TO BE A ZOLA.
YOU CAN BE MY SON...
SHUT UP!
CHOOSE A NAME, SON.
CHOOSE THE ONE THAT FEELS RIGHT...I'LL DIE HAPPY IF I KNOW IT WAS YOUR CHOICE...
FOR YOURSELF.
I...
MY NAME IS...
MY NAME IS... IAN...
D-DAD...
KNEW IT... KNEW YOU'D COME TO SEE...
IT'S OKAY...JUST TAKE A BREATH... PUT THE GUN DOWN...
IT'S ALL GOING TO BE--

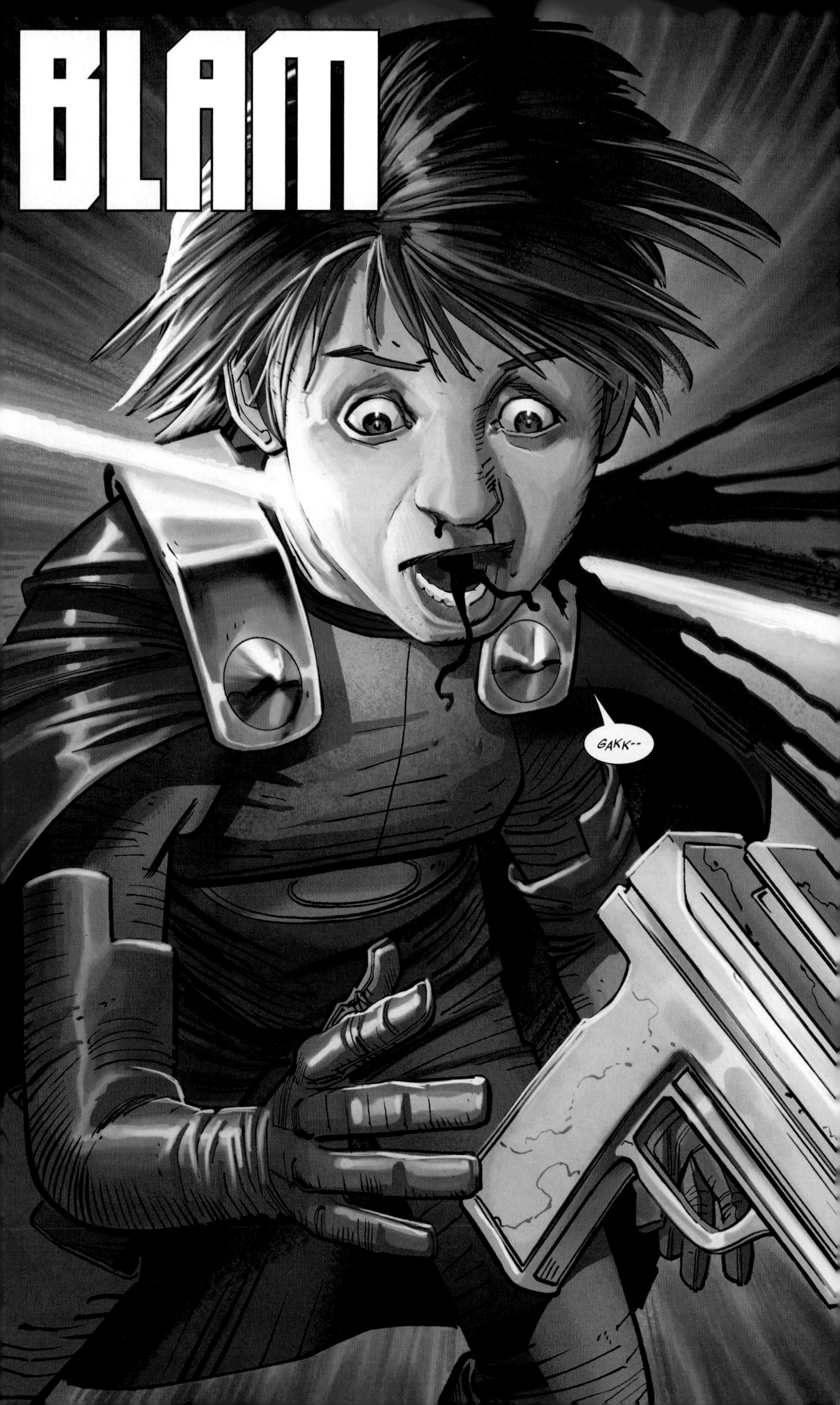
BLAM
GAKK--

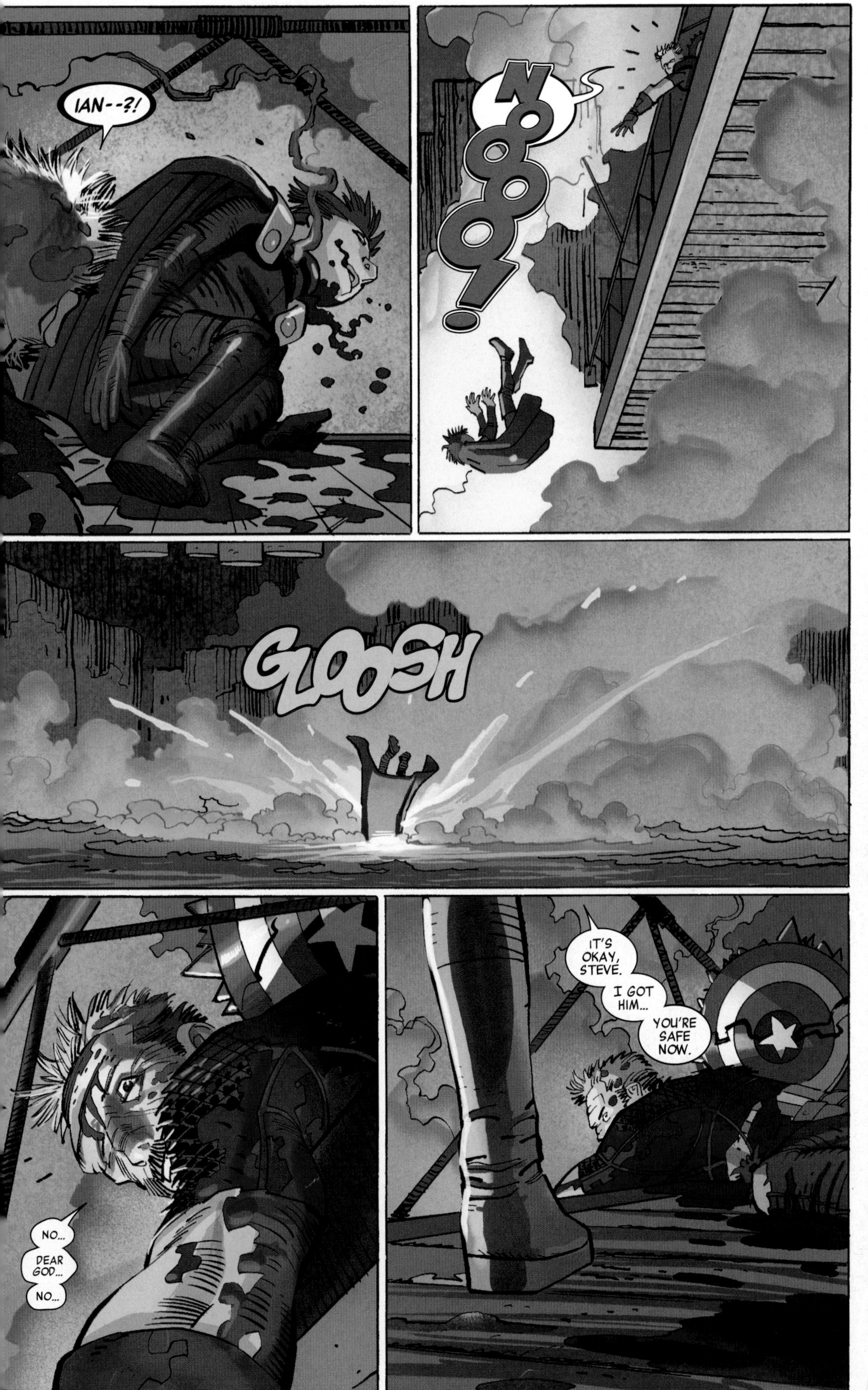
IAN--?!
NOOOO!
GLOOSH
NO...
DEAR GOD...
NO...
IT'S OKAY, STEVE.
I GOT HIM...
YOU'RE SAFE NOW.

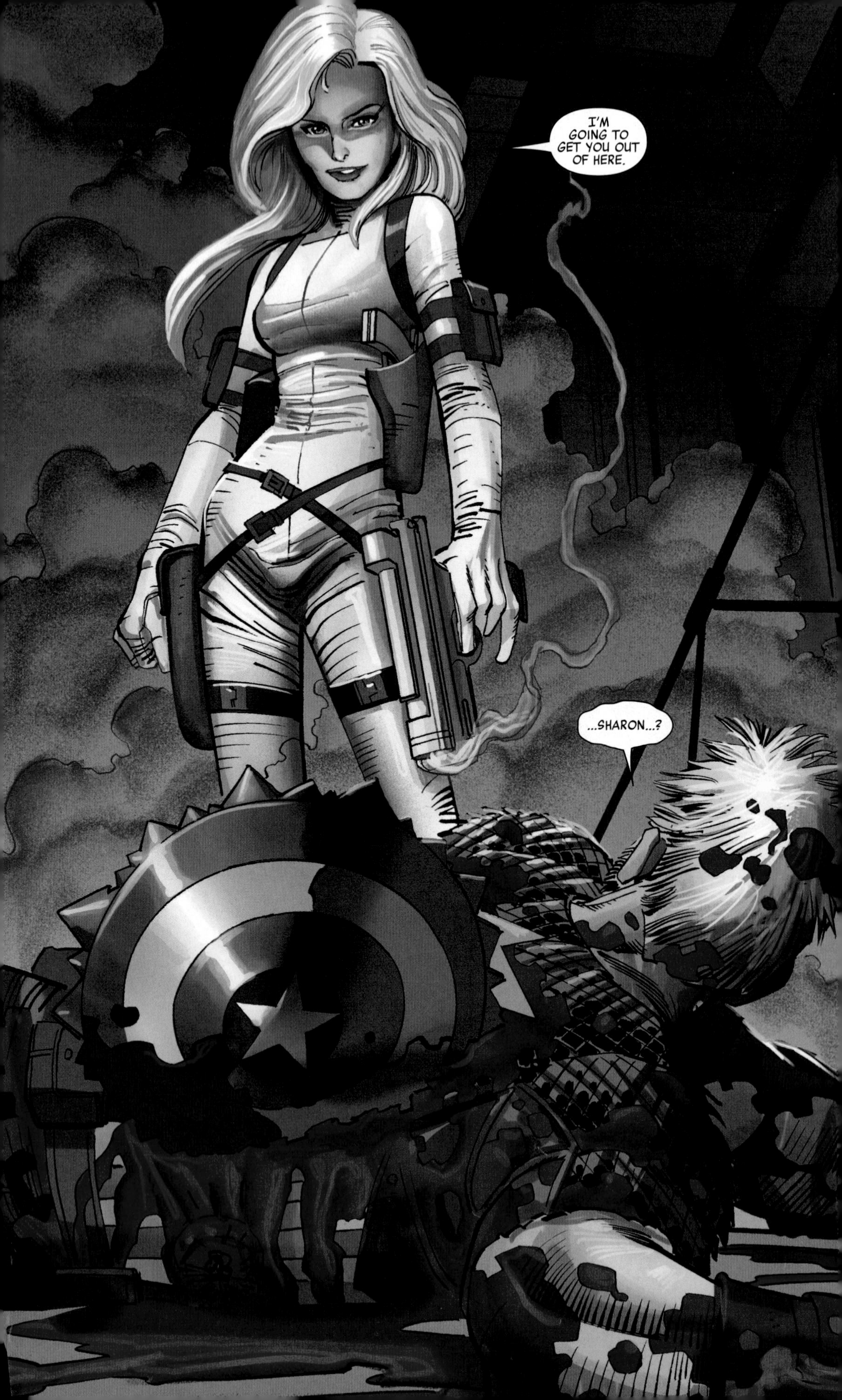
I'M GOING TO GET YOU OUT OF HERE.
...SHARON...?

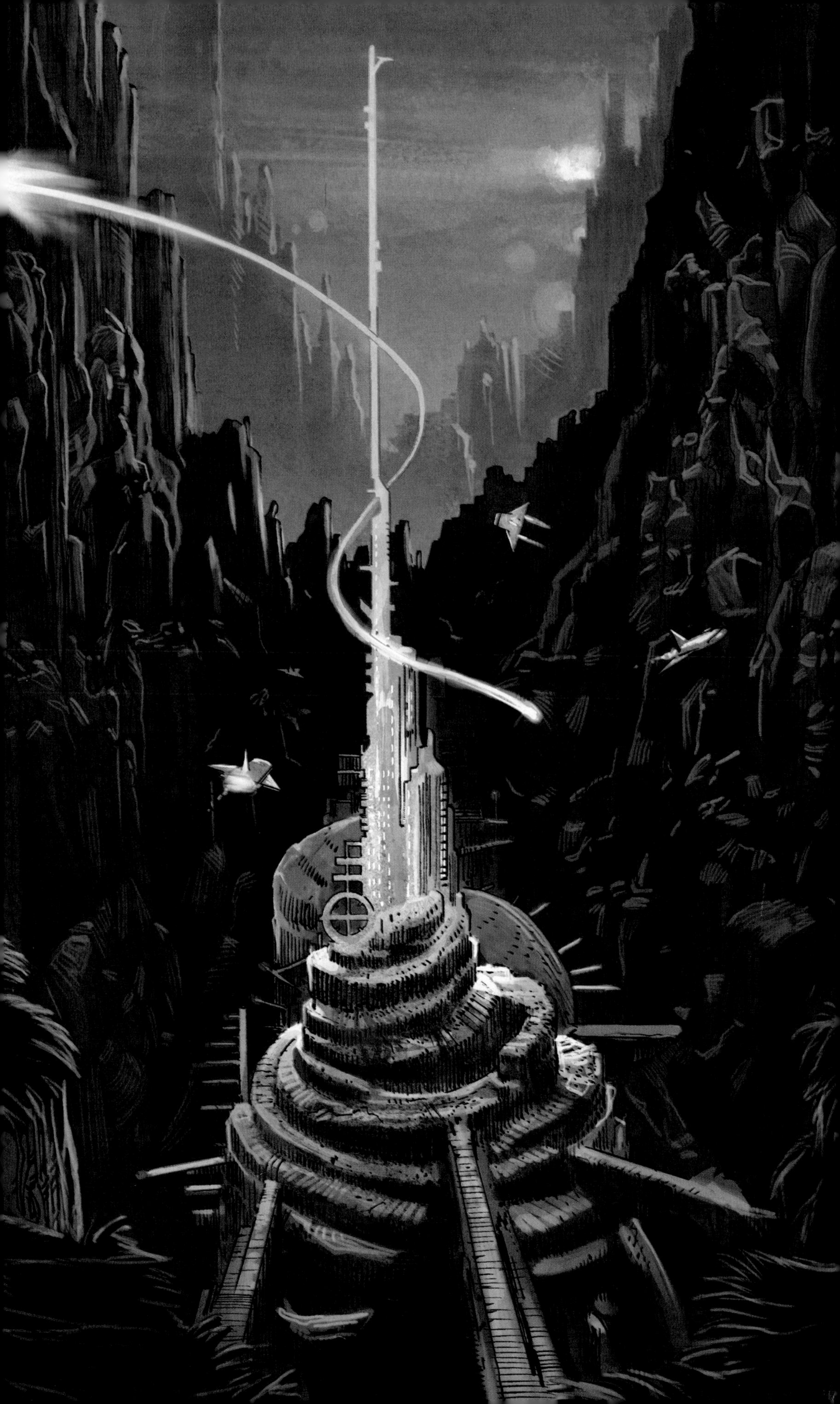

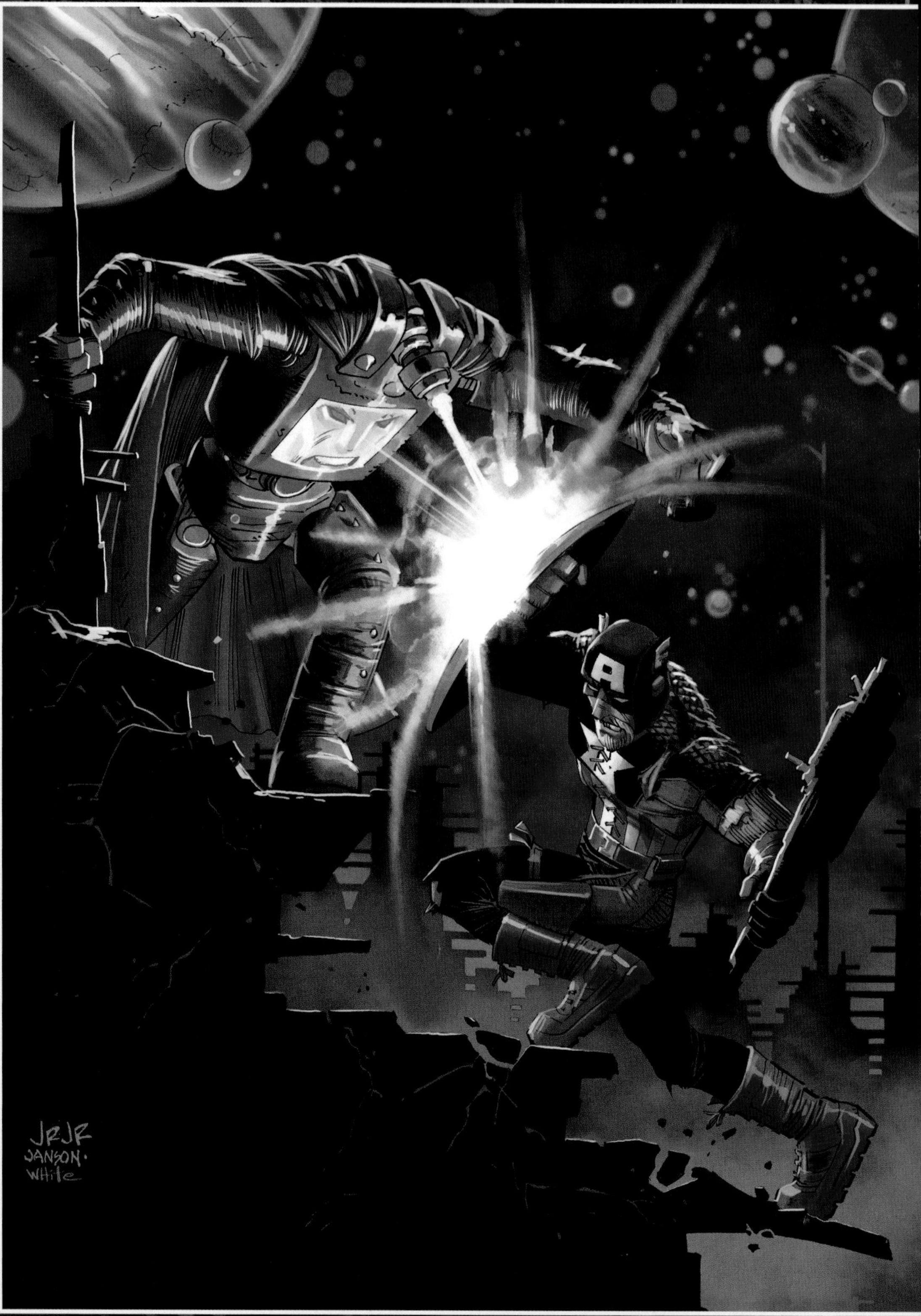
JRJR
JANSON.
White

NINE

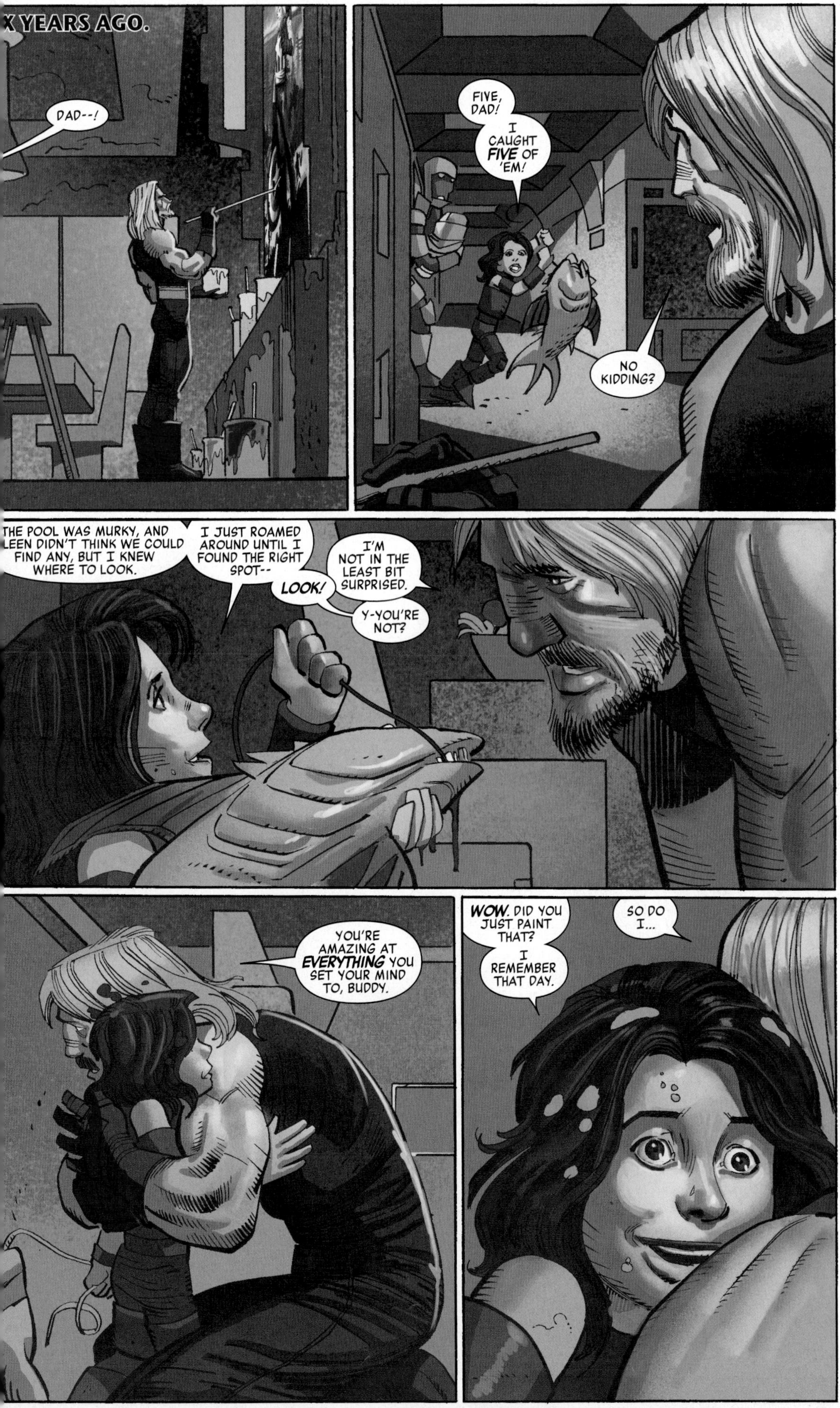

X YEARS AGO.
DAD--!
FIVE, DAD!
I CAUGHT FIVE OF 'EM!
NO KIDDING?
THE POOL WAS MURKY, AND LEEN DIDN'T THINK WE COULD FIND ANY, BUT I KNEW WHERE TO LOOK.
I JUST ROAMED AROUND UNTIL I FOUND THE RIGHT SPOT--
LOOK!
I'M NOT IN THE LEAST BIT SURPRISED.
Y-YOU'RE NOT?
YOU'RE AMAZING AT EVERYTHING YOU SET YOUR MIND TO, BUDDY.
WOW. DID YOU JUST PAINT THAT?
I REMEMBER THAT DAY.
SO DO I...

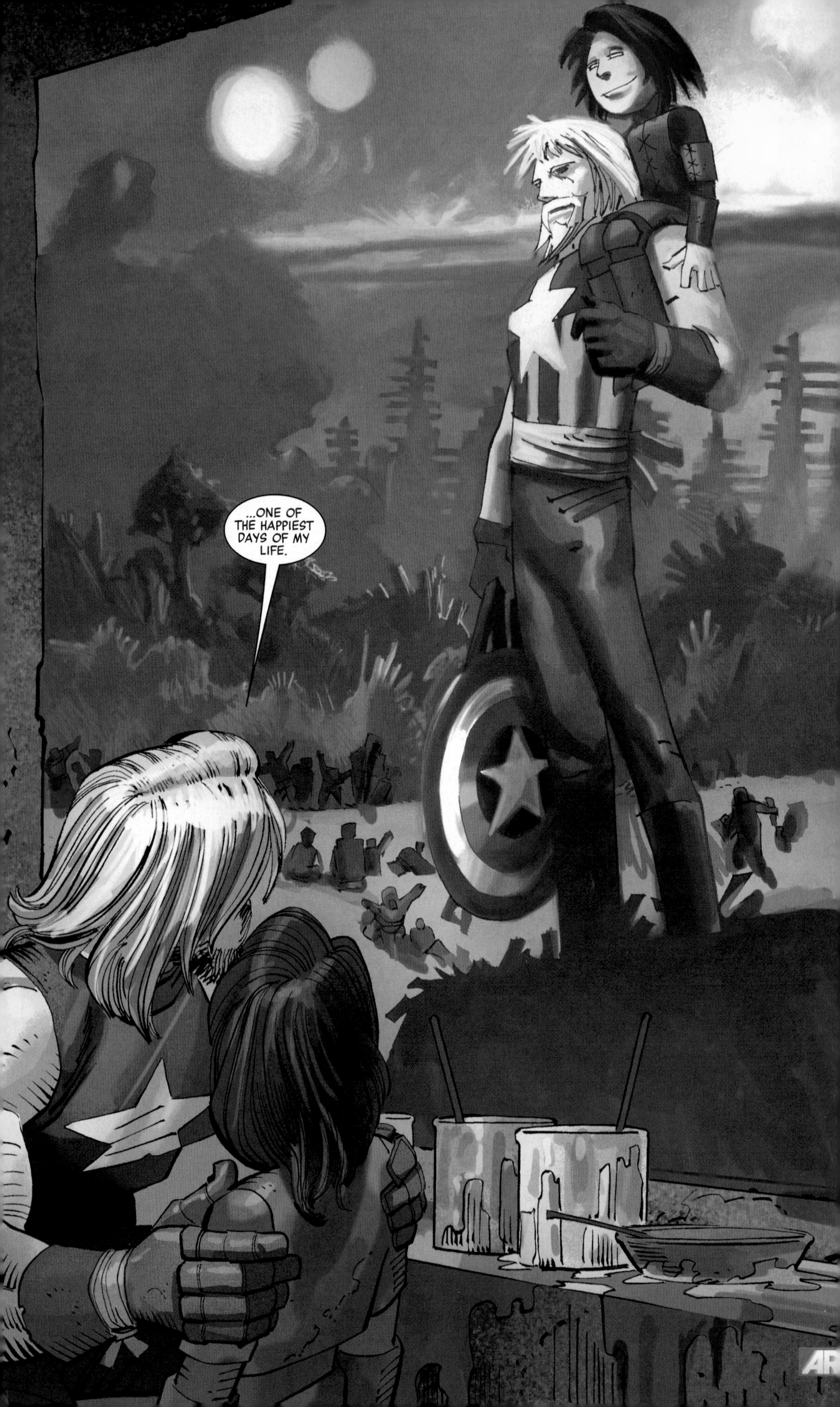
...ONE OF THE HAPPIEST DAYS OF MY LIFE.

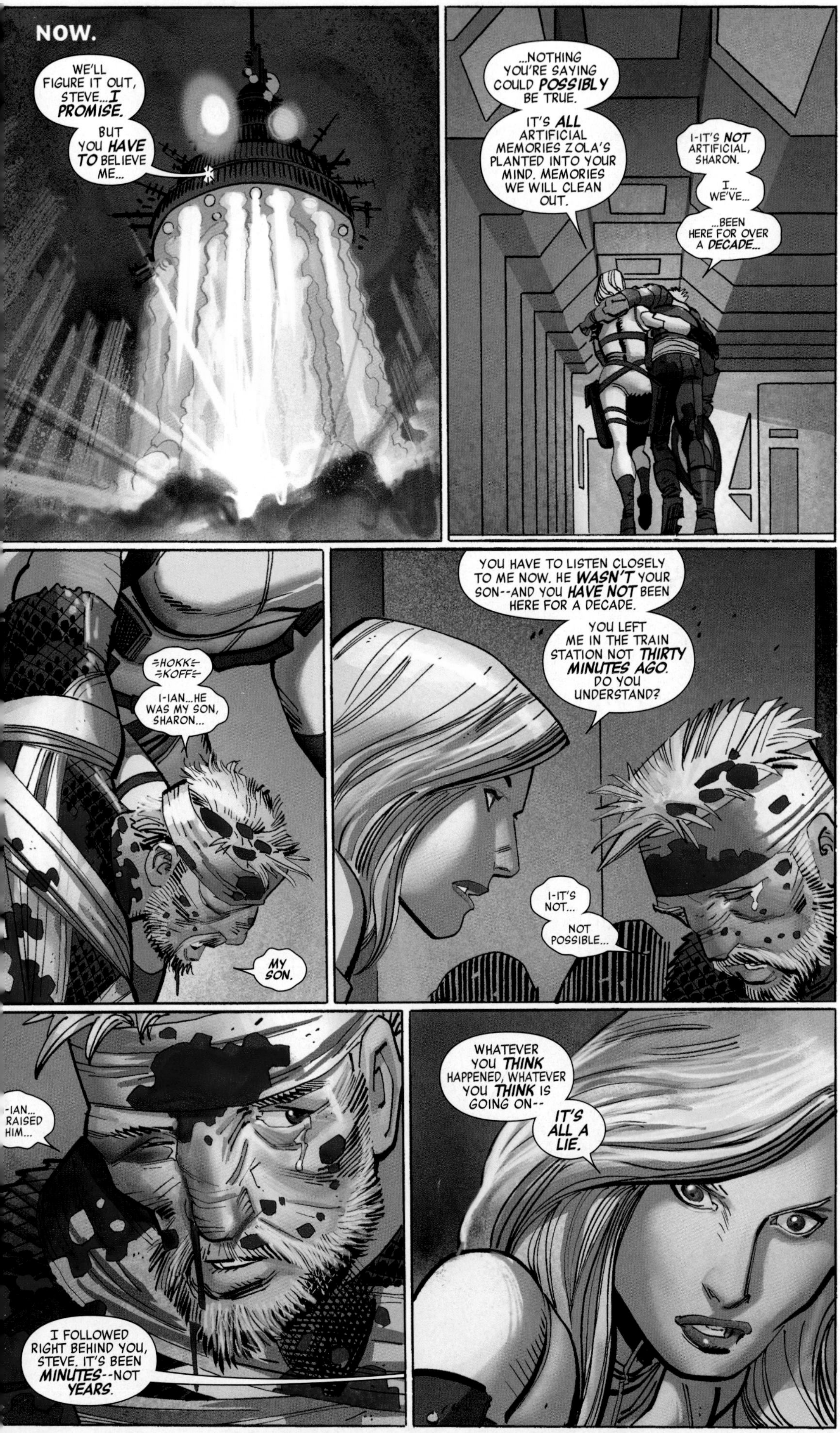
NOW.
WE'LL FIGURE IT OUT, STEVE...I PROMISE.
BUT YOU HAVE TO BELIEVE ME...
...NOTHING YOU'RE SAYING COULD POSSIBLY BE TRUE.
IT'S ALL ARTIFICIAL MEMORIES ZOLA'S PLANTED INTO YOUR MIND. MEMORIES WE WILL CLEAN OUT.
I-IT'S NOT ARTIFICIAL, SHARON.
I... WE'VE...
...BEEN HERE FOR OVER A DECADE...
HOKK KOFF
I-IAN...HE WAS MY SON, SHARON...
MY SON.
YOU HAVE TO LISTEN CLOSELY TO ME NOW. HE WASN'T YOUR SON--AND YOU HAVE NOT BEEN HERE FOR A DECADE.
YOU LEFT ME IN THE TRAIN STATION NOT THIRTY MINUTES AGO. DO YOU UNDERSTAND?
I-IT'S NOT...
NOT POSSIBLE...
-IAN... RAISED HIM...
I FOLLOWED RIGHT BEHIND YOU, STEVE. IT'S BEEN MINUTES--NOT YEARS.
WHATEVER YOU THINK HAPPENED, WHATEVER YOU THINK IS GOING ON--
IT'S ALL A LIE.

WHOEVER YOU THINK HE WAS--HE WAS GOING TO KILL YOU AND I STOPPED HIM.
I'VE BEEN A VICTIM OF ZOLA'S MIND GAMES. I KNOW WHAT YOU'RE DEALING WITH.
NO... IT WAS REAL...
IT--IT CAN'T...
CAN'T BE A LIE...
STEVE, ANGEL, JUST PUT IT OUT OF YOUR MIND--IT DOESN'T MATTER, NOT RIGHT NOW--WE'LL FIGURE IT OUT LATER.
RIGHT NOW THIS PLACE RIGGED TO BL WE HAVE T GET OUT.
WHAT?!
WHAT DO YOU MEAN, IT'S RIGGED TO BLOW UP--?!
I PLANTED PYM-CONDENSED C4 ACROSS THE BASE.
I DON'T THINK YOU UNDERSTAND THE SEVERITY OF THIS.
AS SOON AS I ARRIVED, THE CITY TURNED INTO A FLOATING BATTLE STATION.
AN ARMY OF MUTATES ARE PREPARING TO INVADE AND INFECT MANKIND WITH A ZOLA CONSCIOUSNESS VIRUS.
I SAW ROCKET BIKES--WE HAVE TO GET TO THEM.
TAKE THE TUNNEL BACK TO EARTH AND GET--
THERE!
THEM GET THAT MURDER!
SHRAKOOOM
THEM DIE FOR US--MUTATES' TURN!
EAT THEM GOOD!

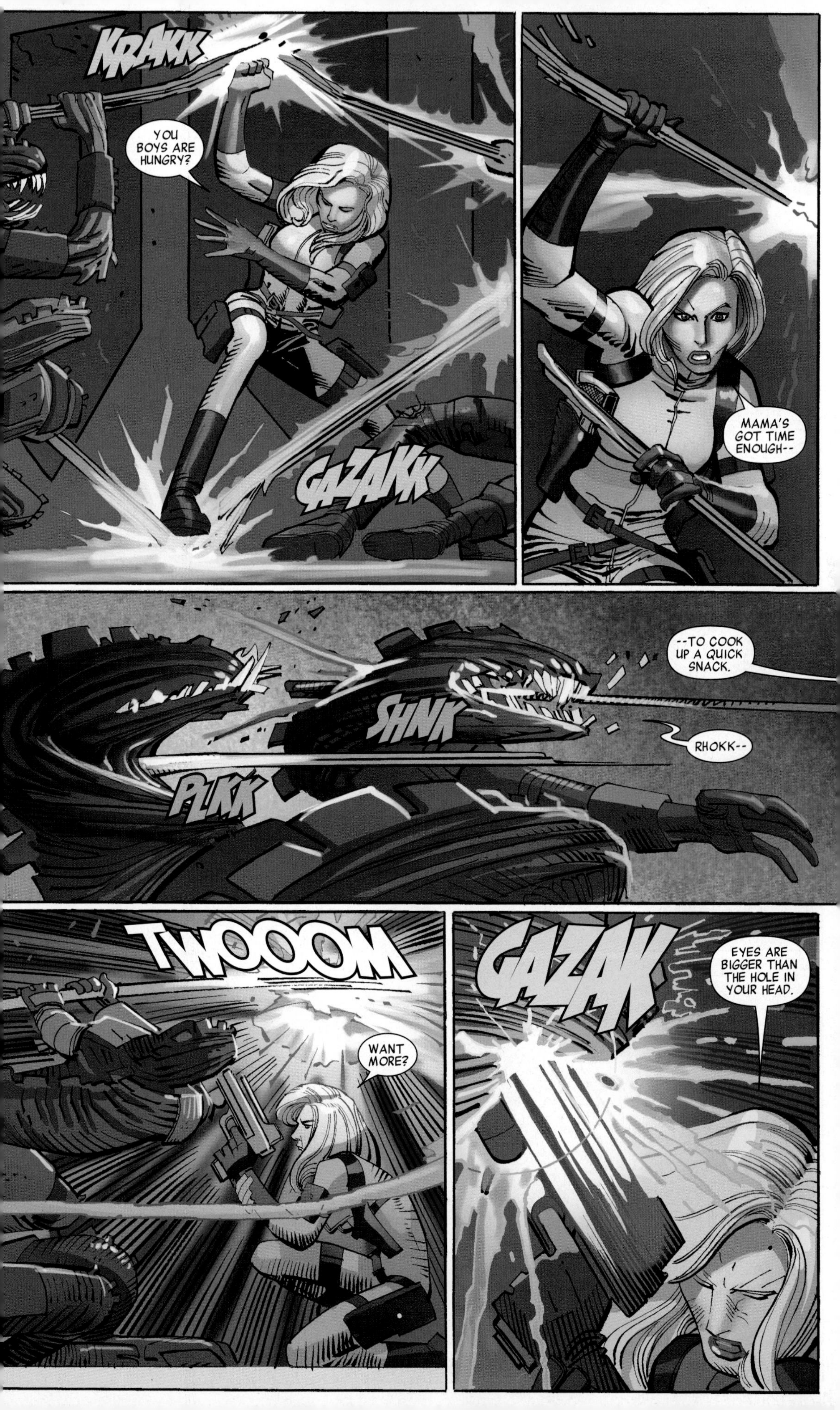
KRAKK
YOU BOYS ARE HUNGRY?
GAZAKK
MAMA'S GOT TIME ENOUGH--
--TO COOK UP A QUICK SNACK.
SHNK
RHOKK--
PLKK
TWOOOM
WANT MORE?
GAZAK
EYES ARE BIGGER THAN THE HOLE IN YOUR HEAD.

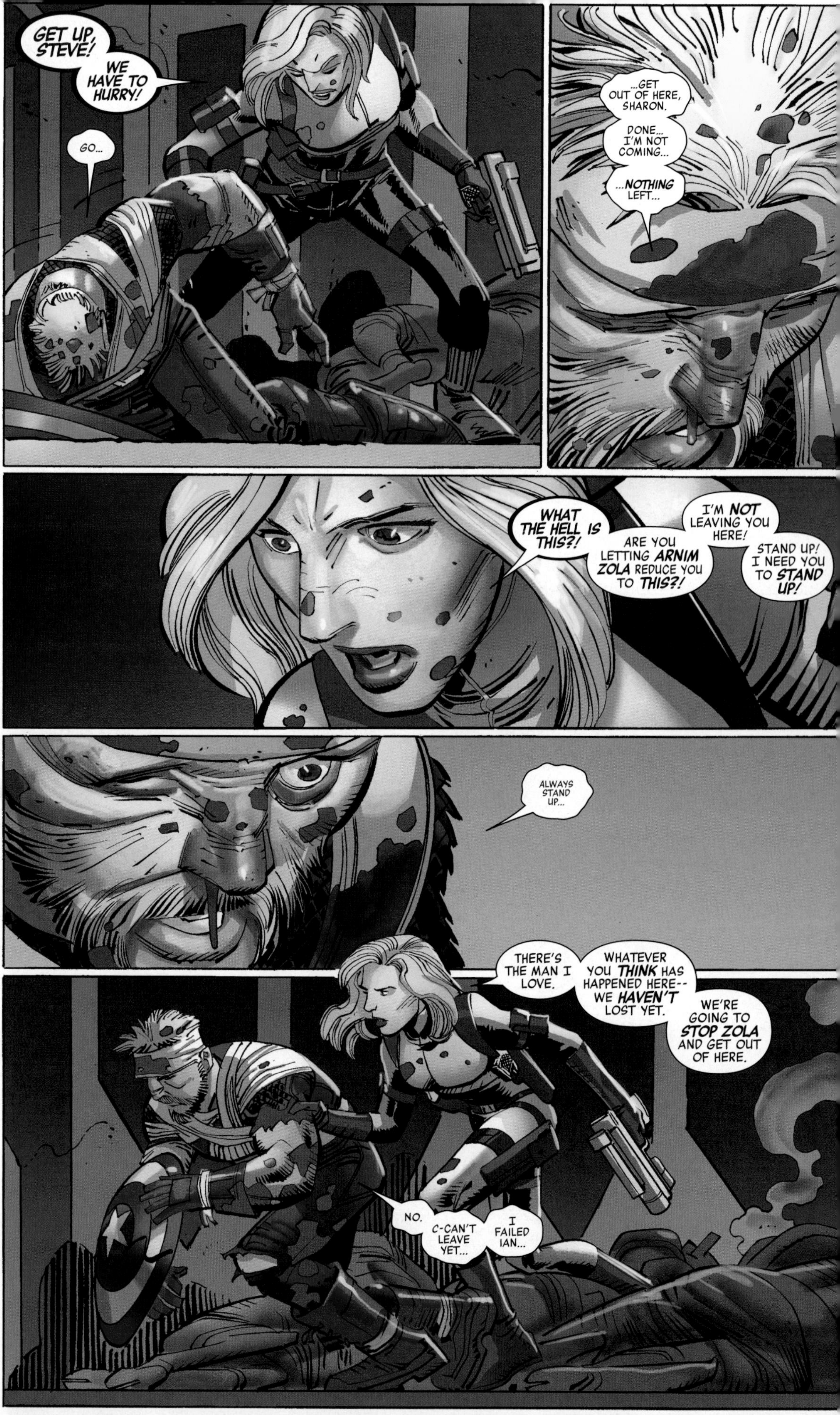
GET UP, STEVE!
WE HAVE TO HURRY!
GO...
...GET OUT OF HERE, SHARON.
DONE... I'M NOT COMING...
...NOTHING LEFT...
WHAT THE HELL IS THIS?!
ARE YOU LETTING ARNIM ZOLA REDUCE YOU TO THIS?!
I'M NOT LEAVING YOU HERE!
STAND UP! I NEED YOU TO STAND UP!
ALWAYS STAND UP...
THERE'S THE MAN I LOVE.
WHATEVER YOU THINK HAS HAPPENED HERE-- WE HAVEN'T LOST YET.
WE'RE GOING TO STOP ZOLA AND GET OUT OF HERE.
NO.
C-CAN'T LEAVE YET...
I FAILED IAN...

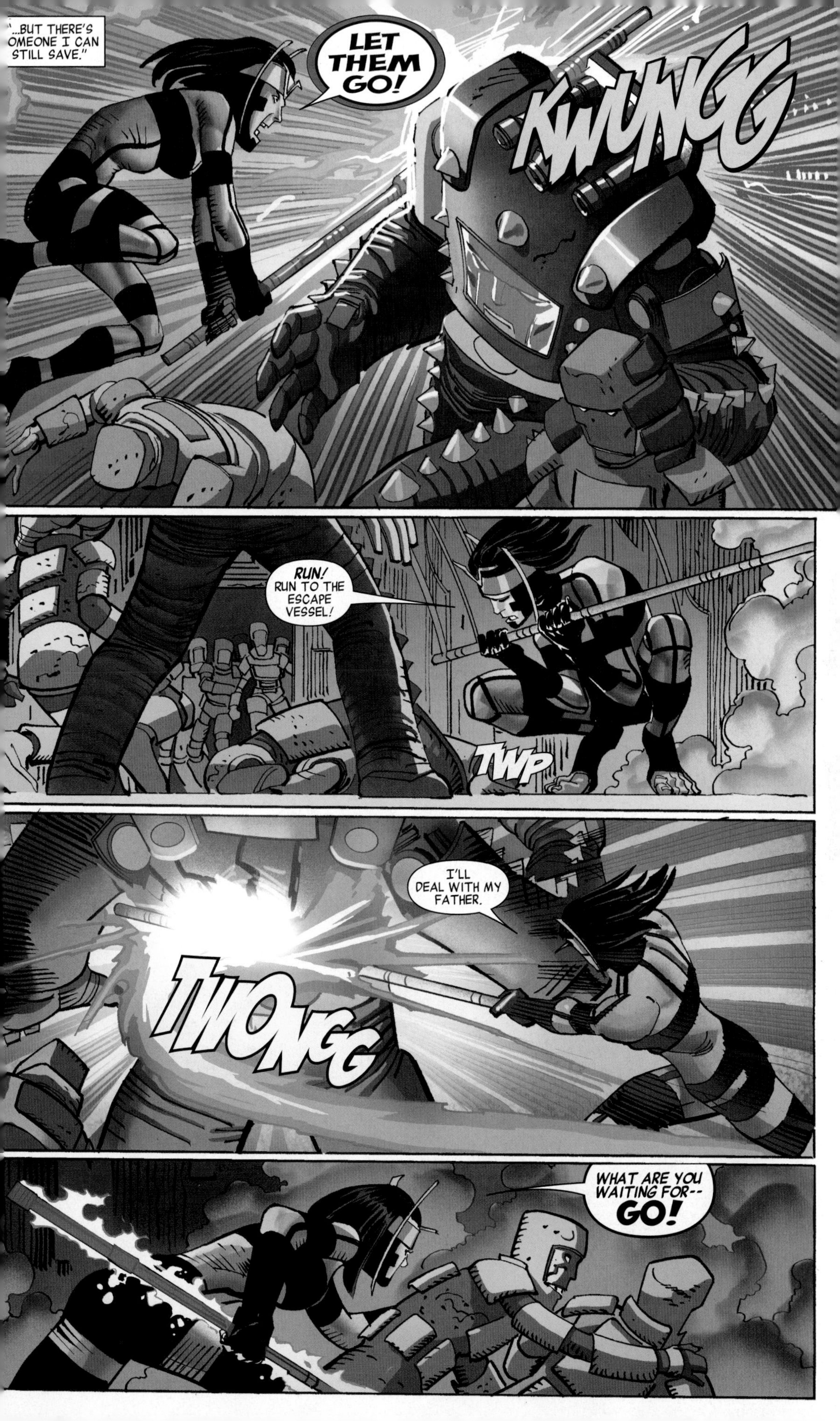
"...BUT THERE'S
OMEONE I CAN
STILL SAVE."
LET THEM GO!
KWUNGG
RUN! RUN TO THE ESCAPE VESSEL!
TWP
I'LL DEAL WITH MY FATHER.
TWONGG
WHAT ARE YOU WAITING FOR-- GO!

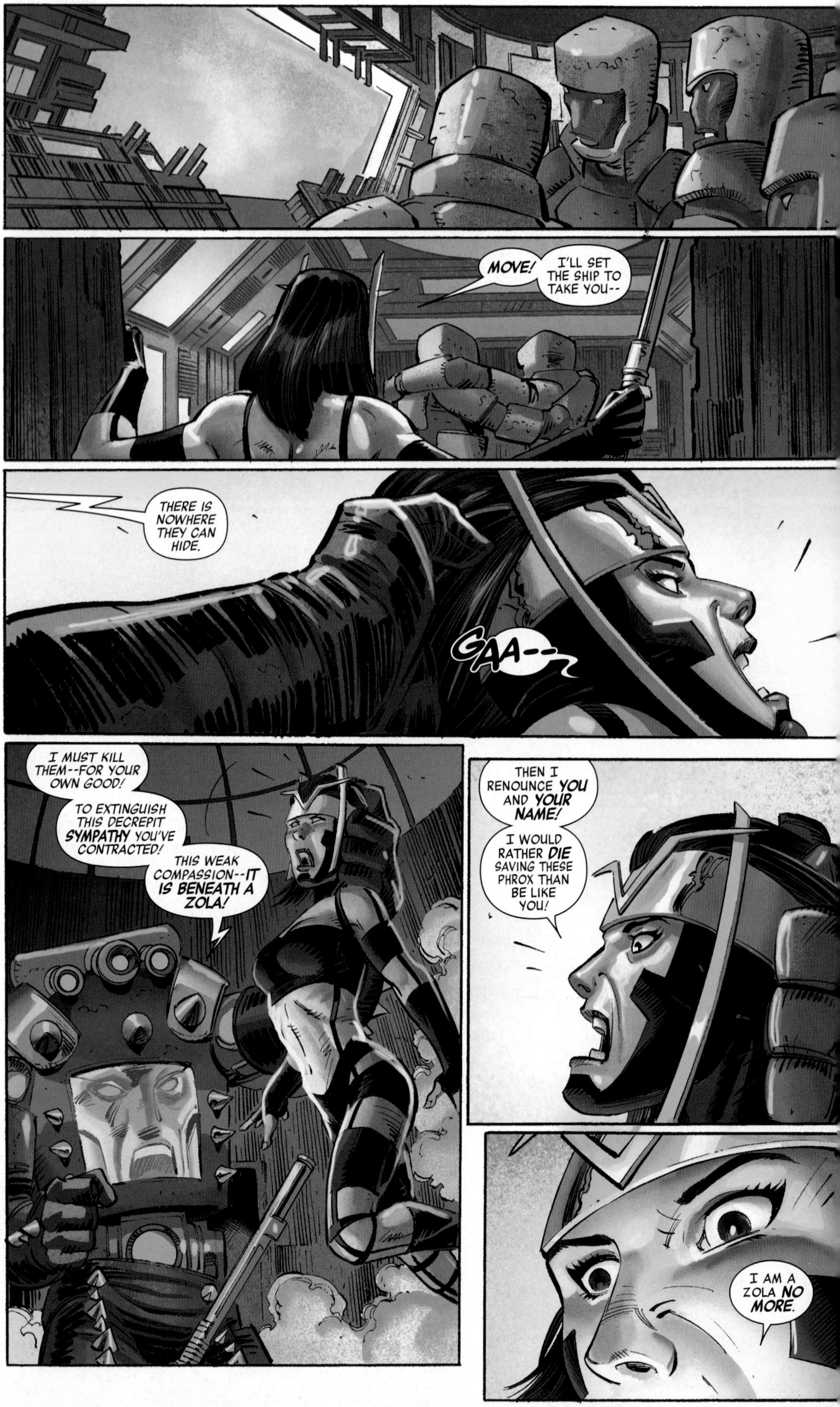
MOVE!
I'LL SET THE SHIP TO TAKE YOU--
THERE IS NOWHERE THEY CAN HIDE.
GAA--
I MUST KILL THEM--FOR YOUR OWN GOOD!
TO EXTINGUISH THIS DECREPIT SYMPATHY YOU'VE CONTRACTED!
THIS WEAK COMPASSION--IT IS BENEATH A ZOLA!
THEN I RENOUNCE YOU AND YOUR NAME!
I WOULD RATHER DIE SAVING THESE PHROX THAN BE LIKE YOU!
I AM A ZOLA NO MORE.

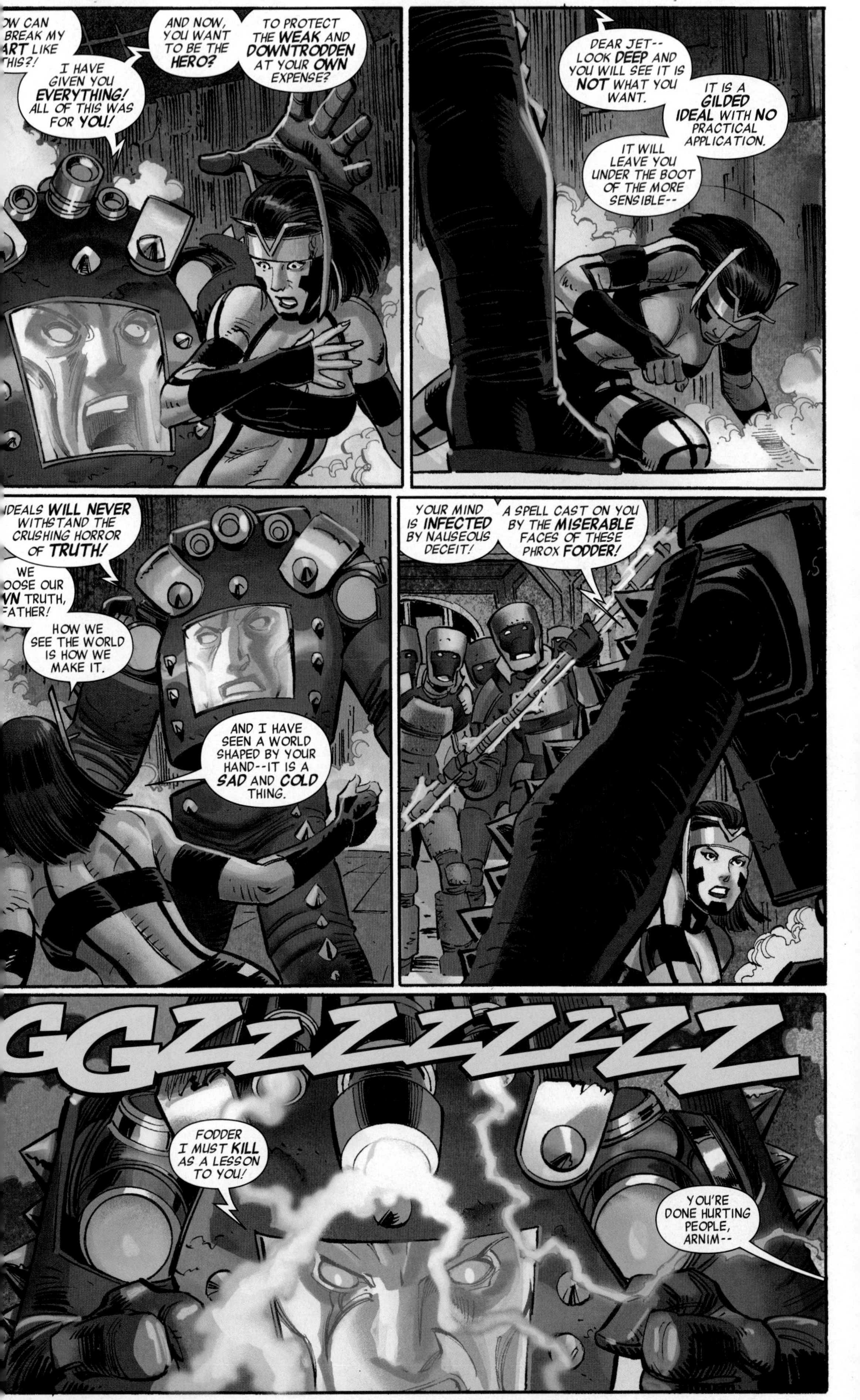

OW CAN BREAK MY ART LIKE THIS?!
I HAVE GIVEN YOU EVERYTHING! ALL OF THIS WAS FOR YOU!
AND NOW, YOU WANT TO BE THE HERO?
TO PROTECT THE WEAK AND DOWNTRODDEN AT YOUR OWN EXPENSE?
DEAR JET-- LOOK DEEP AND YOU WILL SEE IT IS NOT WHAT YOU WANT.
IT IS A GILDED IDEAL WITH NO PRACTICAL APPLICATION.
IT WILL LEAVE YOU UNDER THE BOOT OF THE MORE SENSIBLE--
IDEALS WILL NEVER WITHSTAND THE CRUSHING HORROR OF TRUTH!
WE OOSE OUR VN TRUTH, FATHER!
HOW WE SEE THE WORLD IS HOW WE MAKE IT.
AND I HAVE SEEN A WORLD SHAPED BY YOUR HAND--IT IS A SAD AND COLD THING.
YOUR MIND IS INFECTED BY NAUSEOUS DECEIT!
A SPELL CAST ON YOU BY THE MISERABLE FACES OF THESE PHROX FODDER!
GGZZZZZZZZ
FODDER I MUST KILL AS A LESSON TO YOU!
YOU'RE DONE HURTING PEOPLE, ARNIM--

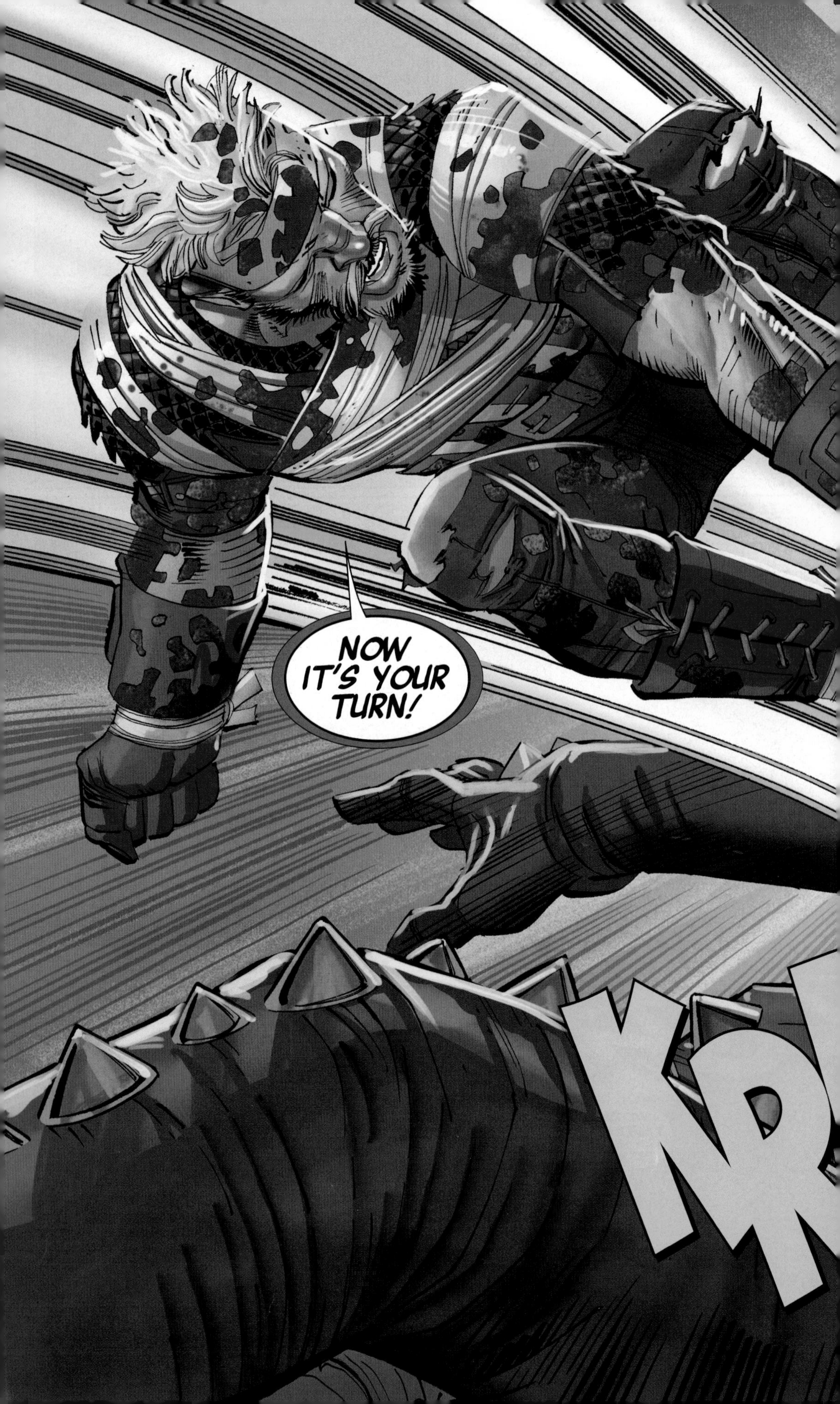
NOW IT'S YOUR TURN!
KR

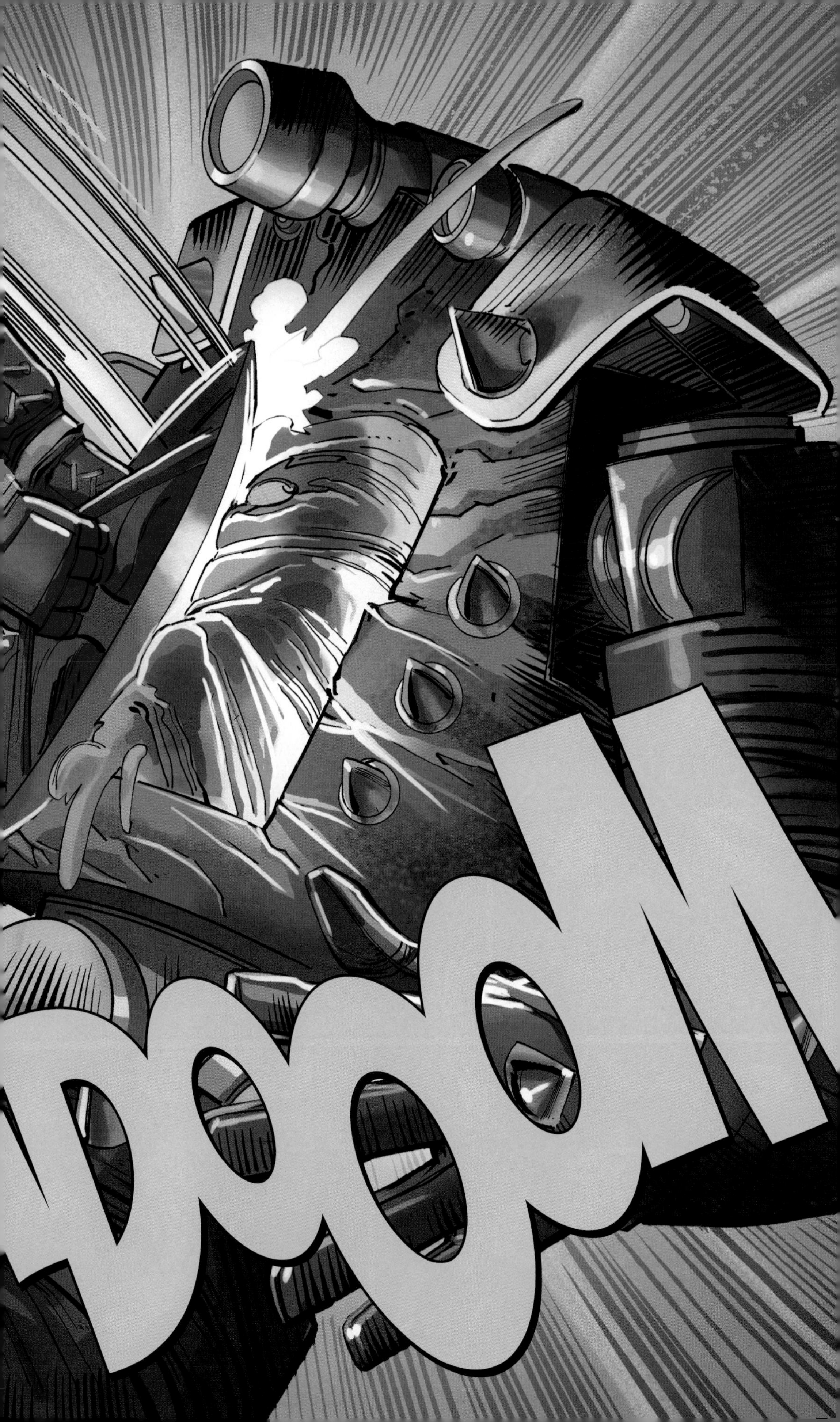
DOOOM

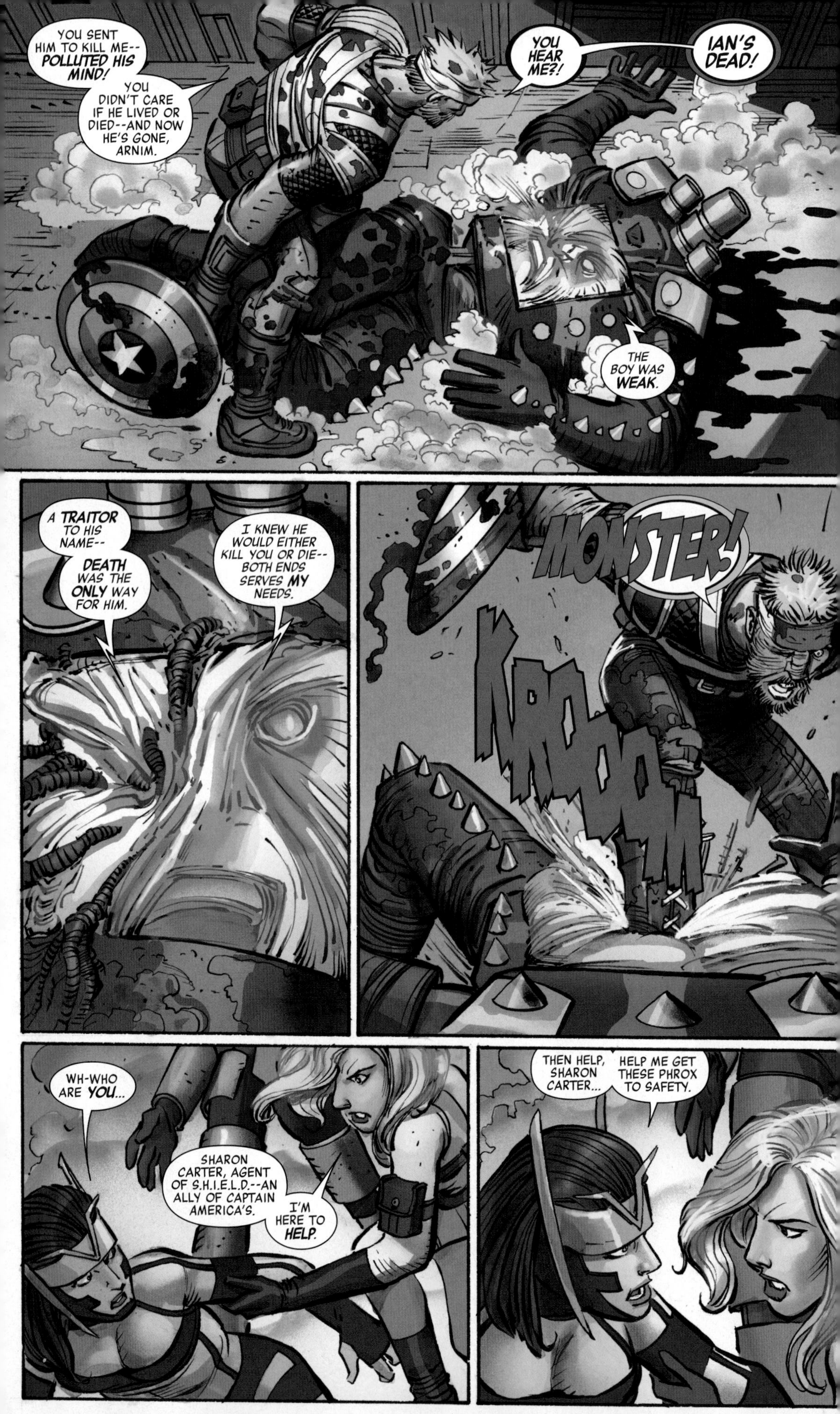

YOU SENT HIM TO KILL ME-- POLLUTED HIS MIND!
YOU DIDN'T CARE IF HE LIVED OR DIED--AND NOW HE'S GONE, ARNIM.
YOU HEAR ME?!
IAN'S DEAD!
THE BOY WAS WEAK.
A TRAITOR TO HIS NAME--
DEATH WAS THE ONLY WAY FOR HIM.
I KNEW HE WOULD EITHER KILL YOU OR DIE-- BOTH ENDS SERVES MY NEEDS.
MONSTER!
KROOOM
WH-WHO ARE YOU...
SHARON CARTER, AGENT OF S.H.I.E.L.D.--AN ALLY OF CAPTAIN AMERICA'S.
I'M HERE TO HELP.
THEN HELP, SHARON CARTER...
HELP ME GET THESE PHROX TO SAFETY.

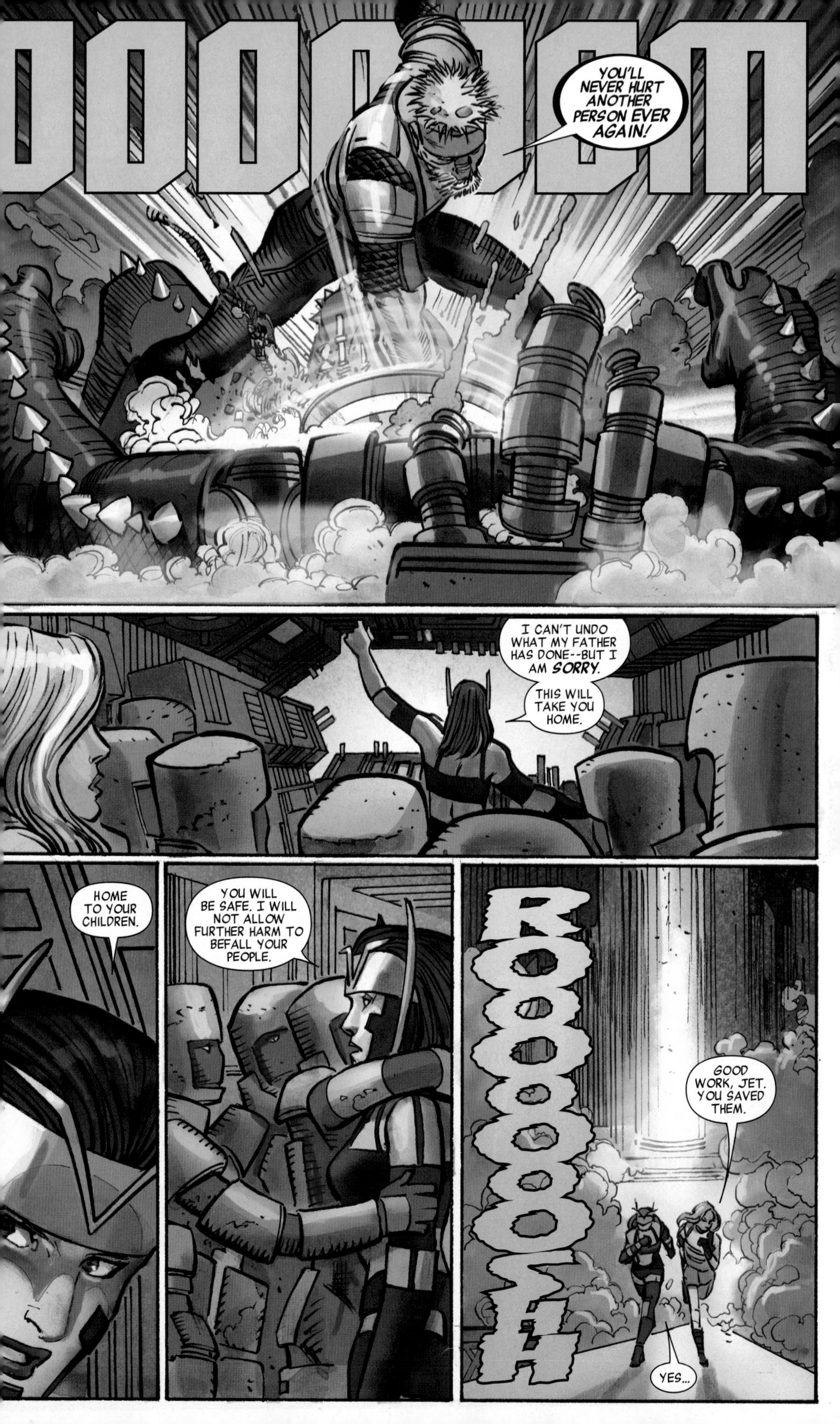
DOOOOOM
YOU'LL NEVER HURT ANOTHER PERSON EVER AGAIN!
I CAN'T UNDO WHAT MY FATHER HAS DONE--BUT I AM SORRY.
THIS WILL TAKE YOU HOME.
HOME TO YOUR CHILDREN.
YOU WILL BE SAFE. I WILL NOT ALLOW FURTHER HARM TO BEFALL YOUR PEOPLE.
ROOOOOOSH
GOOD WORK, JET. YOU SAVED THEM.
YES...

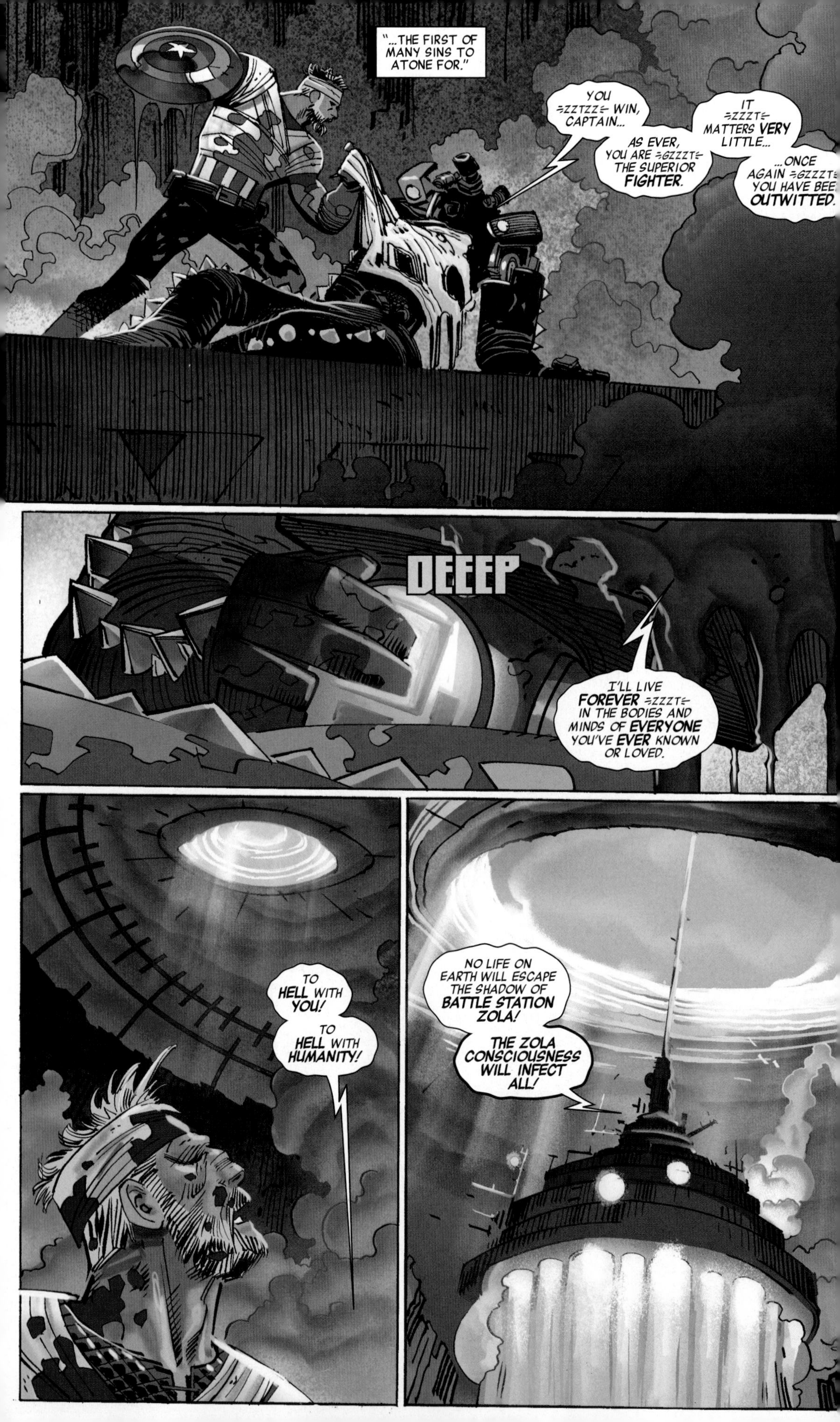
"...THE FIRST OF MANY SINS TO ATONE FOR."
YOU =ZZTZZ= WIN, CAPTAIN...
AS EVER, YOU ARE =GZZZT= THE SUPERIOR FIGHTER.
IT =ZZZT= MATTERS VERY LITTLE...
...ONCE AGAIN =GZZZT= YOU HAVE BEE OUTWITTED.
DEEEP
I'LL LIVE FOREVER =ZZZT= IN THE BODIES AND MINDS OF EVERYONE YOU'VE EVER KNOWN OR LOVED.
TO HELL WITH YOU!
TO HELL WITH HUMANITY!
NO LIFE ON EARTH WILL ESCAPE THE SHADOW OF BATTLE STATION ZOLA!
THE ZOLA CONSCIOUSNESS WILL INFECT ALL!

OOF--!

AND THIS TIME--

--MANKIND WILL **NOT** HAVE CAPTAIN AMERICA TO LEAD A RESISTANCE!

THE PORTAL TEARS OPEN--

--REVEALING THE BLUE SKIES OF HOME.

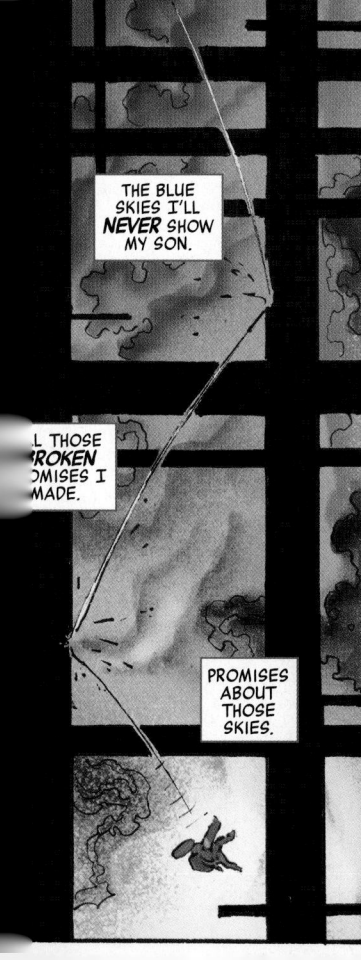

THE BLUE SKIES I'LL **NEVER** SHOW MY SON.

L THOSE ROKEN OMISES I MADE.

PROMISES ABOUT THOSE SKIES.

A BLUE THE ATMOSPHERE HERE **NEVER** SHOWS.

A COLOR THAT REPRESENTED A **DREAM** TO HIM.

IN MY PAINTINGS OF HOME, THOSE BLUE SKIES--

IAN WOULD OFTEN BE LOST IN THEM.

TWUPP

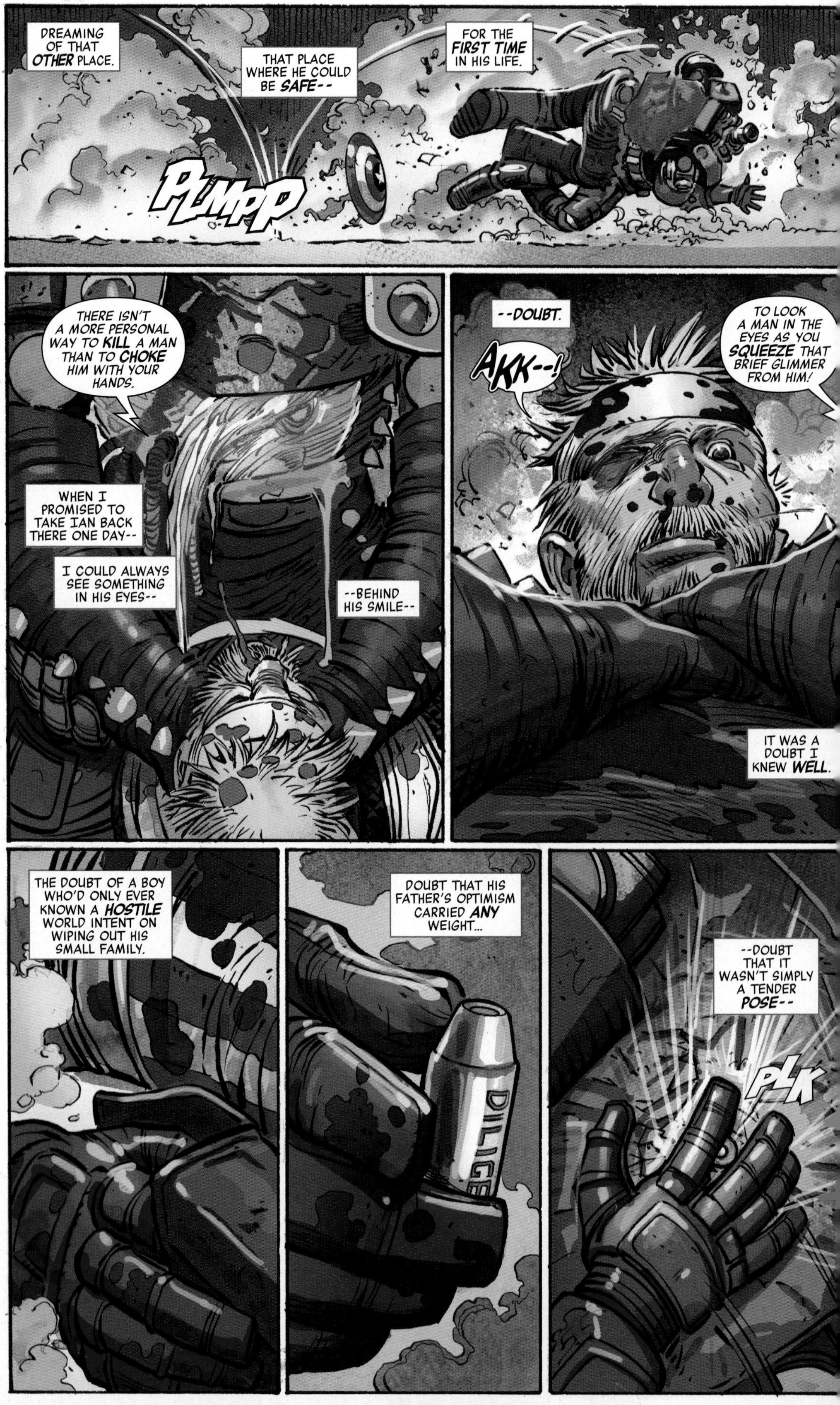
DREAMING OF THAT OTHER PLACE.
THAT PLACE WHERE HE COULD BE SAFE--
FOR THE FIRST TIME IN HIS LIFE.
PLMPP
THERE ISN'T A MORE PERSONAL WAY TO KILL A MAN THAN TO CHOKE HIM WITH YOUR HANDS.
WHEN I PROMISED TO TAKE IAN BACK THERE ONE DAY--
I COULD ALWAYS SEE SOMETHING IN HIS EYES--
--BEHIND HIS SMILE--
--DOUBT.
AKK--!
TO LOOK A MAN IN THE EYES AS YOU SQUEEZE THAT BRIEF GLIMMER FROM HIM!
IT WAS A DOUBT I KNEW WELL.
THE DOUBT OF A BOY WHO'D ONLY EVER KNOWN A HOSTILE WORLD INTENT ON WIPING OUT HIS SMALL FAMILY.
DOUBT THAT HIS FATHER'S OPTIMISM CARRIED ANY WEIGHT...
DILIGE
--DOUBT THAT IT WASN'T SIMPLY A TENDER POSE--
PLK

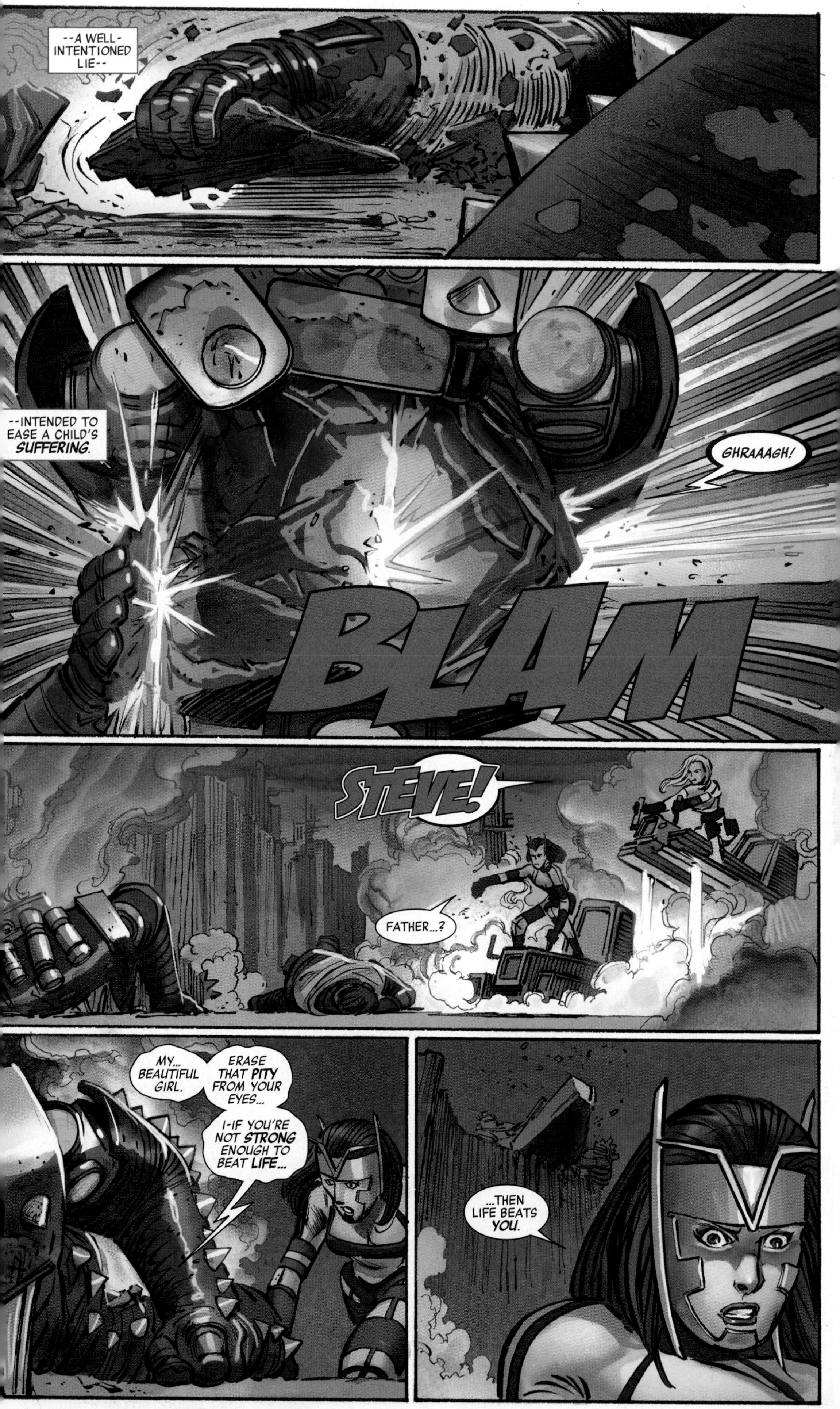
--A WELL-INTENTIONED LIE--
--INTENDED TO EASE A CHILD'S SUFFERING.
GHRAAAGH!
BLAM
STEVE!
FATHER...?
MY... BEAUTIFUL GIRL.
ERASE THAT PITY FROM YOUR EYES...
I-IF YOU'RE NOT STRONG ENOUGH TO BEAT LIFE...
...THEN LIFE BEATS YOU.

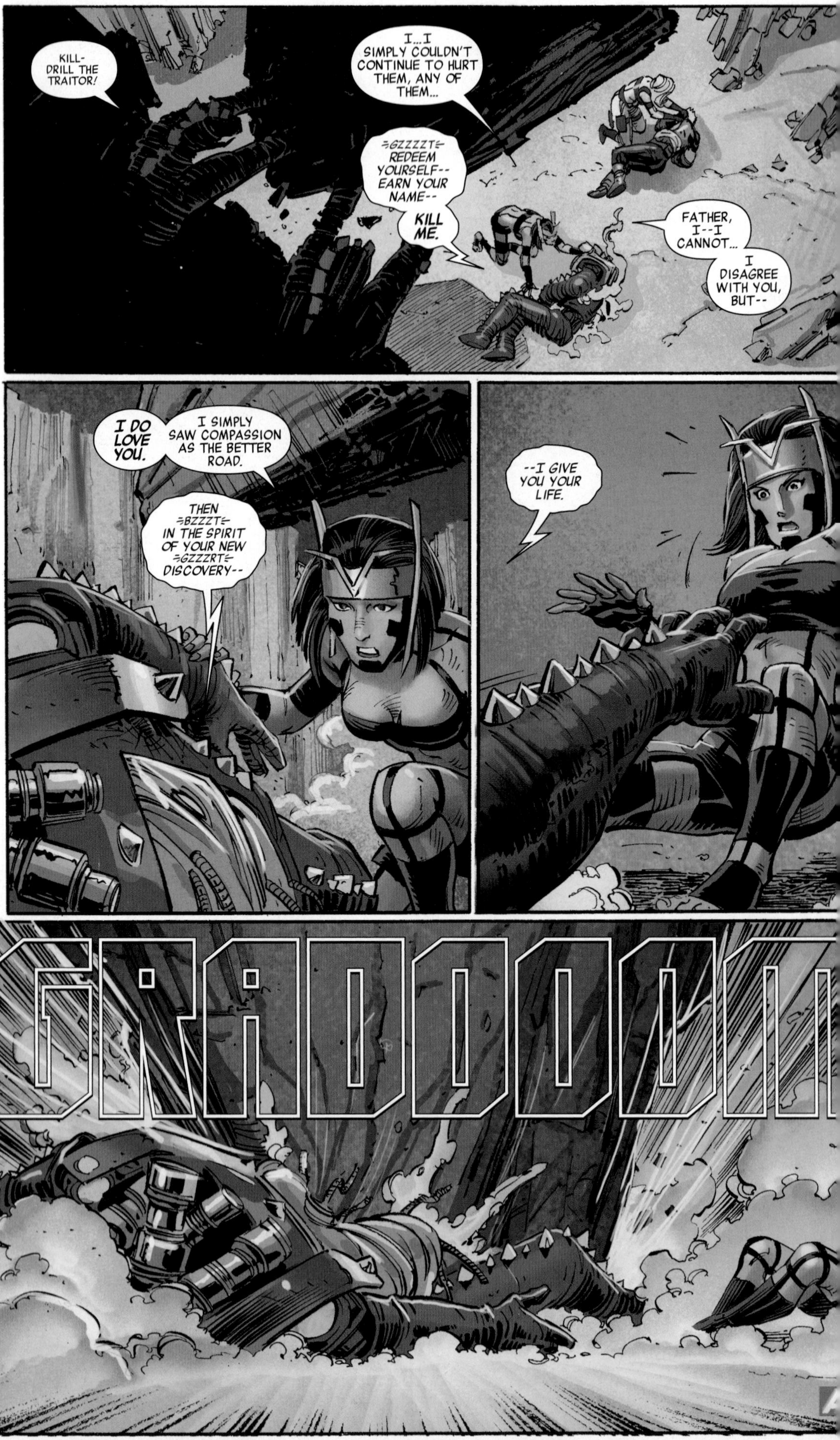
KILL-DRILL THE TRAITOR!
I...I SIMPLY COULDN'T CONTINUE TO HURT THEM, ANY OF THEM...
=GZZZZT= REDEEM YOURSELF-- EARN YOUR NAME--
KILL ME.
FATHER, I--I CANNOT...
I DISAGREE WITH YOU, BUT--
I DO LOVE YOU.
I SIMPLY SAW COMPASSION AS THE BETTER ROAD.
THEN =BZZZT= IN THE SPIRIT OF YOUR NEW =GZZZRT= DISCOVERY--
--I GIVE YOU YOUR LIFE.
GRADOOM

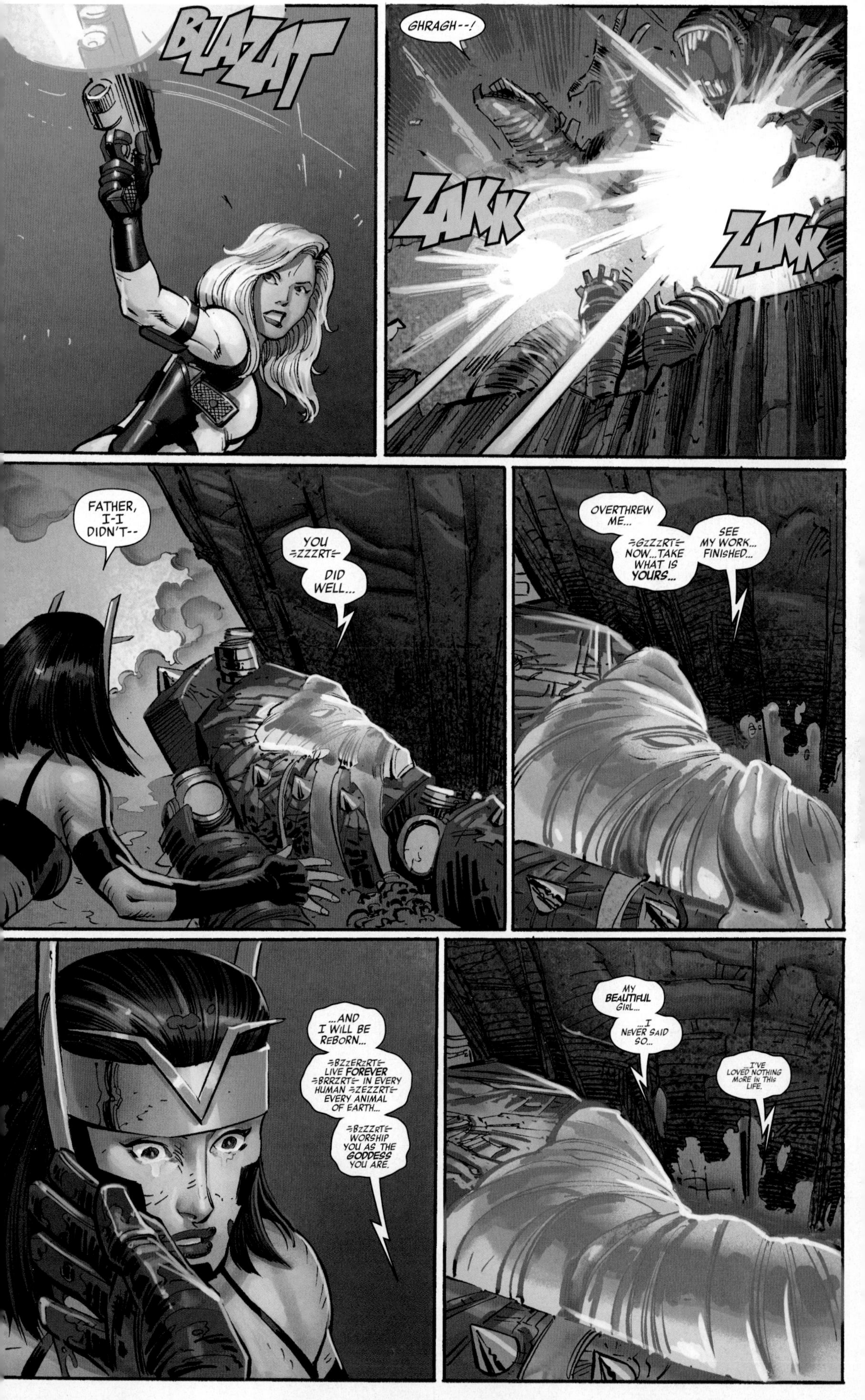
BLAZAT
GHRAGH--!
ZAKK
ZAKK
FATHER, I-I DIDN'T--
YOU =ZZZRT= DID WELL...
OVERTHREW ME...
=GZZZRT= NOW...TAKE WHAT IS YOURS...
SEE MY WORK... FINISHED...
...AND I WILL BE REBORN...
=BZZERZRT= LIVE FOREVER =BRRZRT= IN EVERY HUMAN =ZEZZRT= EVERY ANIMAL OF EARTH...
=BZZZRT= WORSHIP YOU AS THE GODDESS YOU ARE.
MY BEAUTIFUL GIRL...
...I NEVER SAID SO...
...I'VE LOVED NOTHING MORE IN THIS LIFE.

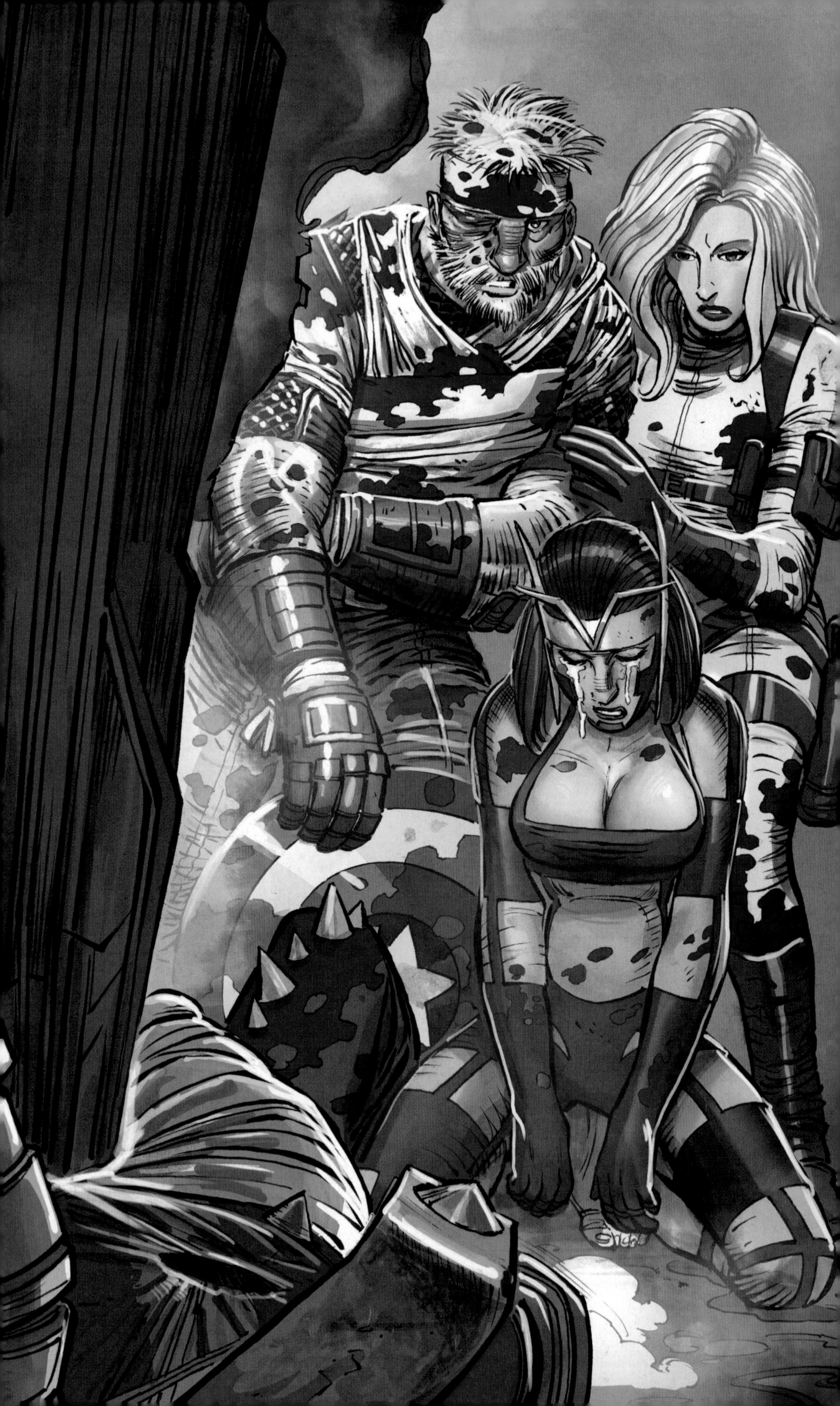

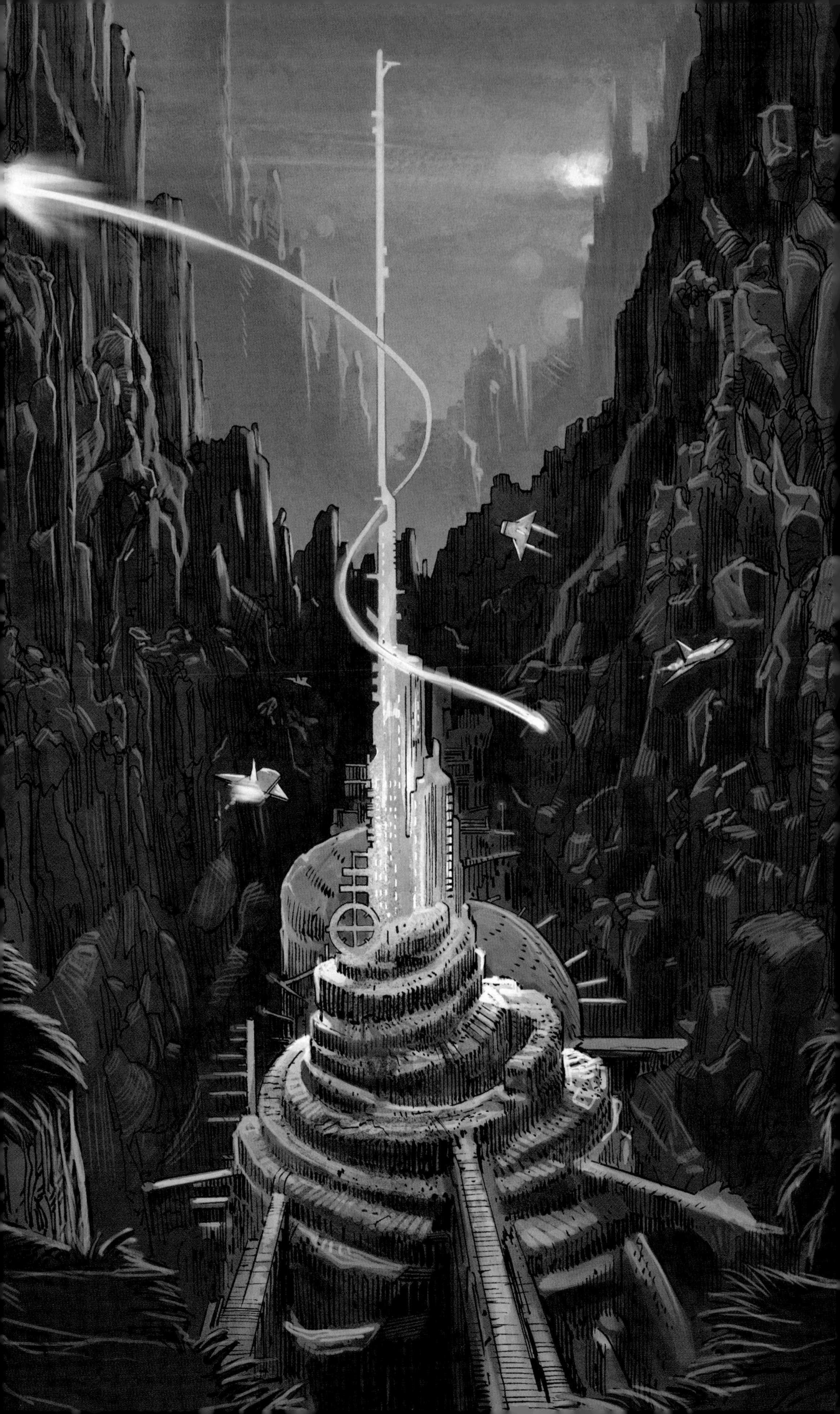

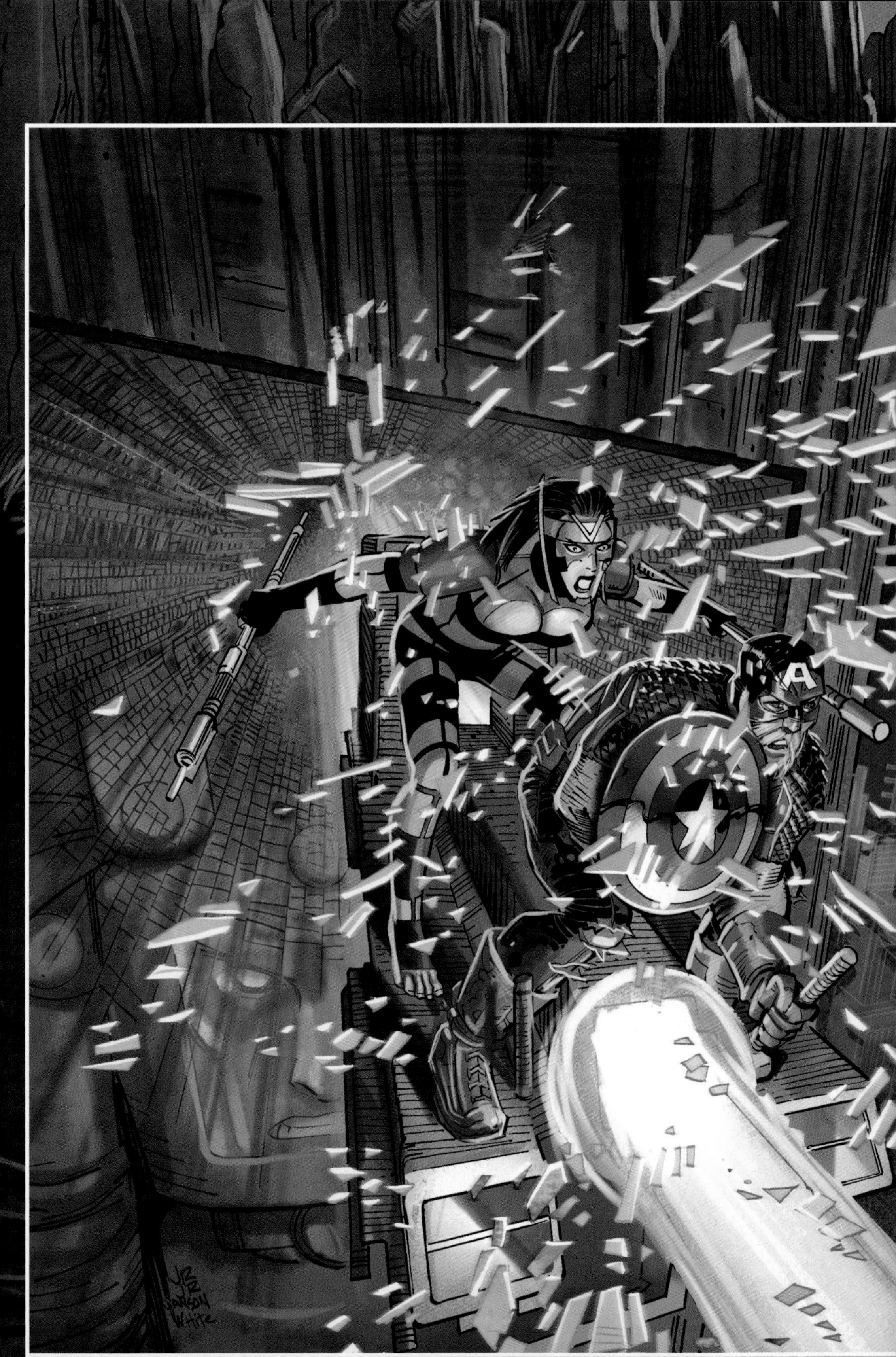

TEN

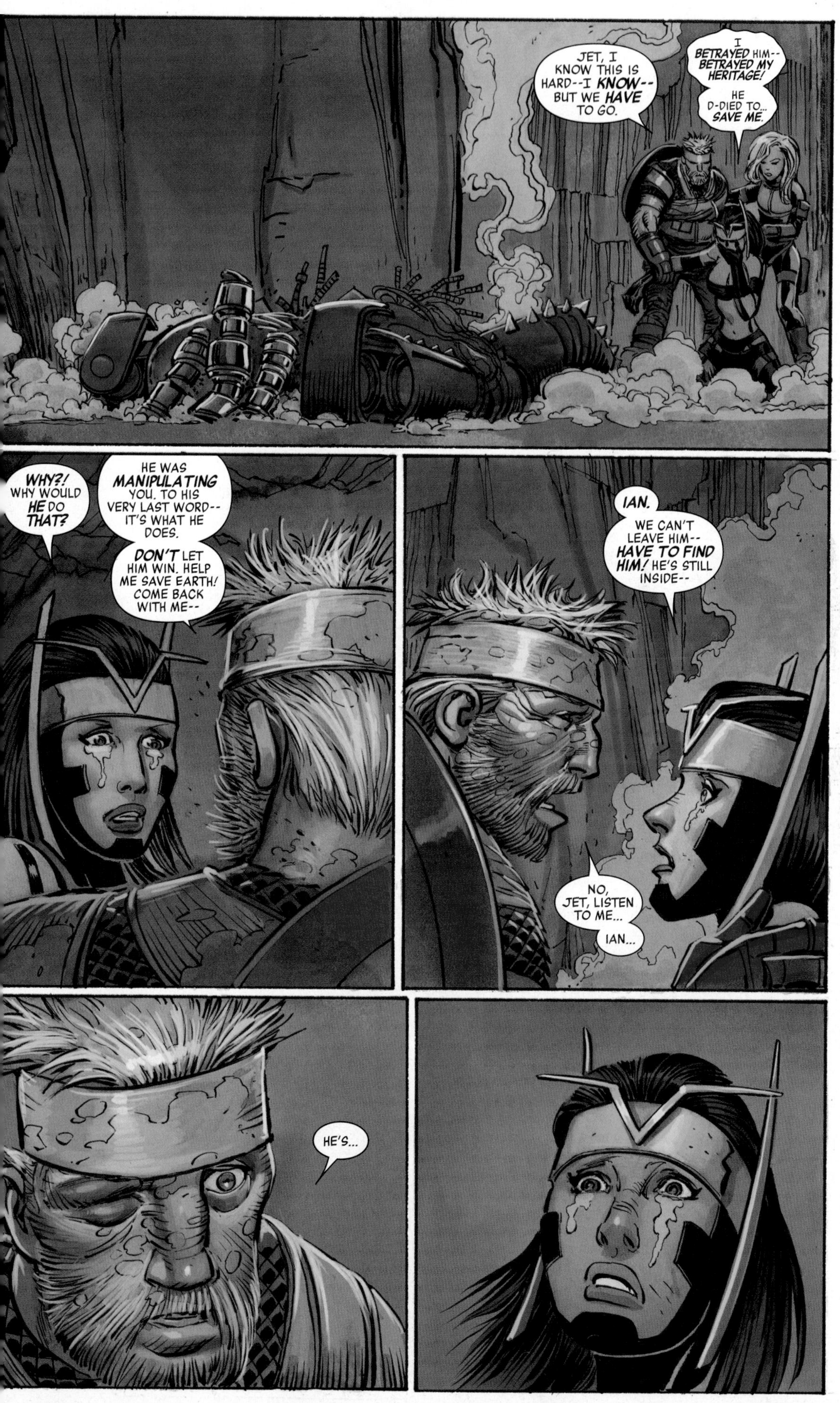
JET, I KNOW THIS IS HARD--I KNOW--BUT WE HAVE TO GO.
I BETRAYED HIM--BETRAYED MY HERITAGE!
HE D-DIED TO... SAVE ME.
WHY?! WHY WOULD HE DO THAT?
HE WAS MANIPULATING YOU. TO HIS VERY LAST WORD--IT'S WHAT HE DOES.
DON'T LET HIM WIN. HELP ME SAVE EARTH! COME BACK WITH ME--
IAN.
WE CAN'T LEAVE HIM--HAVE TO FIND HIM! HE'S STILL INSIDE--
NO, JET, LISTEN TO ME...
IAN...
HE'S...

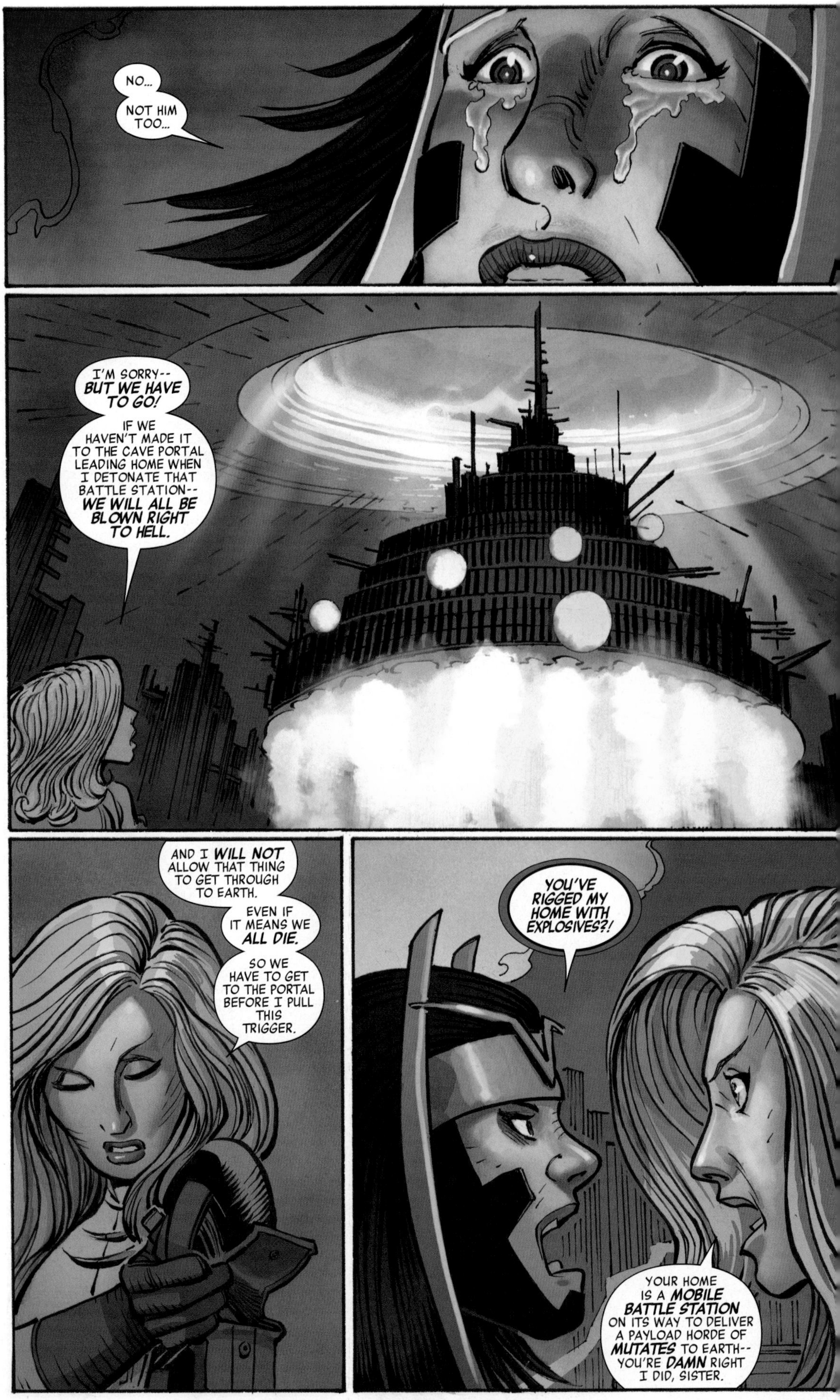
NO...
NOT HIM TOO...
I'M SORRY-- BUT WE HAVE TO GO!
IF WE HAVEN'T MADE IT TO THE CAVE PORTAL LEADING HOME WHEN I DETONATE THAT BATTLE STATION-- WE WILL ALL BE BLOWN RIGHT TO HELL.
AND I WILL NOT ALLOW THAT THING TO GET THROUGH TO EARTH.
EVEN IF IT MEANS WE ALL DIE.
SO WE HAVE TO GET TO THE PORTAL BEFORE I PULL THIS TRIGGER.
YOU'VE RIGGED MY HOME WITH EXPLOSIVES?!
YOUR HOME IS A MOBILE BATTLE STATION ON ITS WAY TO DELIVER A PAYLOAD HORDE OF MUTATES TO EARTH-- YOU'RE DAMN RIGHT I DID, SISTER.

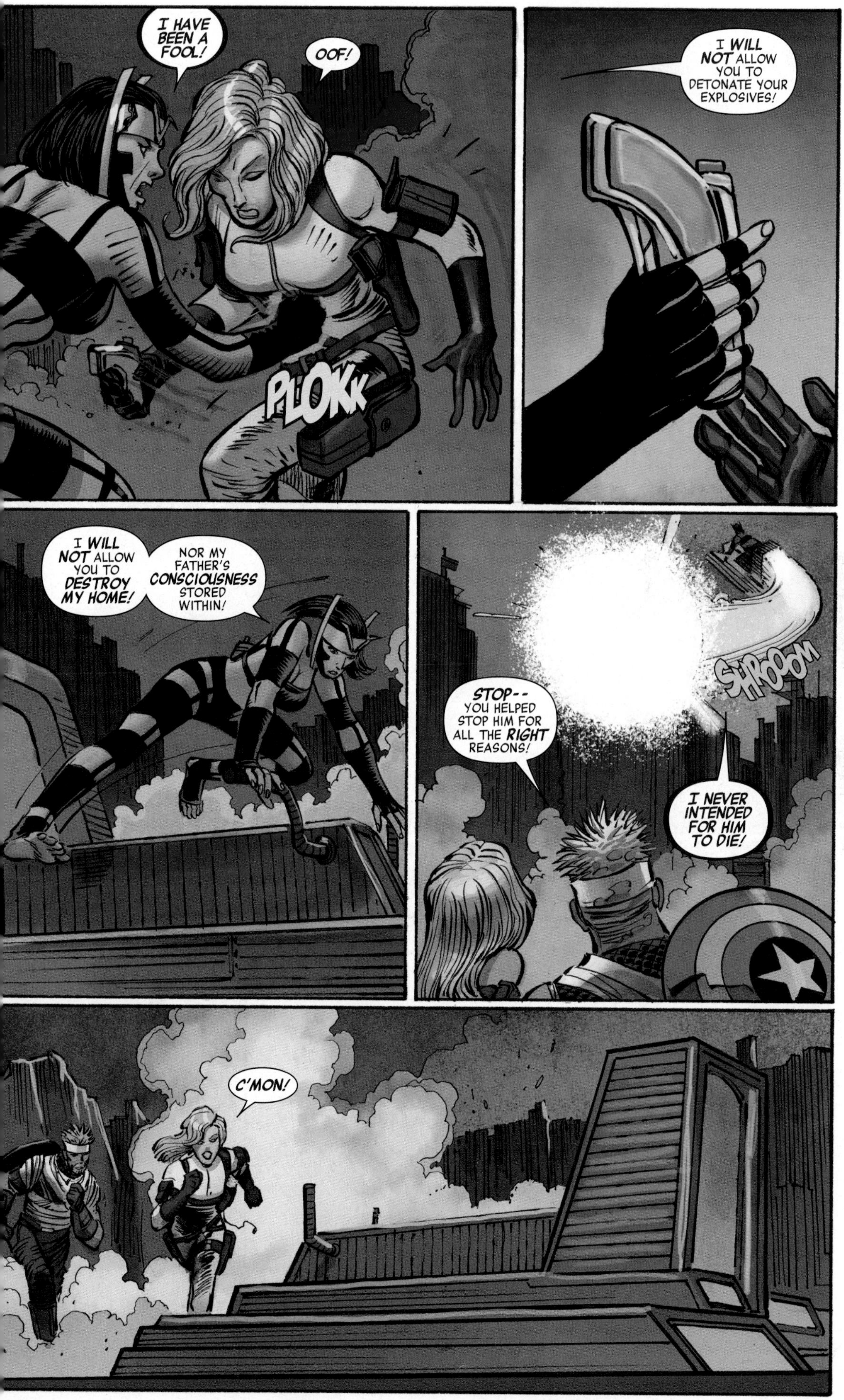
I HAVE BEEN A FOOL!
OOF!
PLOKK
I WILL NOT ALLOW YOU TO DETONATE YOUR EXPLOSIVES!
I WILL NOT ALLOW YOU TO DESTROY MY HOME!
NOR MY FATHER'S CONSCIOUSNESS STORED WITHIN!
SHROOOM
STOP-- YOU HELPED STOP HIM FOR ALL THE RIGHT REASONS!
I NEVER INTENDED FOR HIM TO DIE!
C'MON!

FIND SOME OTHER WAY...

IF SHE DESTROYS THAT DETONATOR--

SHE WON'T-- SHE'S CONFUSED, IN SHOCK--BUT SHE'S SEEN THROUGH ZOLA'S LIES.

BUT WATCHING HIM DIE IN FRONT OF HER--

SHE'S BEEN THROUGH SO MUCH, SHARON--THE DAMAGE DONE TO HER MIND IS UNIMAGINABLE.

BUT SHE KNOWS HE WAS EVIL, KNOWS HE WAS WRONG.

SHE'LL DO THE RIGHT THING GIVEN CHANCE.

JET! STOP--LISTEN TO ME!

IF WE DON'T DESTROY THE BATTLE STATION-- THE COST WILL BE BILLIONS OF INNOCENT LIVES!

YOU KNOW WHAT THOSE MUTATES INTEND TO DO!

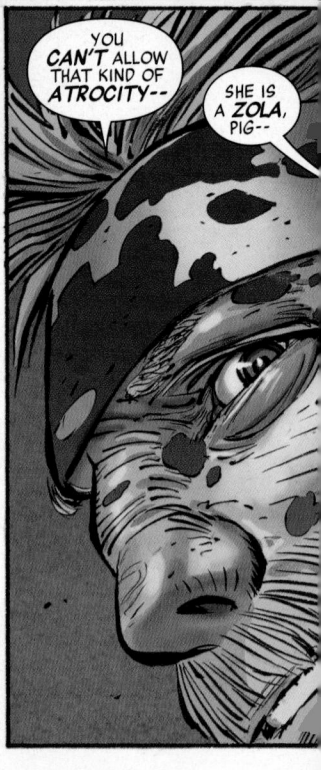

YOU CAN'T ALLOW THAT KIND OF ATROCITY--

SHE IS A ZOLA, PIG--

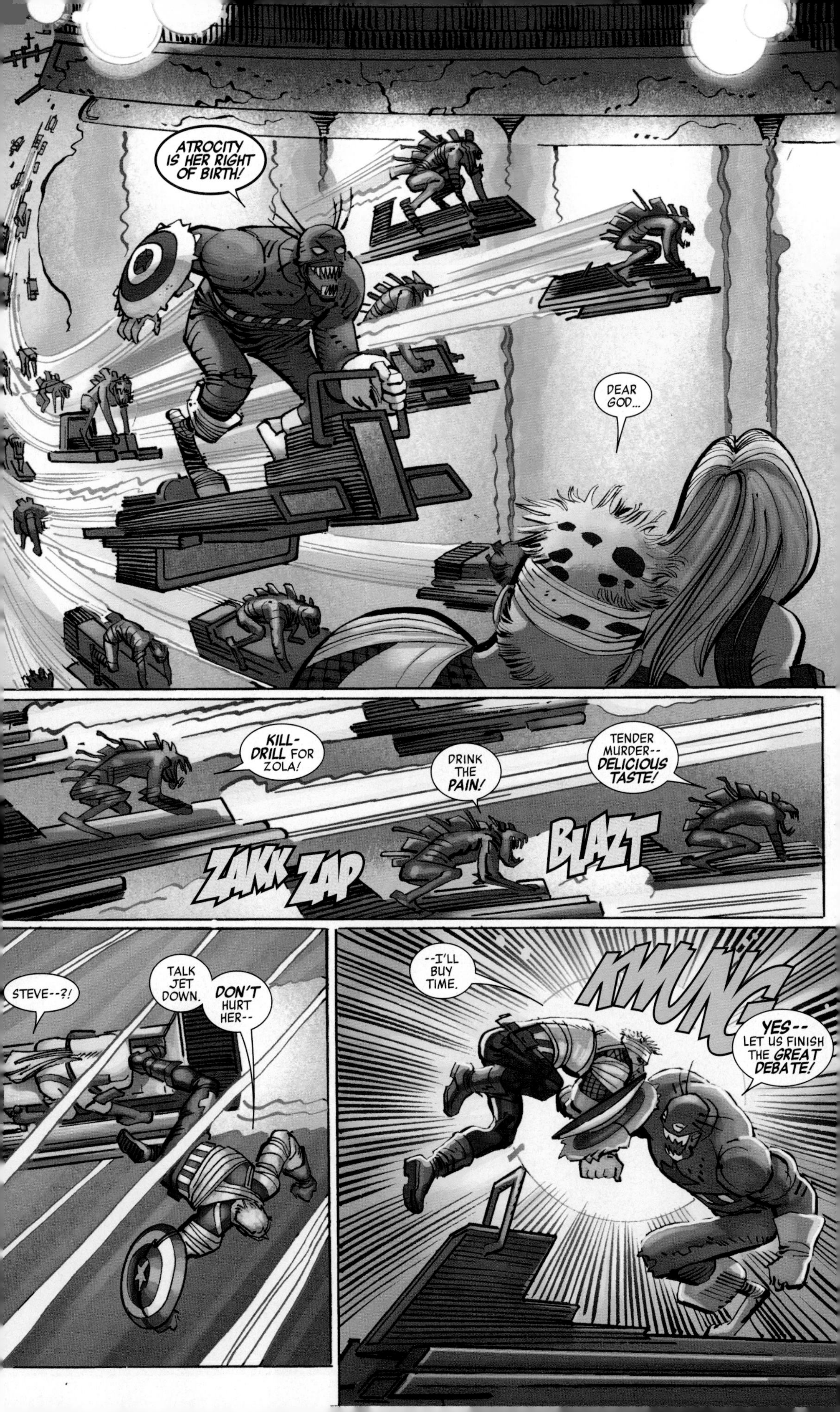
ATROCITY IS HER RIGHT OF BIRTH!
DEAR GOD...
KILL-DRILL FOR ZOLA!
DRINK THE PAIN!
TENDER MURDER--DELICIOUS TASTE!
ZAKK
ZAP
BLAZT
STEVE--?!
TALK JET DOWN.
DON'T HURT HER--
--I'LL BUY TIME.
KWUNG
YES--LET US FINISH THE GREAT DEBATE!

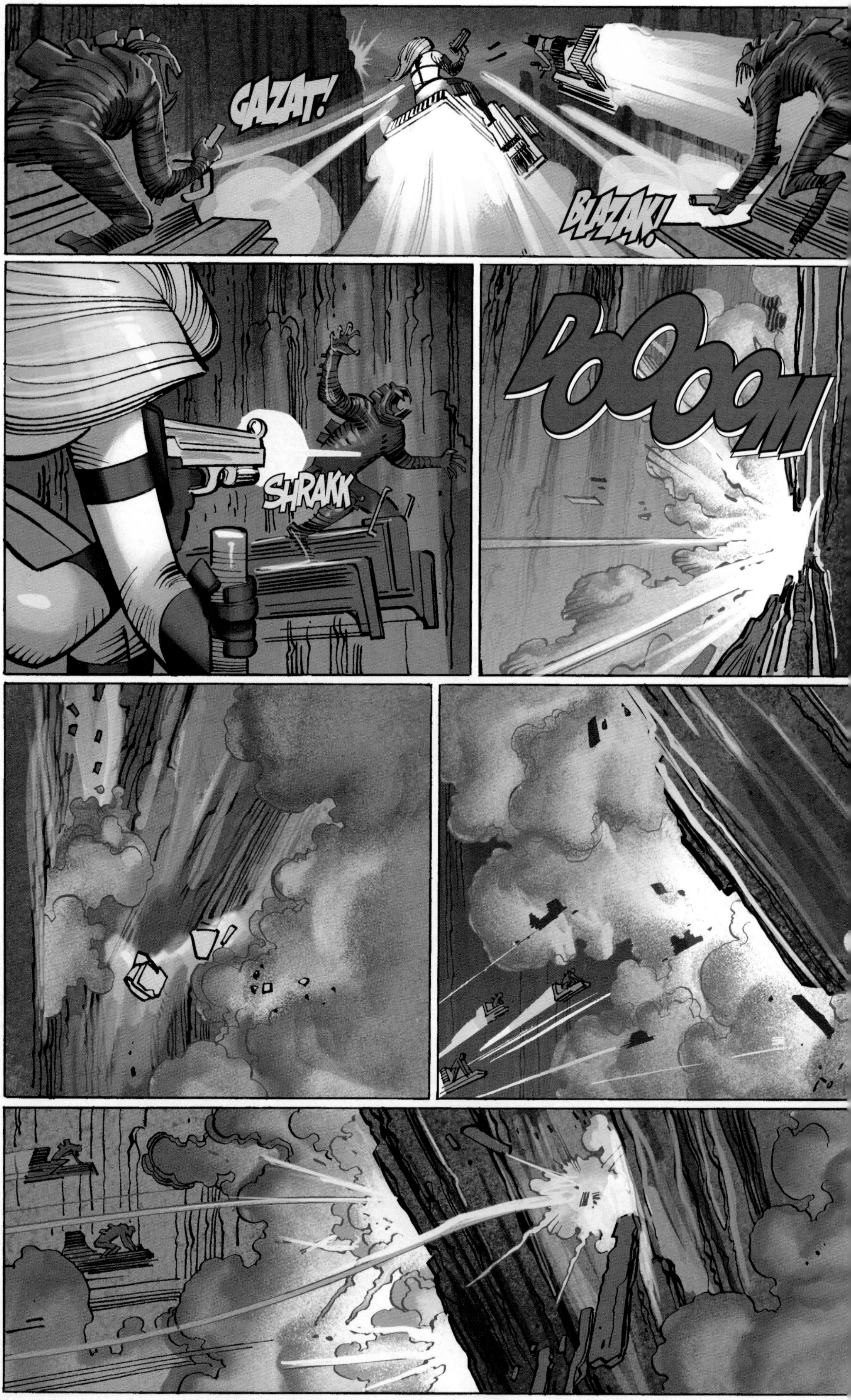
GAZAT!
BLAZAK!
SHRAKK
BOOOOM

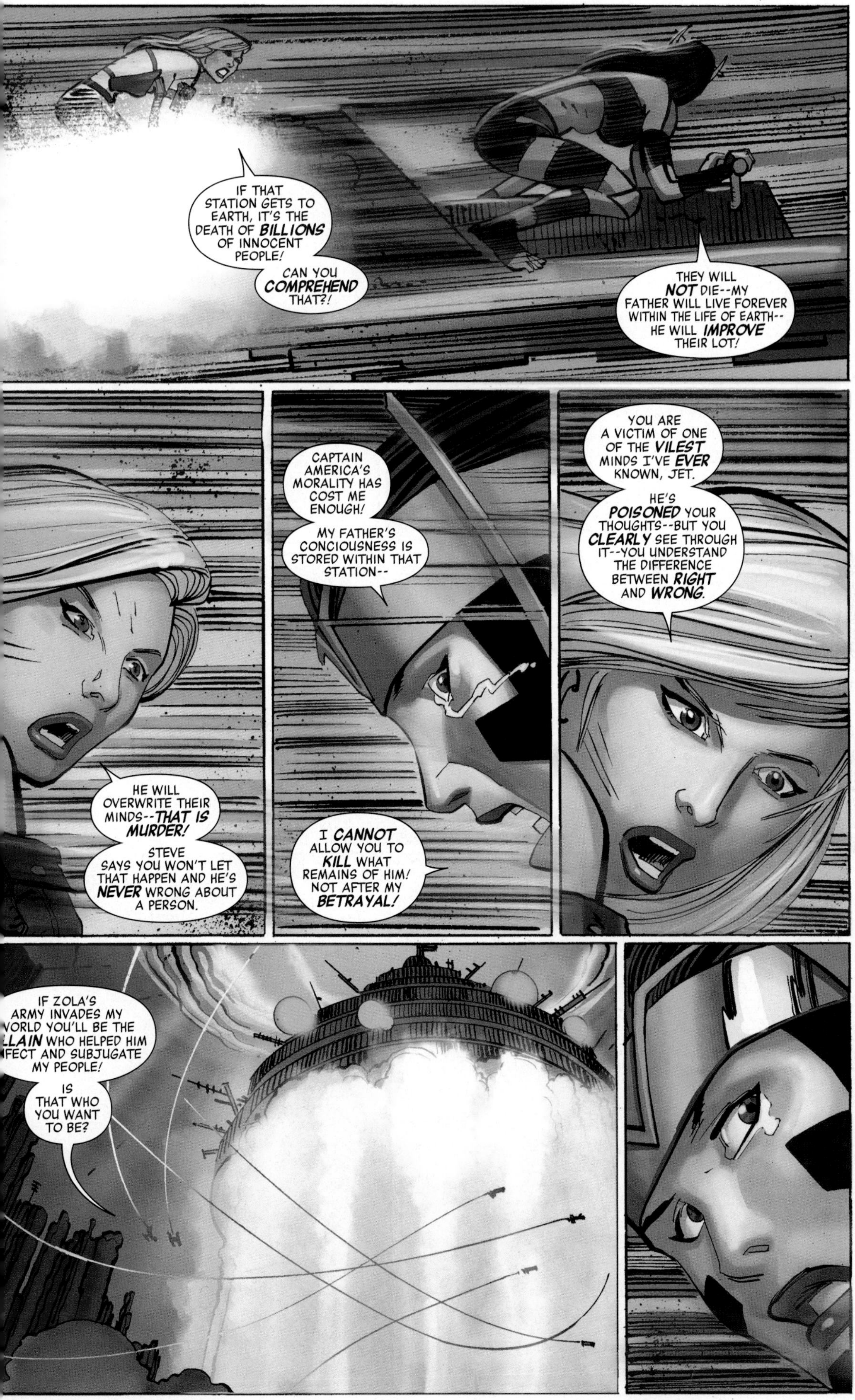

IF THAT STATION GETS TO EARTH, IT'S THE DEATH OF **BILLIONS** OF INNOCENT PEOPLE!
CAN YOU **COMPREHEND** THAT?!
THEY WILL **NOT** DIE--MY FATHER WILL LIVE FOREVER WITHIN THE LIFE OF EARTH--HE WILL **IMPROVE** THEIR LOT!
HE WILL OVERWRITE THEIR MINDS--**THAT IS MURDER!**
STEVE SAYS YOU WON'T LET THAT HAPPEN AND HE'S **NEVER** WRONG ABOUT A PERSON.
CAPTAIN AMERICA'S MORALITY HAS COST ME ENOUGH!
MY FATHER'S CONCIOUSNESS IS STORED WITHIN THAT STATION--
I **CANNOT** ALLOW YOU TO **KILL** WHAT REMAINS OF HIM! NOT AFTER MY **BETRAYAL!**
YOU ARE A VICTIM OF ONE OF THE **VILEST** MINDS I'VE **EVER** KNOWN, JET.
HE'S **POISONED** YOUR THOUGHTS--BUT YOU **CLEARLY** SEE THROUGH IT--YOU UNDERSTAND THE DIFFERENCE BETWEEN **RIGHT** AND **WRONG**.
IF ZOLA'S ARMY INVADES MY WORLD YOU'LL BE THE **LLAIN** WHO HELPED HIM FECT AND SUBJUGATE MY PEOPLE!
IS THAT WHO YOU WANT TO BE?

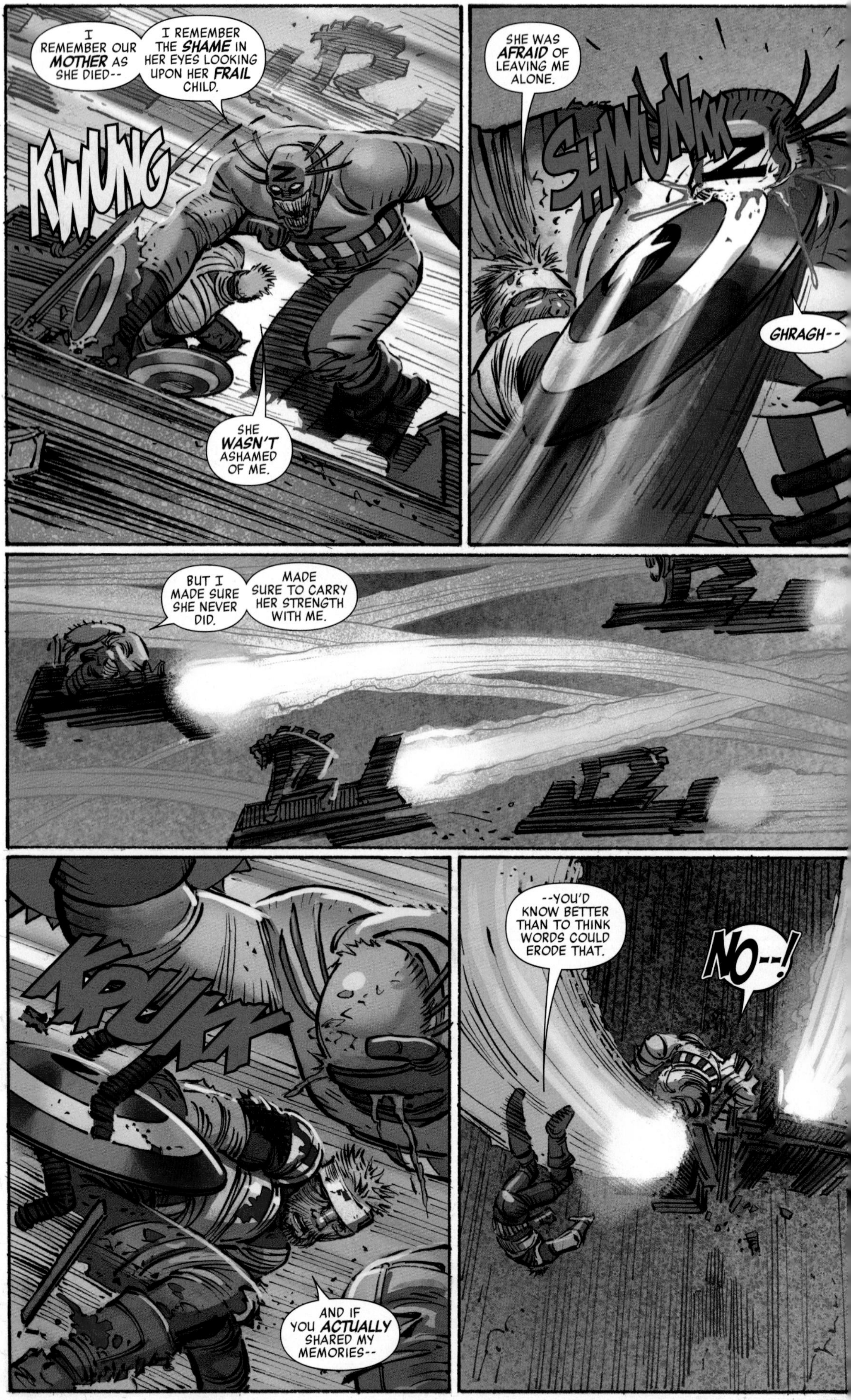

I REMEMBER OUR MOTHER AS SHE DIED--
I REMEMBER THE SHAME IN HER EYES LOOKING UPON HER FRAIL CHILD.
KWUNG
SHE WASN'T ASHAMED OF ME.
SHE WAS AFRAID OF LEAVING ME ALONE.
SHWUNKK
GHRAGH--
BUT I MADE SURE SHE NEVER DID.
MADE SURE TO CARRY HER STRENGTH WITH ME.
KRUNK
AND IF YOU ACTUALLY SHARED MY MEMORIES--
--YOU'D KNOW BETTER THAN TO THINK WORDS COULD ERODE THAT.
NO--!

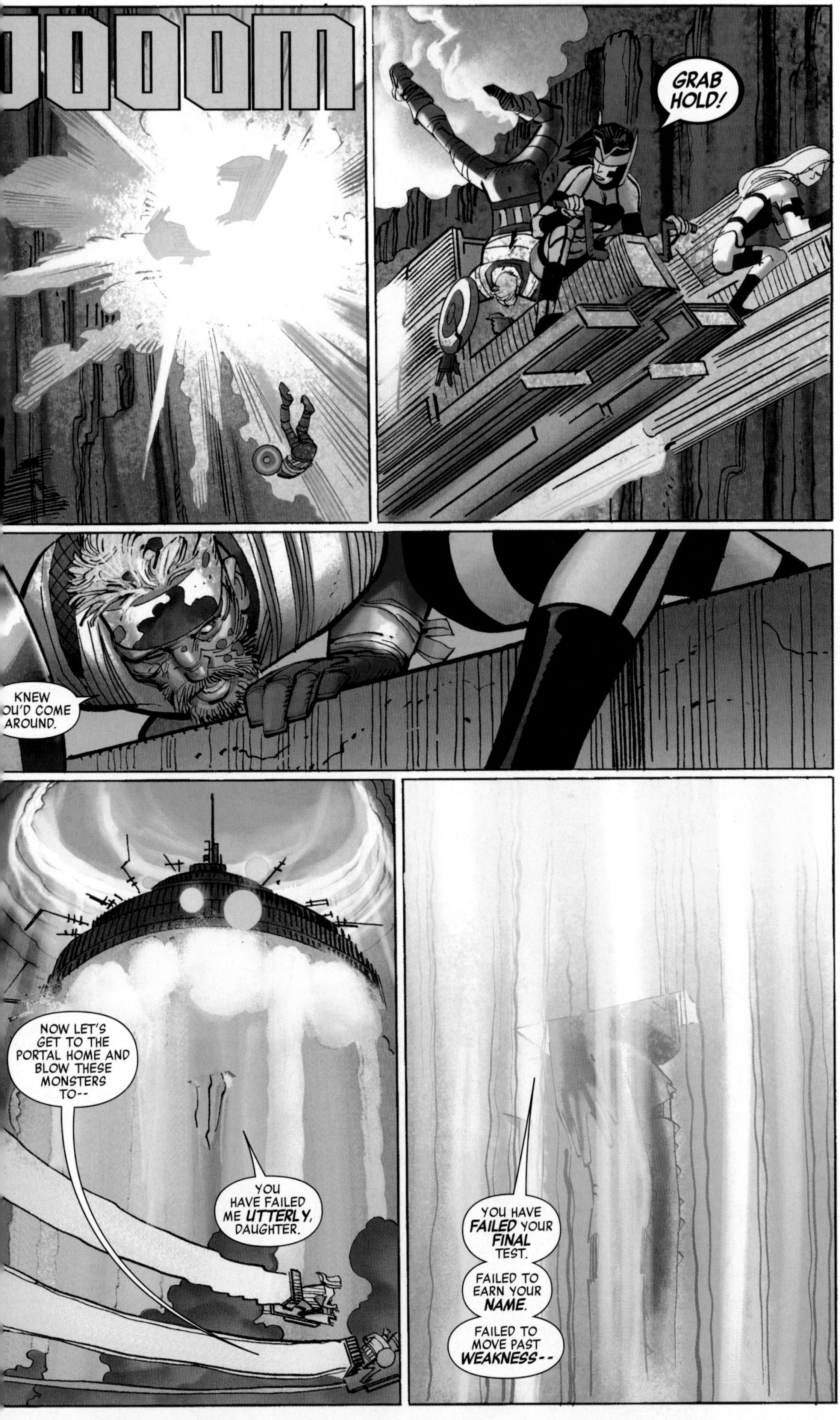
OOOOM
GRAB HOLD!
KNEW YOU'D COME AROUND.
NOW LET'S GET TO THE PORTAL HOME AND BLOW THESE MONSTERS TO--
YOU HAVE FAILED ME UTTERLY, DAUGHTER.
YOU HAVE FAILED YOUR FINAL TEST.
FAILED TO EARN YOUR NAME.
FAILED TO MOVE PAST WEAKNESS--

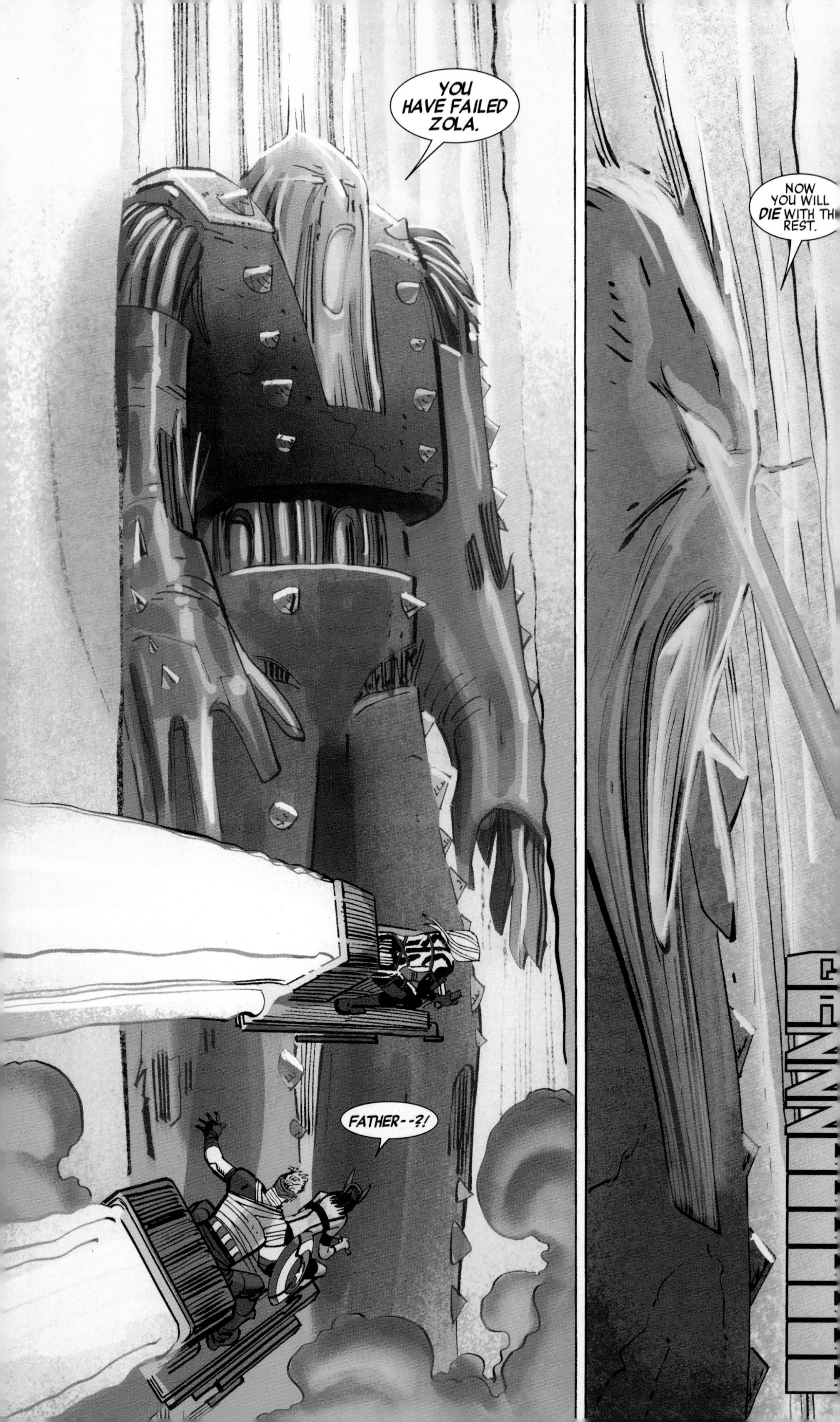
YOU HAVE FAILED ZOLA.
FATHER--?!
NOW YOU WILL DIE WITH TH REST.

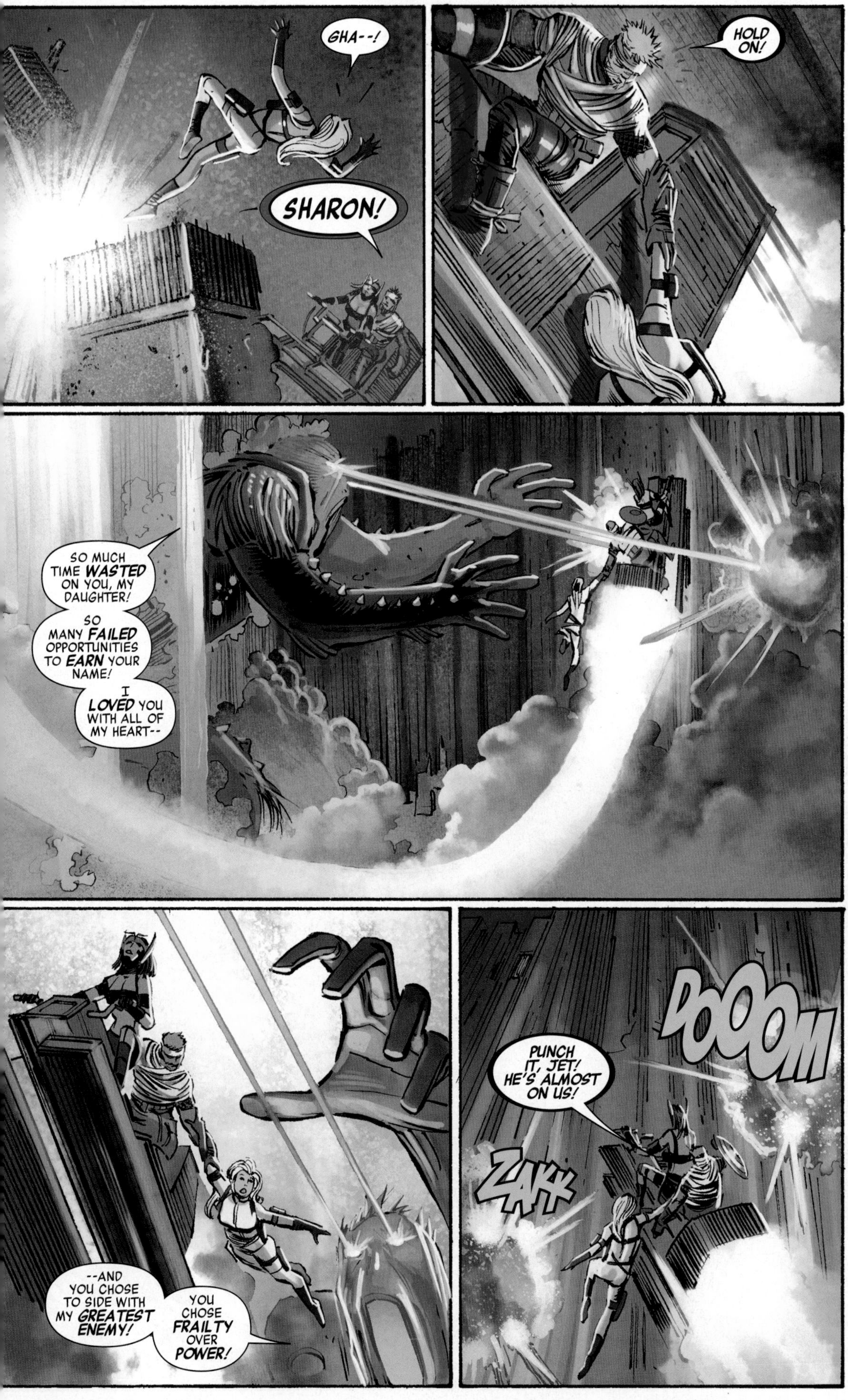
GHA--!
SHARON!
HOLD ON!
SO MUCH TIME WASTED ON YOU, MY DAUGHTER!
SO MANY FAILED OPPORTUNITIES TO EARN YOUR NAME!
I LOVED YOU WITH ALL OF MY HEART--
--AND YOU CHOSE TO SIDE WITH MY GREATEST ENEMY!
YOU CHOSE FRAILTY OVER POWER!
DOOOM
PUNCH IT, JET! HE'S ALMOST ON US!
ZAKK

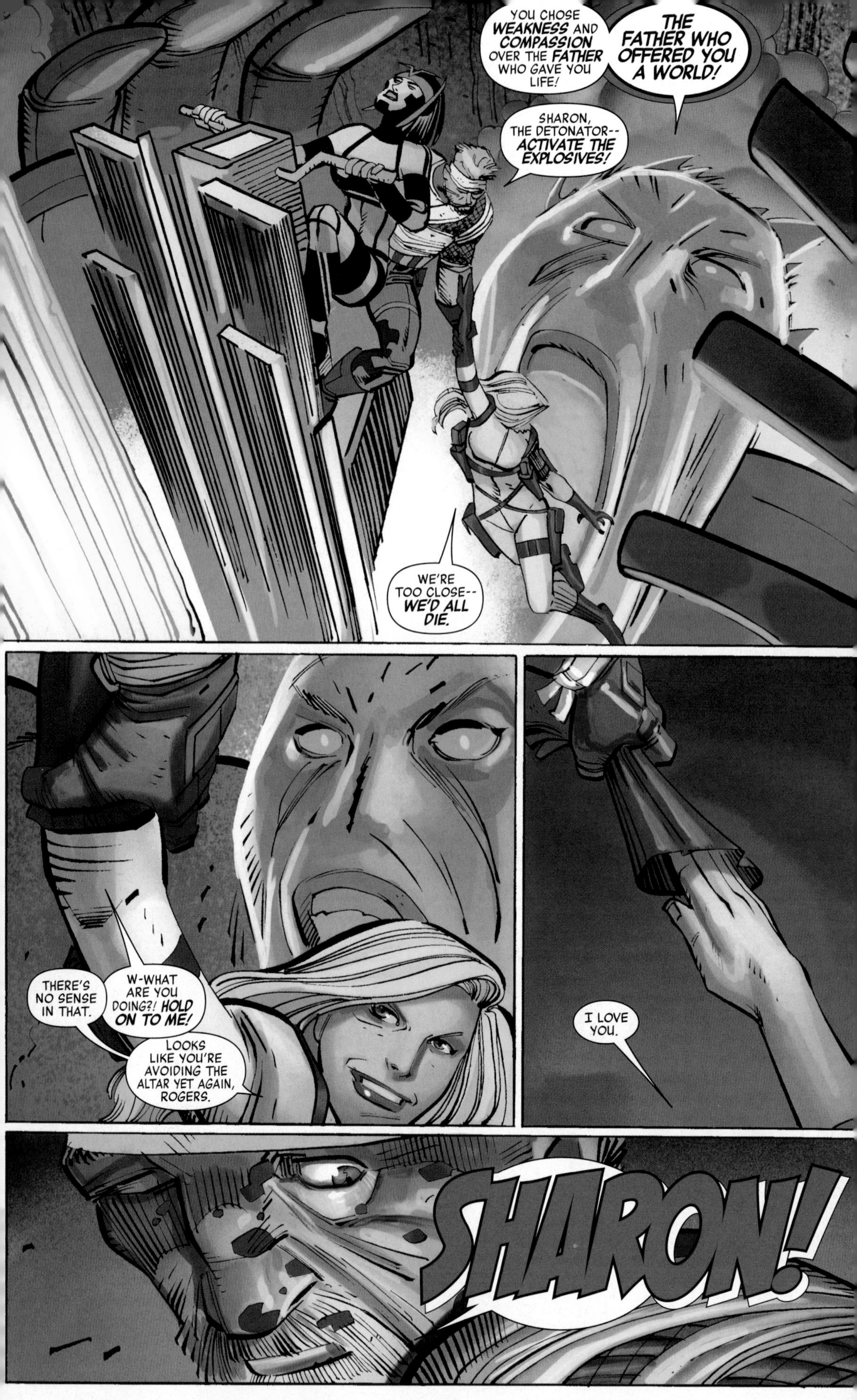

YOU CHOSE WEAKNESS AND COMPASSION OVER THE FATHER WHO GAVE YOU LIFE!
THE FATHER WHO OFFERED YOU A WORLD!
SHARON, THE DETONATOR-- ACTIVATE THE EXPLOSIVES!
WE'RE TOO CLOSE-- WE'D ALL DIE.
THERE'S NO SENSE IN THAT.
W-WHAT ARE YOU DOING?! HOLD ON TO ME!
LOOKS LIKE YOU'RE AVOIDING THE ALTAR YET AGAIN, ROGERS.
I LOVE YOU.
SHARON!

IT'S *GOOD* TO SEE YOU ALIVE, ZOLA.

OUR ENCOUNTER WILL BE QUITE *BRIEF*, AGENT CARTER.

I WAS *DISAPPOINTED* IN THE *LAME* WAY YOU CHECKED OUT.

I KNEW IT WAS TOO HEARTFELT TO BE *GENUINE*.

AND, MOST IMPORTANTLY-- I WAS HOPING TO HAVE A HAND IN THE *KILL*.

GLAZZAT

FOR WHATEVER THE HELL YOU'VE DONE TO STEVE.

GLAZZAT

YHRAGH--!

AND TO WATCH YOU *DIE* KNOWING YOU *FAILED*.

KNOWING STEVE *GOT AWAY*--

D *YOUR* AUGHTER ITH HIM.

TO WATCH YOU *DIE* IN THE SAME EXPLOSION THAT *ERASES* ALL OF YOUR WORK--

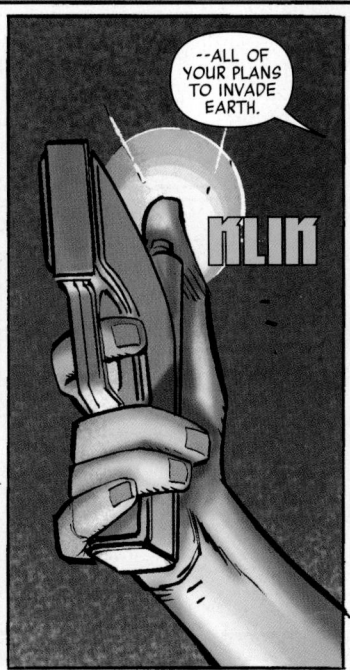

--ALL OF YOUR PLANS TO INVADE EARTH.

KLIK

TURN IT AROUND! WE HAVE TO GET HER!

TURN *THIS DAMNED THING*--

"AND *MOST* IMPORTANTLY--

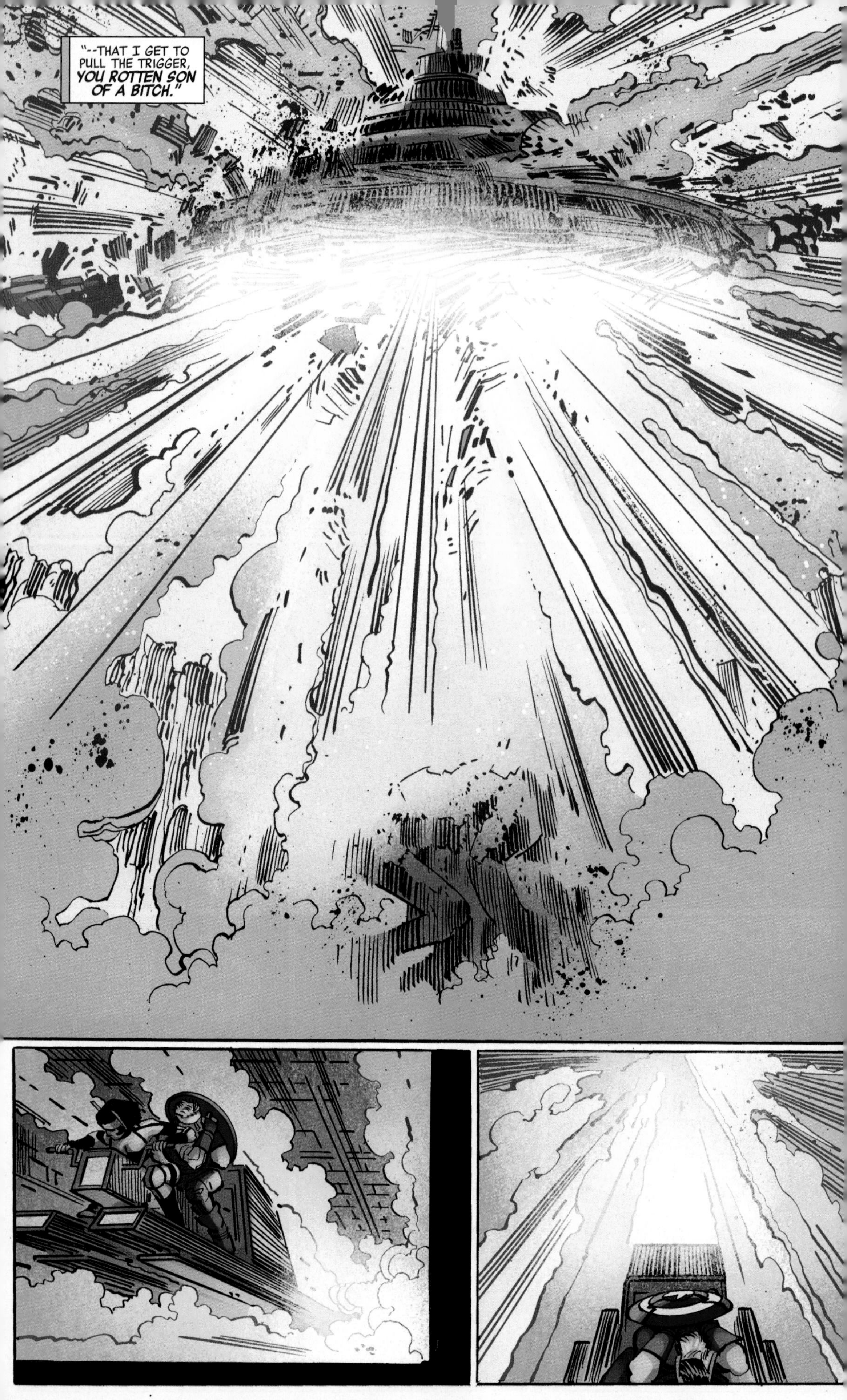
"--THAT I GET TO PULL THE TRIGGER, YOU ROTTEN SON OF A BITCH."

GRADOOOM

SHARON...

SHE'S GONE! THE BLAST WAS TOO GREAT--

THE PORTAL IS **UNSTABLE!**

NO-- NOT LIKE THIS--

I'M NOT LOSING HER TO HIM--

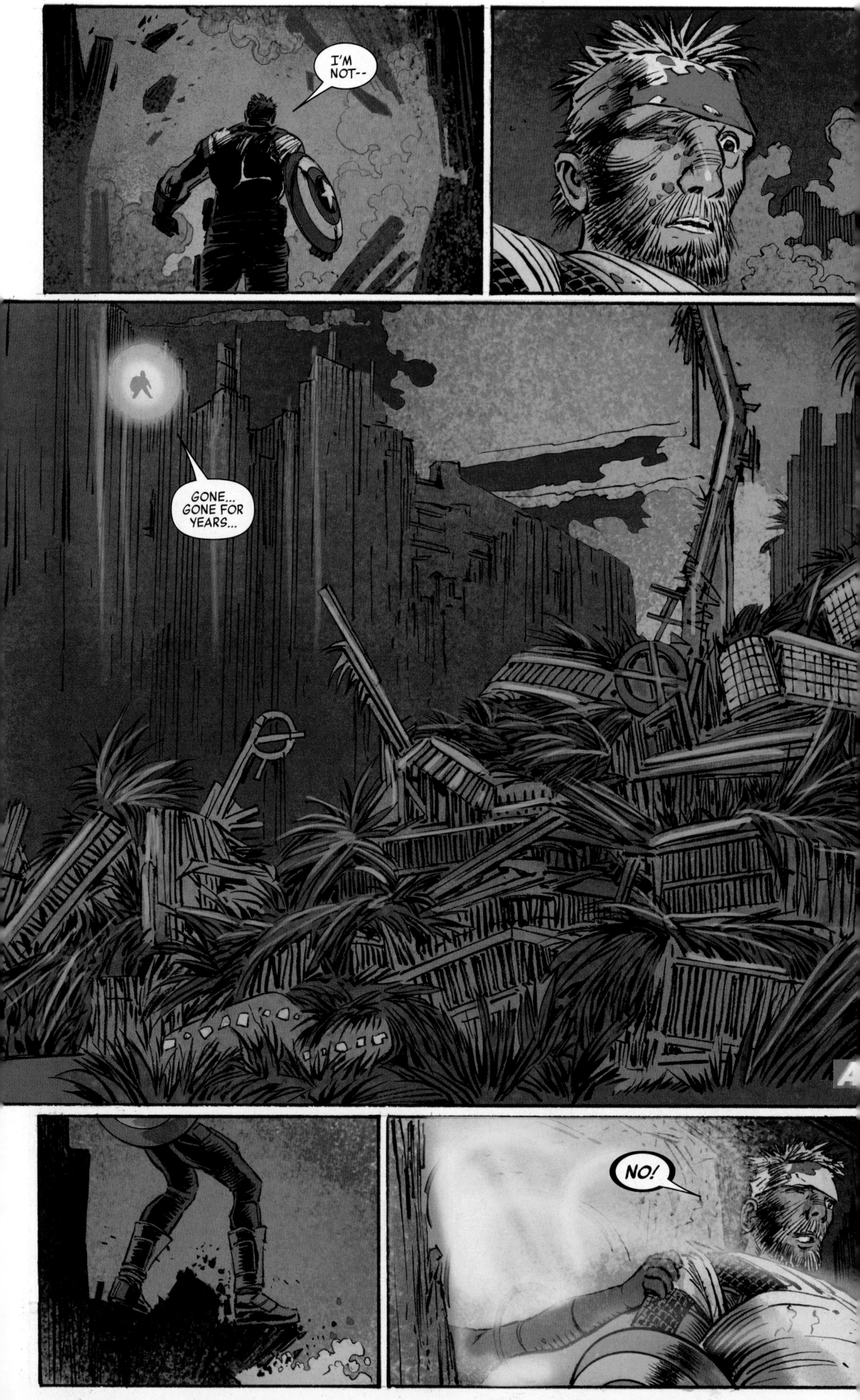

I'M NOT--
GONE... GONE FOR YEARS...
NO!

LET ME GO!

THE TUNNEL IS COLLAPSING!

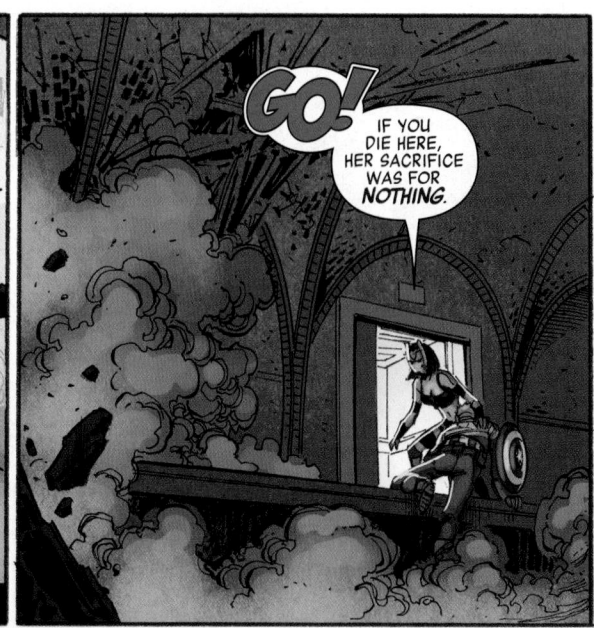

GO!

IF YOU DIE HERE, HER SACRIFICE WAS FOR *NOTHING*.

F-FIND HELP... ...COME BACK.

COME BACK FOR HER...

NO.

SHE IS GONE.

AS IS MY FATHER.

51 ST Street

AND THE PORTAL HOME *DESTROYED*.

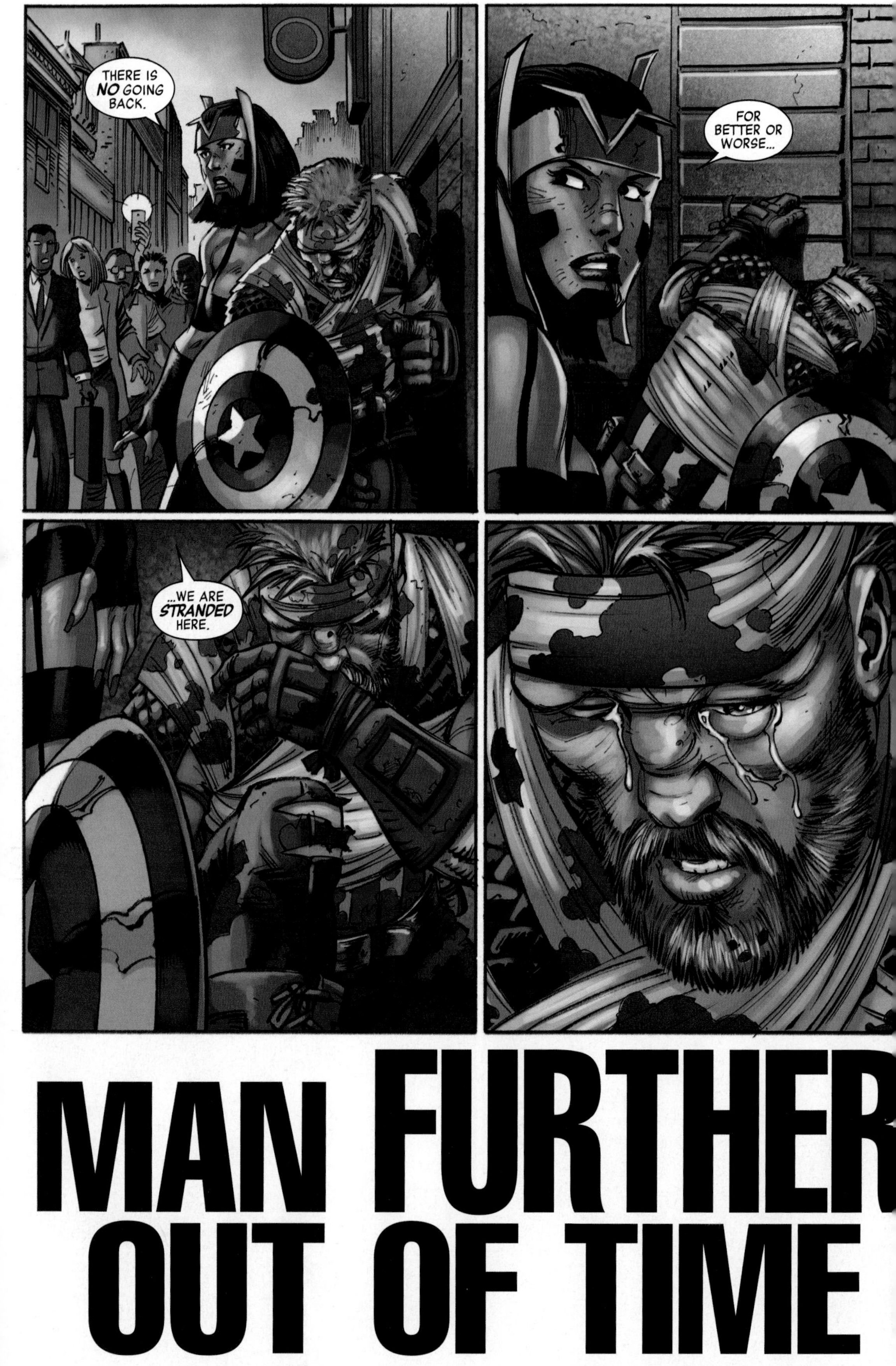
THERE IS NO GOING BACK.
FOR BETTER OR WORSE...
...WE ARE STRANDED HERE.

MAN FURTHER OUT OF TIME

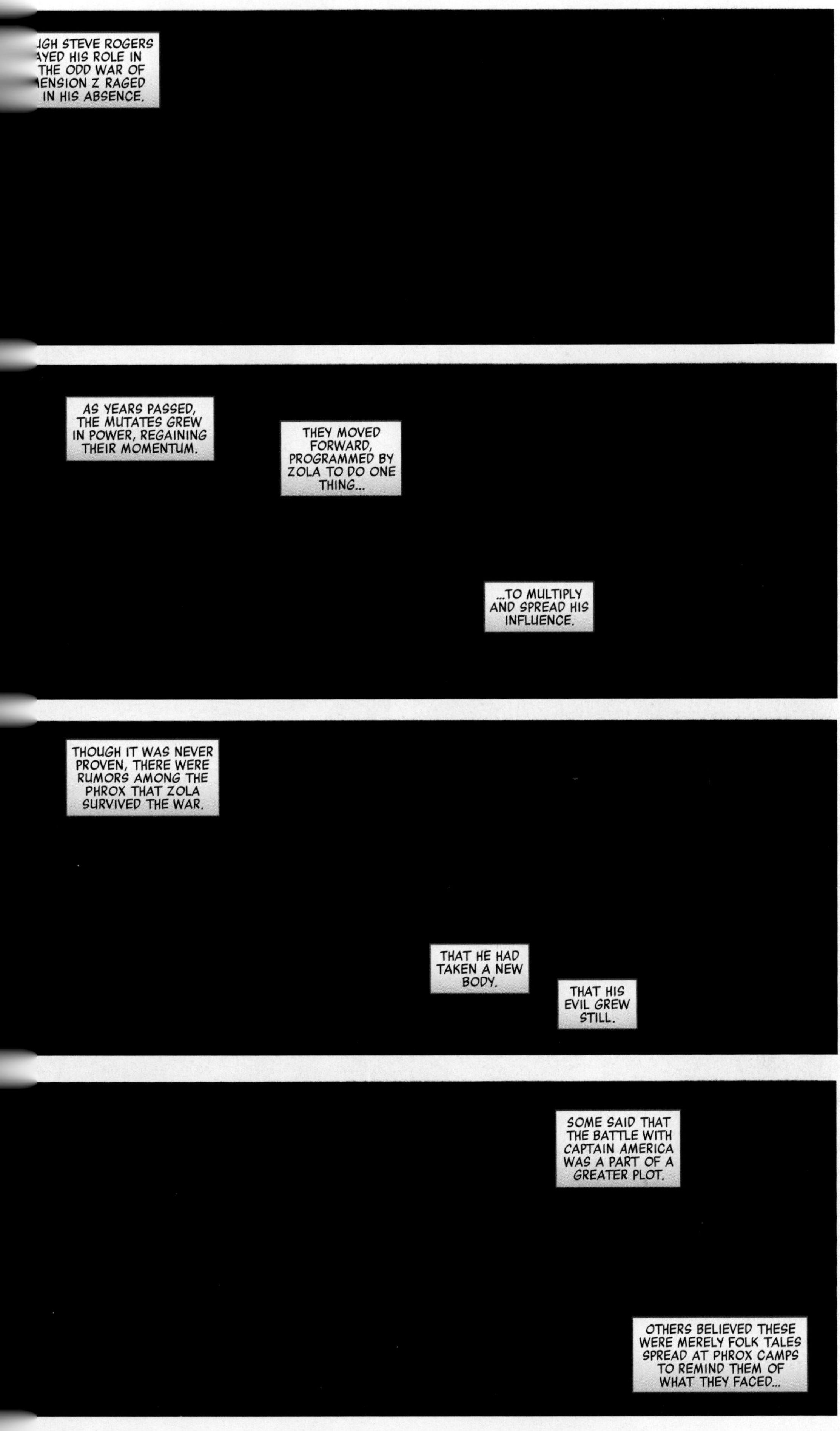
GH STEVE ROGERS AYED HIS ROLE IN THE ODD WAR OF ENSION Z RAGED IN HIS ABSENCE.
AS YEARS PASSED, THE MUTATES GREW IN POWER, REGAINING THEIR MOMENTUM.
THEY MOVED FORWARD, PROGRAMMED BY ZOLA TO DO ONE THING...
...TO MULTIPLY AND SPREAD HIS INFLUENCE.
THOUGH IT WAS NEVER PROVEN, THERE WERE RUMORS AMONG THE PHROX THAT ZOLA SURVIVED THE WAR.
THAT HE HAD TAKEN A NEW BODY.
THAT HIS EVIL GREW STILL.
SOME SAID THAT THE BATTLE WITH CAPTAIN AMERICA WAS A PART OF A GREATER PLOT.
OTHERS BELIEVED THESE WERE MERELY FOLK TALES SPREAD AT PHROX CAMPS TO REMIND THEM OF WHAT THEY FACED...

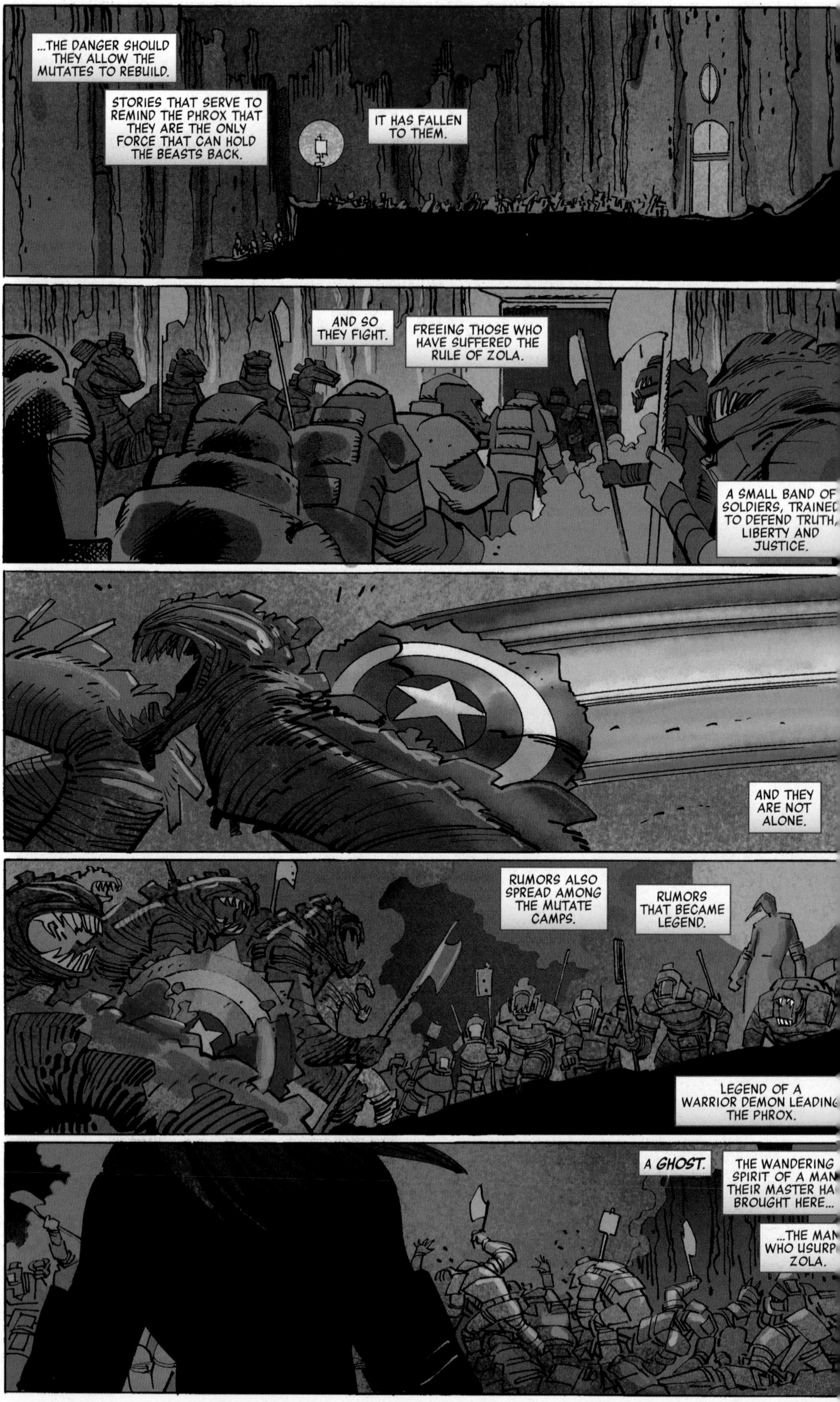
...THE DANGER SHOULD THEY ALLOW THE MUTATES TO REBUILD.
STORIES THAT SERVE TO REMIND THE PHROX THAT THEY ARE THE ONLY FORCE THAT CAN HOLD THE BEASTS BACK.
IT HAS FALLEN TO THEM.
AND SO THEY FIGHT.
FREEING THOSE WHO HAVE SUFFERED THE RULE OF ZOLA.
A SMALL BAND OF SOLDIERS, TRAINED TO DEFEND TRUTH, LIBERTY AND JUSTICE.
AND THEY ARE NOT ALONE.
RUMORS ALSO SPREAD AMONG THE MUTATE CAMPS.
RUMORS THAT BECAME LEGEND.
LEGEND OF A WARRIOR DEMON LEADING THE PHROX.
A *GHOST*.
THE WANDERING SPIRIT OF A MAN THEIR MASTER HA BROUGHT HERE...
...THE MAN WHO USURP ZOLA.

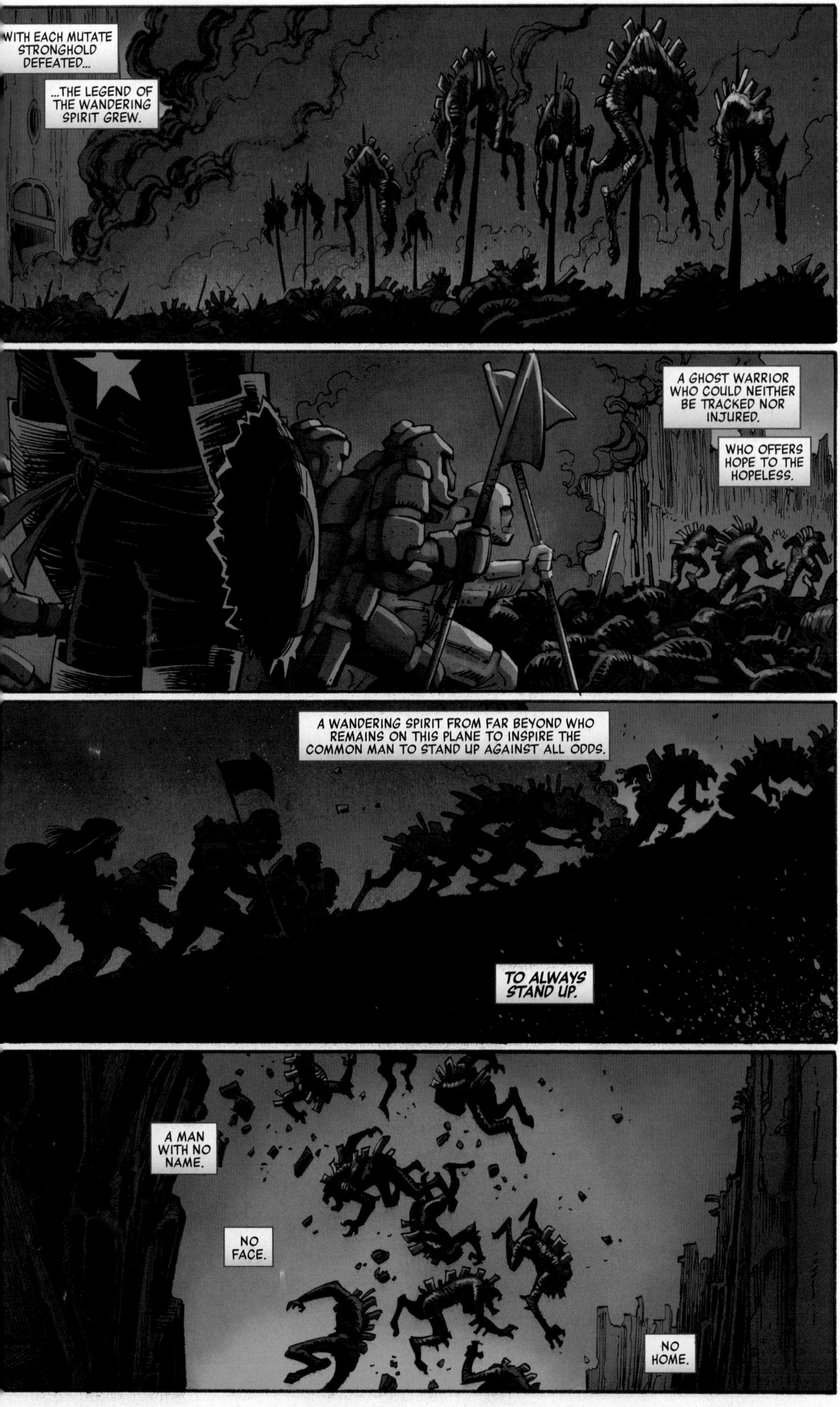
WITH EACH MUTATE STRONGHOLD DEFEATED...
...THE LEGEND OF THE WANDERING SPIRIT GREW.
A GHOST WARRIOR WHO COULD NEITHER BE TRACKED NOR INJURED.
WHO OFFERS HOPE TO THE HOPELESS.
A WANDERING SPIRIT FROM FAR BEYOND WHO REMAINS ON THIS PLANE TO INSPIRE THE COMMON MAN TO STAND UP AGAINST ALL ODDS.
TO ALWAYS STAND UP.
A MAN WITH NO NAME.
NO FACE.
NO HOME.

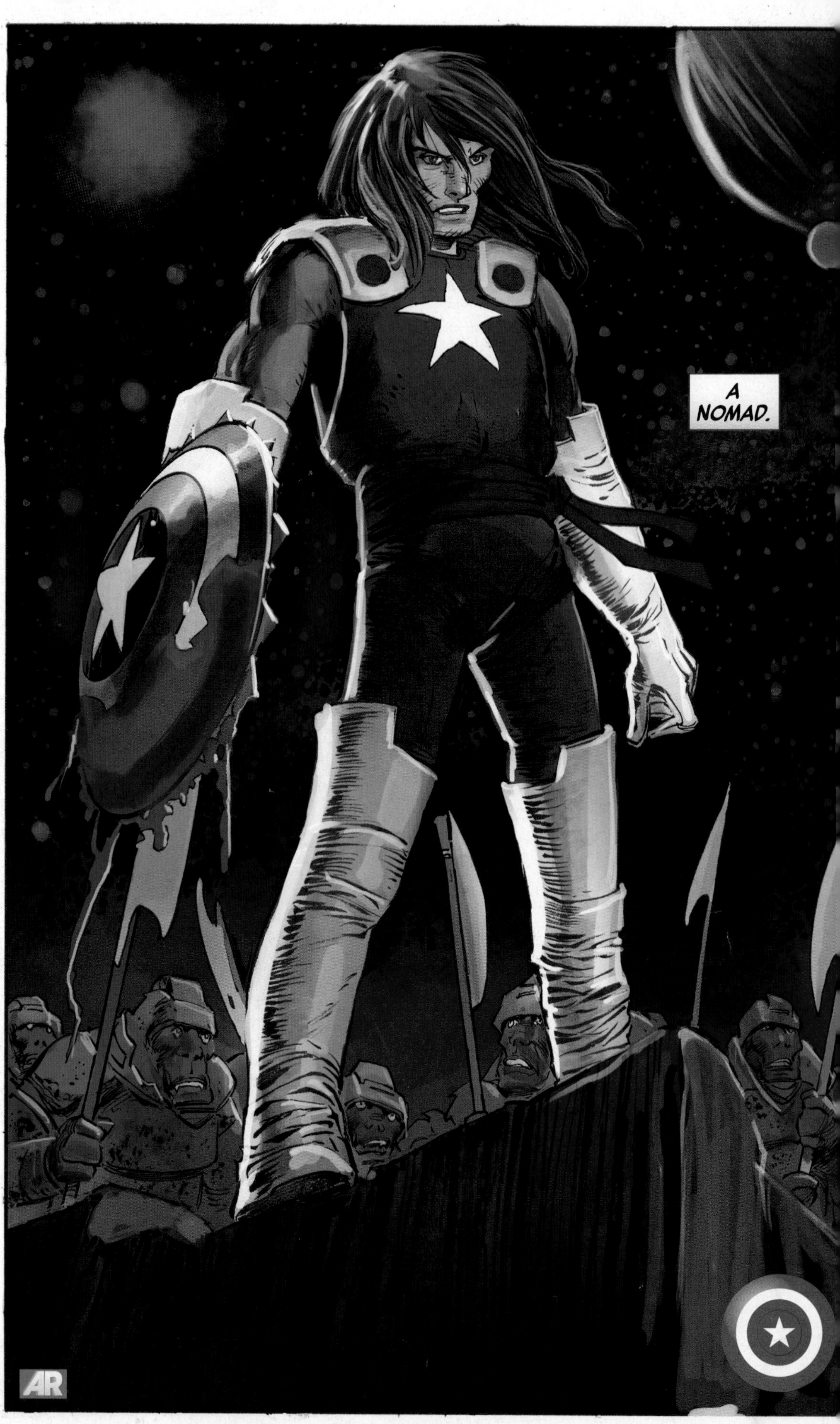
A NOMAD.

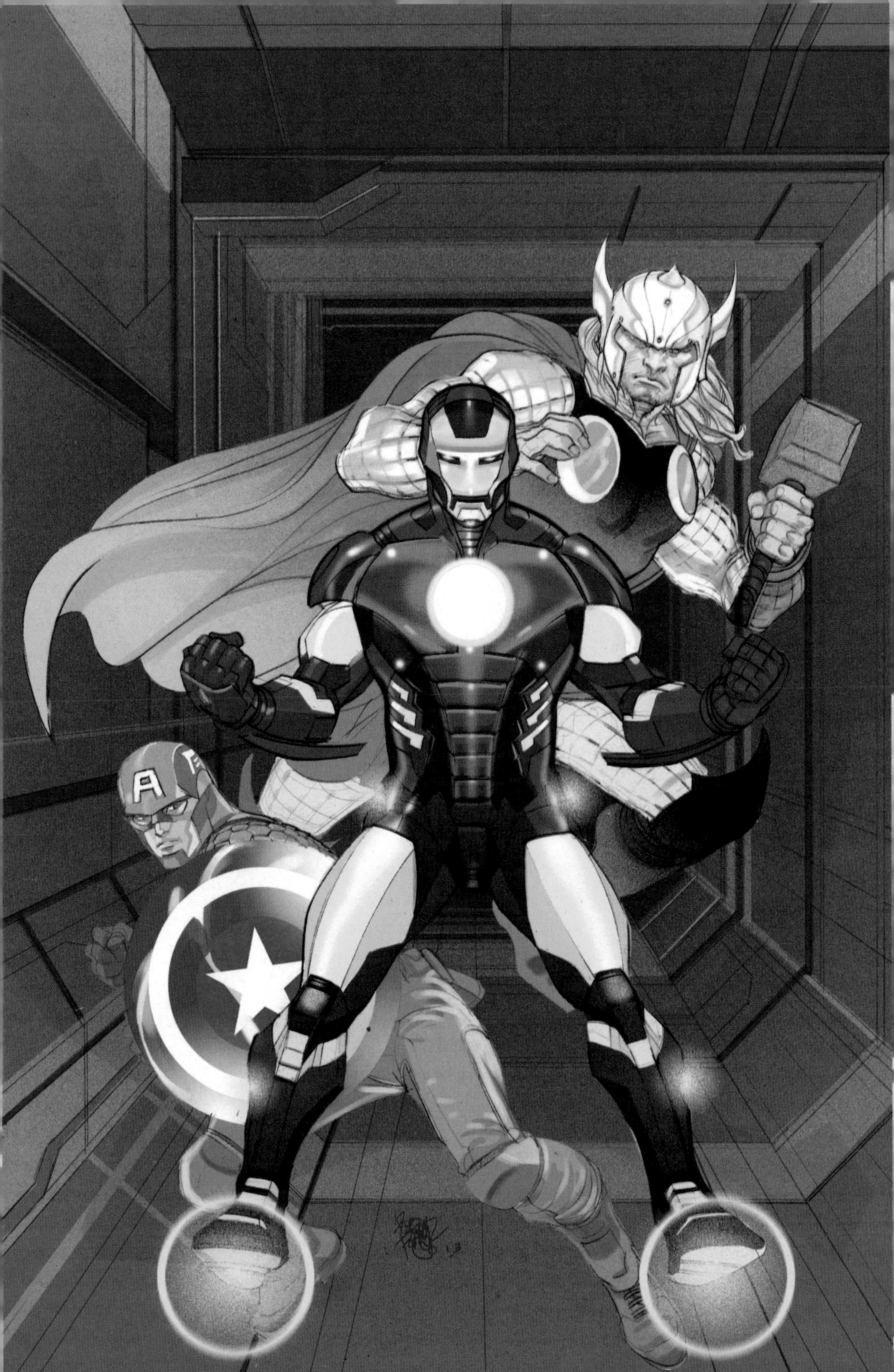

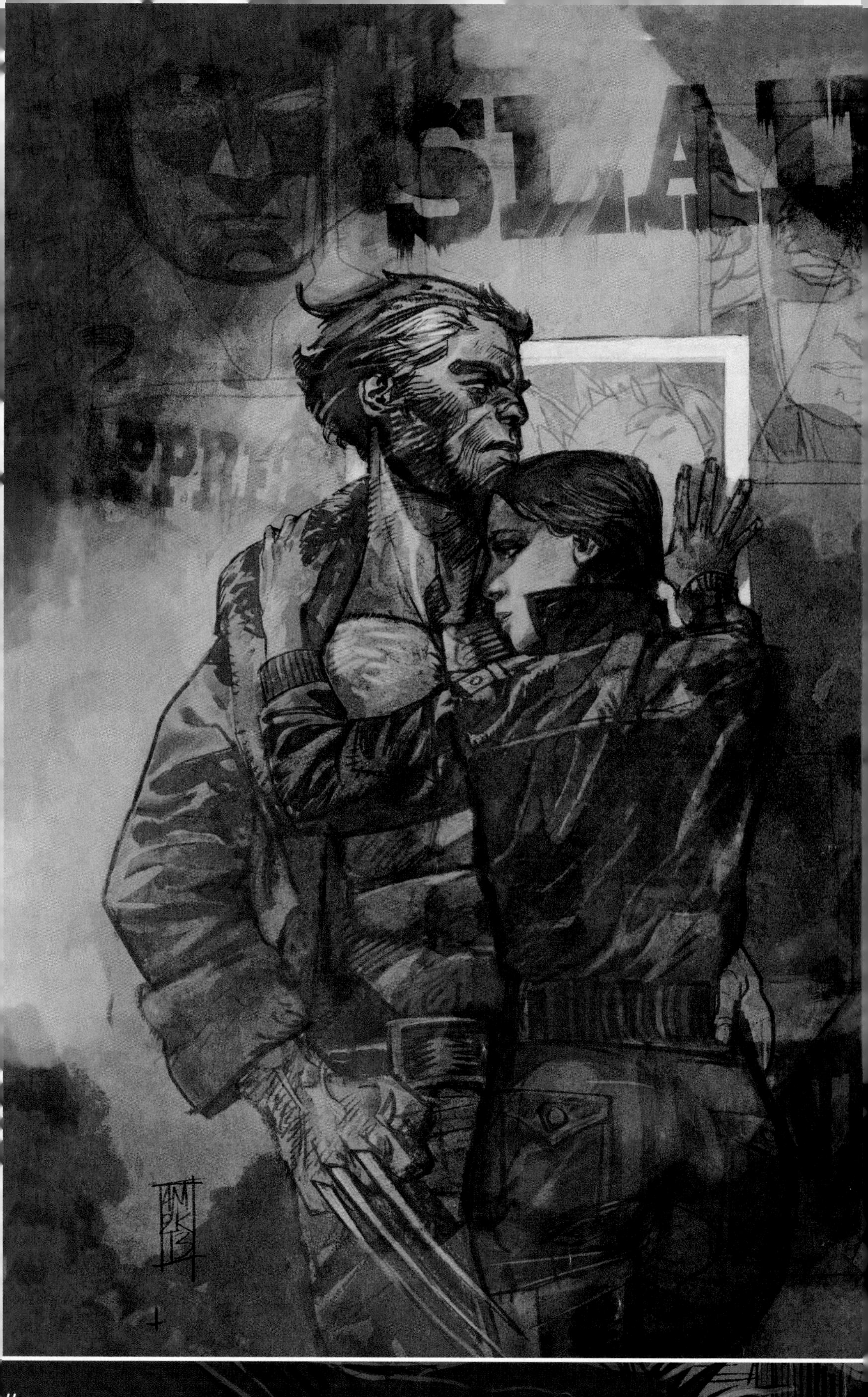

CAPTAIN AMERICA #10
script by RICK REMENDER,
artwork by JOHN ROMITA JR., TOM PALMER, KLAUS JANSON & SCOTT HANNA

PAGE 1

1 - Cap is pulling Jet away from dead Zola.

CAPT. AMERICA
Jet, I know this is hard--**I know**--but we **have** to go.

JET (weeping/weak/wavy)
I **betrayed** him-- **betrayed my heritage!**

He d-died to… **save me**.

2 - Jet is weeping uncontrollably, she turns to Steve, total anguish on her face.

JET
Why?! Why would **he** do **that**?

CAPT. AMERICA
He was **manipulating** you. To his very last word--it's what he does.

CAPT. AMERICA
Don't let him win. Help me save Earth! Come back with me--

3 - Steve holds Jet, comforts her.

JET
Ian.

We can't leave him--**have to find him!** He's still inside--

CAPT. AMERICA
No, Jet, listen to me…

Ian…

4 - Steve is stuttering, unsure. Jet is awake, terrified, demanding answers.

5 - Steve looks up at Jet, his expression sells everything. His sadness so deep it can only mean one thing.

CAPT. AMERICA
He's…

PAGE 2

1 - Jet recoils in horror, her brother is dead.

JET
No…

Not him too…

2 - Sharon looks up to see the giant city battle station of Zolandia drifting up towards the giant portal in the sky leading to Earth.

SHARON
I'm sorry--**but we have to go!**

If we haven't made it to the cave portal home when I detonate that battle station--**we will all be blown right to Hell.**

3 - Sharon pulls out the detonation device, a simple handheld device with a trigger. Maybe it's got the S.H.I.E.L.D. emblem on it.

SHARON
And I **will not** allow that thing to get through to Earth.

Even if it means we **all die.**

So we have to get to the portal before I pull this trigger.

4 - Jet is suddenly furious; she turns to Sharon, barking at her.

JET (stroked/red)
You've rigged my home with explosives?!

SHARON
Your home is a **mobile battle station** on its way to deliver a payload horde of **mutates** to Earth--you're **damn right** I did, sister.

PAGE 3

1 - JET TAKES THE DETONATOR, She is conflicted, but Zola's guilt trip worked.

JET
I have been a fool!

SFX
PLOKK

SHARON
OOF--!

2 - Before Sharon can react, Jet kicks her in the gut, sending her backwards into Cap.

JET
I **will not** allow you to detonate your explosives!

3 - Jet gets on a rocket bike as...

JET
I **will not** allow you to **destroy my home!**

Nor my father's **consciousness** stored within!

4 - Cap and Sharon collect themselves. Jet rockets away on the bike.

CAPT. AMERICA
STOP-- You helped stop him for all the **right** reasons!

JET
I never intended for him to die!
SFX
SHROOOM

5 - Cap and Sharon hop on the other bike to give chase.

SHARON
C'mon!

PAGE 4

1 - Jet rocketing up towards the floating city.

JET
Find some other way…

2 - On Cap and Sharon on a rocket bike chasing Jet. Sharon pilots it, Cap on the back.

SHARON
If she destroys that detonator--

CAPT. AMERICA
She **won't**--she's confused, in shock--but she's seen through Zola's lies.

SHARON
But watching him **die** in front of her--

3 - Closer on Cap, thoughtful.

CAPT. AMERICA
She's been through so much, Sharon--the damage done to her mind is **unimaginable**.

But she knows he was **evil**, knows he was **wrong**.

She'll do the **right** thing given a chance.

4 - Cap and Sharon closing in. Cap is standing, ready to jump off his rocket bike and onto Jet's.

CAPT. AMERICA
JET! Stop--**listen to me!**

If we don't destroy the battle station--the cost will be **billions** of innocent lives!

You know what those mutates intend to do!

5 - Close on Cap's face, total shock and fear.

CAPT. AMERICA
You **can't** allow that kind of **atrocity**--

CAPT. ZOLANDIA (OP)
She is a **Zola**, pig--

PAGE 5

1 - IMPACT - Bad times - Reverse camera - Behind Steve and Sharon's rocket bike, to reveal what Steve was frightened of. The last remaining Captain of Zolandia leads an army of Mutates from out of the city rocketing towards them. Dozens of mutates on rocket bikes, weapons at the ready. Captain Zolandia is on a big war bike, bigger than the other rocket bikes we've seen.

CAPT. ZOLANDIA
Atrocity is her right of birth!

CAPT. AMERICA
Dear God...

2 - Mutates unleash hell to stop Cap and Sharon, lasers blasting all over.

MUTATE 1
Kill-drill for Zola!

MUTATE 2
Drink the **pain**!

MUTATE 3
Tender murder--**Delicious taste**!

SFX (add to the guns)
ZAKK ZAP BLAZT

3 - Sharon quickly turns her rocket bike to avoid laser blasts; Cap is leaping off of the bike, in mid air.

SHARON
Steve--?!

CAPT. AMERICA
Talk Jet down.

Don't hurt her--

4 - Cap lands on the giant war machine driven by a surprised Captain Zolandia!

CAPT. AMERICA
--I'll buy time.

SFX
KWUNG

CAPT. ZOLANDIA
YES--Let us finish the **great debate**!

PAGE 6

1 - Sharon chasing Jet. Rocketing through the canyon the city was once nuzzled in. Mutates now chasing Sharon, shooting at her.

SFX
GAZAT! BLAZAK!

SFX
PNG! SNKG!

2 - Sharon rams her bike into a mutate biker next to her.

SFX
SHRAKK

3 - The bike crashes into the canyon wall and explodes. It crashes right into a hunk of cliff that is now breaking off, falling.

SFX
DOOOOM

4 - Another 3 mutates are behind Sharon, they can see they are suddenly in a bad spot as the building-sized hunk of falling cliff broken free is now falling down in front of them, about to crush them.

5 - IMPACT - Sharon rocketing towards us as the giant piece of cliff wall falls and explodes on the mutates chasing behind her.

PAGE 7

1 - SHARON pulls up next to Jet, yelling at her.

SHARON
If that station gets to Earth, it's the death of **billions** of innocent people!

Can you **comprehend** that?!

JET
They will **not** die--my father will live forever within the life of Earth--he will **improve** their lot!

2 - Jet is crying, totally distraught and conflicted.

SHARON
He will overwrite their minds--**that is murder!**

Steve says you won't let that happen and he's **never** wrong about a person.

3 - JET.

JET
Steve's morality has cost me enough!

My Father's consciousness is stored within that station--

JET
I **cannot** allow you to **kill** what remains of him! Not after my **betrayal**!

4 - SHARON convinces Jet.

SHARON
You're a victim of one of the **vilest** minds I've **ever** known, Jet.

He's **poisoned** your thoughts--but you **clearly** see through it--you understand the difference between **right** and **wrong**.

5 - Two shot as they rocket through the canyon. Zolandia rising towards the portal in the sky in the BG.

SHARON
If Zola's army invades my world you'll be the **villain** who helped him infect and subjugate my people!

Is **that** who you want to be?

6 - On Jet, looking at Sharon, her face tells us she is beginning to see her point.

[silent]

PAGE 8

1 - CUT TO - Cap fighting Captain Zolandia on his burly war bike. Both men standing, balancing on the precarious bike as it rockets through the canyon. Mutates on rocket bikes on either side, guns trained on Cap, waiting for a shot.

CAPT. ZOLANDIA
I remember our **mother** as she died--

SFX
KWUNG

I remember the **shame** in her eyes looking upon her **frail** child.

CAPT. AMERICA
She **wasn't** ashamed of me.

2 - Cap leaps over the attacking Captain Zolandia, jumping in the direction of the bike's controls.

CAPT. AMERICA
She was **afraid** of leaving me alone.

SFX
SHWUNKK

CAPT. ZOLANDIA
GHRAGH--

3 - Cap kicks the handlebars, violently turning the bike.

CAPT. AMERICA
But I made sure she never did.

Made sure to carry her strength with me.

4 - Cap kicks the handlebars, violently turning the bike.

CAPT. AMERICA
And if you **actually** shared my memories--

SFX
KRUKK

5 - IMPACT - The giant war bike veers sharp right, seconds away from colliding with one of the mutates. Big hero shot - Cap has jumped off of the war bike, in the direction of the second mutate.

CAPT. AMERICA
--you'd know better than to think words could erode that.

CAPT. ZOLANDIA
NO--!

PAGE 9

1 - Cap catches the bottom and uses the second mutate bike as a swing, as the other two collide and blow up behind him.

SFX
DOOOM

2 - Cap releases, falling now, mid air, Sharon and Jet rocketing towards him from the BG.

JET
GRAB HOLD!

3 - Cap lands on the back of Jet's bike.

CAPT. AMERICA
Knew you'd come around.

4 - CUT TO - The City is lifting up, entering the portal to Earth. Giant metal doors sliding open at the bottom of the flying city.

CAPT. AMERICA
Now let's get to the portal home and blow these monsters to--

GODZOLA (from inside opening door)
You have failed me **utterly**, daughter.

5 - Giant door opens on the bottom of the city. GODZOLA'S feet have begun to emerge, basically we're about to drop a Godzilla sized Zola out of the bottom of the city and onto our heroes.

GODZOLA (from inside opening door)
You have **failed** your **final** test.

Failed to earn your **name**.

Failed to move past **weakness**--

PAGE 10

Seeing this as 2 page tall vertical panels to sell the scope of the giant Zola.

1 - ½ Splash - GODZOLA EMERGES FROM the giant doors on the bottom of the CITY!

GODZOLA
You have failed Zola.

JET
Father--?!

2 - ½ Splash - GODZOLA lands in the canyon - Jet and Sharon just managing to maneuver their rocket bikes to avoid the giant robot falling down toward them.

GODZOLA
Now you will **die** with the rest.

SFX
GAZZZEEEEEEEE

PAGE 11

1 - GODZOLA fires a laser blast that hits Sharon's bike.

SHARON
GHA--!

SFX
DOOOOM

CAPT. AMERICA
SHARON!

2 - Sharon is in mid air having leapt off of the bike before it blew up.

CAPT. AMERICA (stroked/red/bold)
HOLD ON!

3 - Sharon grabs Cap's hand, she's being pulled on the back of Jet and Cap's bike. Enormous Godzola chasing behind them.

GODZOLA
So much time **wasted** on you, my daughter!

So many **failed** opportunities to **earn** your name!

I **loved** you with all of my heart--

4 -Angle from behind - Jet turns the rocket bike up, rocketing towards the cave entrance leading back to Earth.

GODZOLA
--and you chose to side with my **greatest enemy!**

You chose **frailty** over **power**!

5 - Sharon hangs onto Cap's arm, it's precarious.

CAPT. AMERICA
Punch it, Jet! He's almost on us!

SFX
ZAKK
DOOOM

PAGE 12

1 - Double page-wide vista - Front on Cap, JET AND SHARON'S rocket bike flying UP THE sheer FACE OF THE MOUNTAIN. Enormous Godzola is right behind them, filling the BG, his giant hand reaching for them. If someone doesn't do something ASAP they are done for! ZOLA's seconds away from grabbing and crushing them.

GODZOLA
You chose **weakness** and **compassion** over the **Father** who gave you life!

(BIG/bold/red/stroked)
The father who offered you a world!

CAPT. AMERICA
Sharon, The detonator--**activate the explosives!**

SHARON
We're too close--**we'd all die.**

2 - Sharon looks at Steve and smiles. Giant Zola hand looming in the BG.

SHARON
There's no sense in that.

CAPT. AMERICA
W-what are you doing! **Hold on to me!**

SHARON
Looks like you're avoiding the altar yet again, Rogers.

3 - SHARON doesn't waste a second--she pulls her glove off, leaving it in Cap's clenched fist as she falls back and away off the bike and towards giant GODZOLA.

SHARON
I love you.

4 - Tiny Sharon empties her gun into giant Zola's face, it causes the giant Zola pain, he ceases his attack on the rocket bike.

CAPT. AMERICA (bold/stroked red/impact)
SHARON!

PAGE 13

1 - Sharon lands, riding on the top of Zola's giant hand or somewhere on him. She did it, she bought them time.

SHARON
It's **good** to see you alive, Zola.

GODZOLA
Our encounter will be quite **brief**, Agent Carter.

2 - Tight on Sharon - looking back at Cap one last time. She is holding the detonator device now.

SHARON
I was **disappointed** in the **lame** way you checked out.

SFX
GLAZZAT

SHARON
I knew it was too heartfelt to be **genuine**.

And, most importantly--I was hoping to have a hand in the **kill**.

3 -

SHARON
For whatever the hell you've done to Steve.

SFX
GLAZZAT

GODZOLA
YHRAGH--!

SHARON
And to watch you **die** knowing you **failed**.

Knowing Steve **got away**--

4 -

SHARON
--and **your daughter** with him.

To watch you **die** in the same explosion that **erases** all of your work--

5 -

SHARON
--all of your plans to invade Earth.

SFX
-KLIK-

6 - On Cap, last time he sees Sharon, he knows what she's about to do.

CAPT. AMERICA
Turn it around! We have to get her!

TURN THIS DAMNED THING--

SHARON (CAP)
"And **most** importantly--"

PAGE 14

1 - Impact - The floating battle city blows up.

SHARON (CAP)
"--that I get to pull the trigger, **you rotten son of a bitch.**"

2 - The enormous blast is chasing right behind Jet and Cap as they rocket into the tunnel to Earth!

3 - CUT TO - Int. Tunnel - CAP AND JET ROCKET THROUGH PORTAL, fire from the detonation chasing them down the dark tunnel. Seconds away from being incinerated!

PAGE 15

1 - Behind the rocket now as it is almost consumed by flames, it is just a few feet away from flying into the swirling portal. Fire all around them--

2 - CUT TO - Earth - subway tunnel - Jet and Cap come rocketing out of the swirling portal back into the Earth side of the train tracks we saw in issue 1.

SFX
GRADOOOM

3 - Their rocket bike crashes, Cap leaping off, frantic.

CAPT. AMERICA (weak/small)
Sharon…

4 - Cap runs back to the gateway, the tunnel is collapsing all around them, the ceiling falling down, Jet yelling for him to stop!

JET
She's gone, Steve! The blast was too great--

The portal is **unstable**!

5 - Cap runs through the portal.

CAPT. AMERICA
No--not like this--

I'm not losing her to him--

PAGE 16

1 - IMPACT - Dimension Z - angle behind Cap - wide angle reveal - Cap is standing on a ledge; he almost fell over it, looking at the canyon that was once home to the city of Zolandia. But now, at least 5 years have passed in Zolandia. In the canyon we see the old, burnt-out and moss-covered remains of the crashed Zolandia war station/city and also the burnt-out husk of the rusting, moss-covered giant Godzola.

JRJR note: The blast blew apart the tunnel leading to the portal, so Steve is standing precariously on a foot of remaining cliff here, he almost goes over.

CAPT. AMERICA
I'm not--

2 - On Cap.

3 - ON Cap's feet - the few feet of cliff he's standing on is crumbling away.

CAPT. AMERICA
No…

4 - CUT TO - INT. SUBWAY TUNNEL, EARTH - Jet watches as Cap leaps back through the portal into the Earth subway tunnel. The tunnel is falling down around them. The tunnel is about to collapse.

5 - On Cap.

PAGE 17

1 - Jet pulling Cap away from the portal, running through the collapsing tunnel. She is pulling him away from the portal, there is no time!

CAPT. AMERICA (stroked/impact)
Let me go!

JET
The tunnel is collapsing!

2 - TRAIN STATION - They run towards an elevator door, the same one Steve and Sharon came down in a million years ago. The station is coming down all around them.

JET
GO!

If you die here, her sacrifice was for **nothing**.

3 - They make it into the elevator.

CAPT. AMERICA (weak/wavy)
F-find help…

…come back.

Come back for her…

JET
No.

4 - INT. ELEVATOR - Bloody, sooty, and broken Jet and Cap in silence.

JET
She is gone.

5 - BUSY SUBWAY STATION - Jet and Cap emerge, stagger from a doorway into a busy subway station, they are in total shock, and pedestrians look at them with curiosity. This is the same doorway Cap and Sharon entered to go down.

JET
As is my Father.

6 - They walk up/pull themselves up the staircase leading to the streets above. Pedestrians looking at them with shock, they are both beaten and bloody, a total mess.

JET
And the portal home **destroyed**.

PAGE 18

1 - TIMES SQUARE - Jet and Cap stand, having emerged from the subway station, they are looking around. For Cap, this is the first time home in 13 years. For Jet, this is her first time here ever.

> JET
> There is **no** going back.

2 - Jet stands, looking around in total astonishment. Cap is behind her, falling to his knees, broken.

> JET
> For better or worse…

3 - Pull in on Cap - Cap falls forward, weeping, head hung low, now on his hands and knees.

> JET
> …We are **stranded** here.

4 - Pull in closer - Cap lifts his face up to show he is crying. Still on his hands and knees. Staring straight ahead, dead inside, a man who just escaped the war of his life.

5 - Page-wide white space for the issue's title and credits.

> MAN FURTHER OUT OF TIME
> Remender - Romita - Janson - White etc

PAGE 19

4 page-wide horizontal panels - all black - no art -

1 -

> THIRD PERSON (CAP)
> Though Steve Rogers played his role in it, the odd war of Dimension Z raged on in his absence.

2 -

> THIRD PERSON (CAP)
> As years passed, the Mutates grew in power, regaining their momentum.

> THIRD PERSON (CAP)
> They moved forward, programmed by Zola to do one thing...

> THIRD PERSON (CAP)
> …To multiply and spread his influence.

3 -

> THIRD PERSON (CAP)
> Though it was never proven, there were rumors among the Phrox that Zola survived the war.

THIRD PERSON (CAP)
That he had taken a new body.

THIRD PERSON (CAP)
That his evil grew still.

4 -

THIRD PERSON (CAP)
Some said that the war with Captain America was a part of a greater plot.

THIRD PERSON (CAP)
Others believed these were merely folk tales spread at Phrox camps to remind them of what they faced…

PAGE 20

5 page-wide horizontal panels of the same size and shape.

1 - Dimension Z - A Zola mutate outpost.

THIRD PERSON (CAP)
…The danger should they allow the Mutates to rebuild.

Stories that serve to remind the Phrox that they are the only force that can hold the beasts back.

It has fallen to them.

2 - Pull in - Mutates usher Phrox in shackles towards a doorway to a Zola FACTORY like the one we saw before, a Phrox processing facility.

THIRD PERSON (CAP)
And so they fight.

Freeing those who have suffered the rule of Zola.

A small band of soldiers, trained to defend truth, liberty and justice.

3 - The Captain Zolandia serrated shield hurls through the air.

THIRD PERSON (CAP)
And they are not alone.

4 - The serrated shield sticks into the face of a mutate, as suddenly a bunch of Phrox rebels attack.

THIRD PERSON (CAP)
Rumors also spread among the Mutate camps.

Rumors that became legend.

Legend of a warrior demon leading the Phrox.

5 - Zola factory Phrox processing facility burns, black smoke drifts, our liberation army fighting mutates, our human hero still silhouetted against a large alien moon. On a wall outside of the facility we see a white star painted.

THIRD PERSON (CAP)
A ghost.

The wandering spirit of a man their master had brought here…

…the man who usurped Zola.

PAGE 21

5 page-wide horizontal panels of the same size and shape.

1 - Phrox men and women chase mutates away from the burning station, led by a man in the shadows holding the serrated Zolandia shield.

THIRD PERSON (CAP)
With each mutate stronghold defeated…

…The legend of the wandering spirit grew.

2 - The Zola facility burning. Dead mutates on pikes. A white star painted on their faces.

THIRD PERSON (CAP)
A ghost warrior who can neither be tracked nor injured.

Who offers hope to the hopeless.

3 - a battlefield - Phrox warriors stand around a sea of dead mutates. the remaining mutates are running away. The human leader still in shadows, leading the charge, but we can see the white star on his chest and on his shield.

THIRD PERSON (CAP)
A wandering spirit from far beyond who remains on this plane to inspire the common man to stand up against all odds.

To always stand up.

4 - The mutates drop off of the cliff they were running up, they are terrified.

THIRD PERSON (CAP)
A man with no name.

No face.

No home.

PAGE 22

Splash - Big action shot of Ian. He's leaping off of the hill, holds the serrated shield of Captain Zolandia, ready for attack. He's now 23 years old, wearing a rusted old version of the Zola armor he "died" in, but it has a white star painted on the chest now. This is the son of Captain America. Behind him the sky is full of moons and planets. The mutates in the foreground are all turning around, moments away from being taken down by the NOMAD.

THIRD PERSON (CAP)
A Nomad.

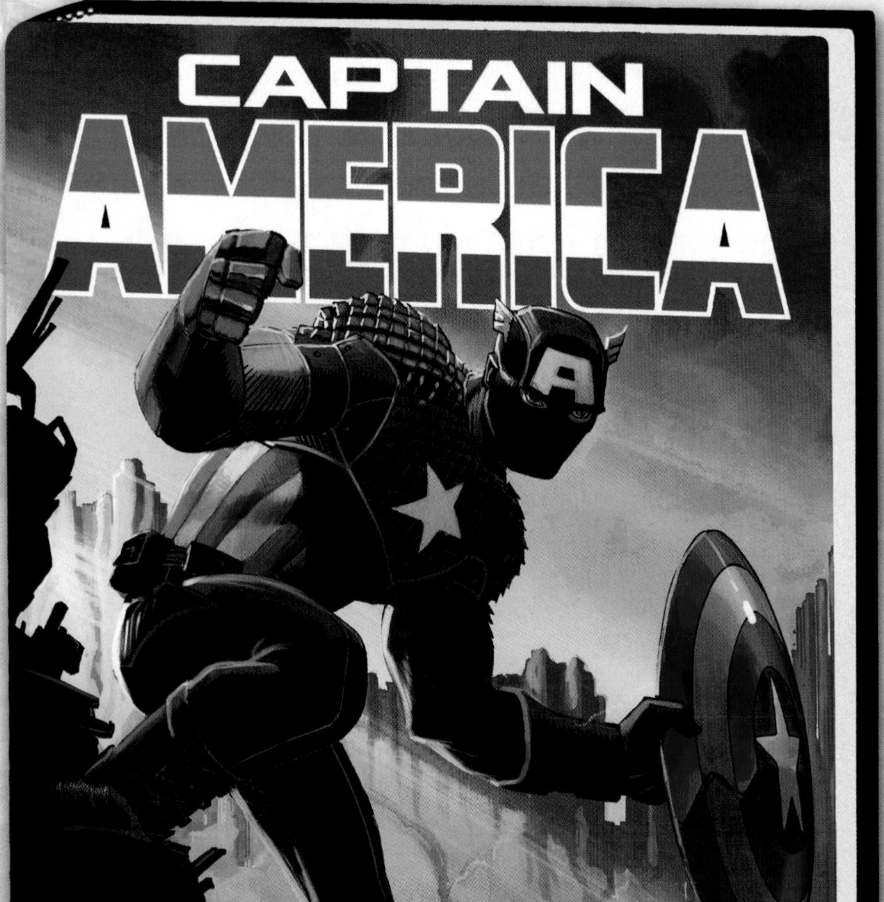

TO ACCESS THE FREE *MARVEL AUGMENTED REALITY APP* THAT ENHANCES AND CHANGES THE WAY YOU EXPERIENCE COMIC

1. **Download the app for free via** marvel.com/ARapp
2. **Launch the app on your camera-enabled Apple iOS® or Android™ device***

3. **Hold your mobile device's camera ov** any cover or panel with the **AR** grap
4. **Sit back and see the future of comics in action!**

*Available on most camera-enabled Apple iOS® and Android™ devices. Content subject to change and availability.

CAPTAIN AMERICA **AR** INDEX